The Development of Civil Society in Central Asia

INTRAC NGO Management and Policy Series

The Development of Civil Society in Central Asia

By
Janice Giffen and Lucy Earle
with Charles Buxton

INTRAC NGO Management and Policy Series No. 17

International NGO Training and Research Centre
An INTRAC Publication

INTRAC:

A Summary Description
INTRAC, the International NGO Training and Research Centre, was set up in 1991 to provide specially designed training, consultancy and research services to organisations involved in international development and relief. Our goal is to improve NGO performance by exploring policy issues and by strengthening management and organisational effectiveness.

First published in 2005 in the UK by
INTRAC
PO Box 563
Oxford
OX2 6RZ
United Kingdom

Tel: +44 (0)1865 201851
Fax: +44 (0)1865 201852
e-mail: info@intrac.org
website: www.intrac.org

Copyright © INTRAC 2005

ISBN 1-897748-75-2

Designed and produced by
Jerry Burman
Tel: +44 (0)1803 409754

Printed in Great Britain by
Antony Rowe Ltd., Eastbourne, Sussex

Contents

Acknowledgements

The authors and research teams would like to thank the Social Science Research Unit (SSRU) of the UK's Department for International Development (DFID) whose generous funding supported this project.

The fieldwork stage of the research project was managed from Oxford by Simon Heap, formerly of INTRAC. The research teams in each country worked closely with him in the early stages of the project. In Kazakhstan the team included Aigerim Ibrayeva, Aliya Kabdieva, Dina Sharipova and Saule Dissenova; in Kyrgyzstan, Baakyt Baimatov and Bermet Stakeeva; in Uzbekistan Shukhrat Abdullaev, Oksana Abdullaeva and Aziz Tatybayev and in Tajikistan, Hofiz Boboroyov. They were provided valuable support by INTRAC's regional staff, in particular from Lola Abdusalyamova, Charles Buxton and Simon Forrester, and the process as a whole was facilitated by Anne Garbutt, who had overall responsibility for INTRAC's Central Asia Programme.

The authors of this publication are grateful for the insightful and helpful comments provided by INTRAC staff members Brian Pratt and Oliver Bakewell as the final draft was drawn up, and for earlier support from David Marsden, INTRAC associate and former Research Director. We would like to extend particular thanks to our external reader, Babken Babajanian of the London School of Economics and Political Science. His careful reading of the text and the sharing of his knowledge of the region and of civil society issues have been much appreciated. Finally, our thanks to Jacqueline Smith, INTRAC Publishing Manager, for her dedicated proofreading and attention to detail.

Acronyms

ACTED	Agence d'Aide à la Coopération Technique et au Développement
ASDP	Agencies for the Support of the Development Process
ASTI	Association of Scientific and Technical Intelligentsia (Tajikistan)
ASTP	analytical skills training programme
BWA	Business Women's Association
CAIP	Community Action Investment Programme (Mercy Corps)
CAP	community action planning
CASDIN	Central Asian Sustainable Development Information Network
CASE	Centre for Action Against Social Exclusion
CBO	community-based organisation
CDC	Community Development Centres
CDD	Community Driven Development (World Bank); also Committee for/on District Development
CDF	Comprehensive Development Framework (World Bank)
CDWUU	Community Drinking Water Users' Union
CGAP	The Consultative Group to Assist the Poor
CHF	Community Habitat Finance
CIB	Centre Interbilim (Kyrgyzstan)
CIC	Community Initiative Council (Mercy Corps)
CIS	Commonwealth of Independent States
CIVICUS	The World Alliance for Citizen Participation
CSI	Civil Society Index
CSO	civil society organisation
CSSC	Civil Society Support Centre
DCCA	Development Cooperation in Central Asia
DFID	Department for International Development (UK)
DPT	Democratic Party of Tajikistan
EBRD	European Bank for Reconstruction and Development
ECOSAN	IWA Specialist Group "Ecological Sanitation"
ESCOR	United Nations Economic and Social Council Resolution
ETSP	education and training support programme
FSU	former Soviet Union
GDP	gross domestic product
GONGO	government-oriented or official NGO
ICAP	INTRAC's (DFID-funded) Central Asia Programme
ICNL	International Center for Not-for-Profit Law
IDS	Institute of Development Studies (University of Sussex)

1

ILO	International Labour Organization
IMU	Islamic Movement of Uzbekistan
INGO	international NGO
IRPT	Islamic Renaissance Party of Tajikistan
KIMEP	Kazakhstan Institute of Management, Economics and Strategic Research
LSE	London School of Economics
MDG	Millennium Development Goal
MIP	Mahalla Initiative Programme
MSDSP	Mountain Societies Development Support Programme (Aga Khan Foundation)
NDI	US National Democratic Institute for International Affairs
NGO	non-governmental organisation
NGOSO	NGO support organisation
NKO	Russian term for non-commercial or non-governmental organisation
NNO	non-governmental non-profit organisations
NPRS	National Poverty Reduction Strategy
NSOSO	NGO-society organisation
OSCE	Organization for Security and Cooperation in Europe
PCA	participatory community appraisals
PCI	Peaceful Communities Initiative (Mercy Corps)
PDP	People's Democratic Party
PRA	participatory rural appraisal
PRS	Poverty Reduction Strategy (Kyrgyzstan)
PRSP	Poverty Reduction Strategy Paper (World Bank)
ROSCA	rotating savings association
SDPT	Social Democratic Party of Tajikistan
SHGA	Self Help Group Association (UNDP)
SSRU	Social Science Research Unit, Institute of Education
UNAIDS	Joint United Nations Programme on HIV/AIDS
UNDP	United Nations Development Programme
UNHCR	United Nations High Commission for Refugees
UNICEF	United Nations Children's Fund
UNRISD	United Nations Research Institute for Social Development
UNV	United Nations Volunteers
USAID	US Agency for International Development
UTO	United Tajik Opposition
VO	village organisation

Introduction

After centuries as outposts of foreign empires, the countries of Central Asia found themselves sovereign, independent states for the first time in 1991 after the break-up of the USSR. At the time, analysts from across the world predicted a transition to liberal economic and democratic systems for the countries of the Former Soviet Union and Eastern Europe. The Central Asian states of Kazakhstan, Kyrgyzstan, Tajikistan, Turkmenistan and Uzbekistan attracted particular interest from Western governments and international institutions. The region had been isolated from the rest of the world during the Soviet period and has been of considerable geo-political importance and sensitivity for thousands of years. With the end of the Cold War, there was noticeable international concern to ensure that these fledgling nation states overcame a history of instability to emerge as peaceful democracies.

Until relatively recently Central Asian societies were traditionally based on kinship structures and, with varying degrees of importance, on Islam. After colonisation by Tsarist Russia in the nineteenth and early twentieth centuries, these societies then underwent huge changes as the Soviet structures of government and administration were imposed upon them. Whilst the Soviet system introduced new forms of public association, many of the old traditional structures survived, existing both in parallel and in a type of symbiotic relationship with the new socialist models of social organisation.

Then, at the beginning of the 1990s, these countries experienced another upheaval, with independence thrust upon them after the fragmentation of the Soviet Union. Since then, the governments of all five Central Asian states have begun a process of nation-building, drawing on elements of pre-Soviet culture whilst (perhaps with the exception of Turkmenistan) attempting to forge a place for themselves in the modern world. What complicated this project was a general economic collapse that occurred across the region in the early 1990s. The Central Asian states, suddenly deprived of Soviet era markets and subsidies, lost 40–50 per cent of their gross domestic product. Levels of poverty increased rapidly as a result.

Much current external interest in this part of the world arises from the status of the Central Asian states as 'transition' countries. For many this transition is premised upon a shift away from a centrally controlled to a liberal market economy. Others place priority on the transition to a democratic style of governance. But these goals are generally understood to be mutually dependent and in both cases the development of a strong, independent civil society is seen as a necessary condition for their achievement. As such, institutions such as the World Bank and European Union, international non-governmental organisations (NGOs) and the governments of donor countries in the West have stressed the key role that a 'strong civil society' should play in this transition.

Clearly, any analysis of the current state of civil society in Central Asia must take account of all of the historical influences mentioned above. However, perceptions of what civil society is, what it can achieve and how it should be encouraged vary considerably amongst policy makers, academics and practitioners, both inside and outside of the region. Furthermore, the dominance of certain policy priorities of the main international actors in the region have narrowed working definitions of civil society. As a result of this, particular organisational forms have been privileged, whilst the role of other potentially influential and resourceful bodies and institutions has been overlooked or misinterpreted. Problems of definition have been further compounded by a lack of understanding of the nature of society in these countries and at times a tendency to simplify the complex social interactions and practices that have evolved in the region over centuries, as a result of shifting patterns of power and control. Inevitably the promotion of certain models of civil society by international agencies has impacted upon the way in which people in the region have come to conceptualise civil society in their own countries.

Whilst civil societies in Western democratic countries have developed over a lengthy period of time, international actors working in Central Asia are hoping to promote these changes in a matter of decades or less. In this project it sometimes seems that the substance of civil society has been lost in an emphasis on form. This is evident, for example, in a tendency to 'count' the number of NGOs that have emerged since independence in the region, and to use this type of statistical data as an indicator of an increasingly 'dynamic' and 'vibrant' civil society.

On the positive side, there has been a steady and exciting, if uneven, growth of civil society organisations and activities in the five countries of the region. Some of the organisations that began work after 1991 were entirely new; others were hybrids of Soviet or pre-Soviet predecessors. They were all working in an unpredictable and often chaotic environment, very many of them dependent on external sources of support.

* * *

It was against this backdrop of change and uncertainty, together with growing international interest in the region, that INTRAC first began work in the Central Asian states in 1994. INTRAC's programmes in Central Asia have centred on support to the NGO and civil society sector. They have worked on a wide range of issues and with many types of organisation but the principal focus has been on partnership with social sector NGOs. The emphasis on social justice set out in INTRAC's mission statement brings together a concern for participation and democratisation with the determination to assist poverty reduction. Its flexible, pragmatic approach to civil society strengthening, as employed in Central Asia since the mid 1990s, is reflected on the research side by an emphasis on empirical analysis of developments in this sphere. This means investigating phenomena as they present themselves rather than adhering to set ideas as to the nature of civil society. The programmes have sought appropriate ways to assist a wide range of groups and actors, so as to strengthen their ability to work together to promote social change and influence policy in favour of poor and marginalised populations.

This book is based on a series of research studies undertaken by local research institutes, academics and NGOs in Kazakhstan, Kyrgyzstan, Tajikistan and Uzbekistan between 1999 and 2003. The studies had a dual aim: first, to deepen understanding of the dynamics of civil society development in these countries, and second, to strengthen local institutions' research capacity in data collection and analysis. Drawing on the findings of these studies and placing them within the wider body of programmatic experience and research undertaken by INTRAC and its local partners since 1994, this book provides insight into the way in which civil society has developed during the period of Central Asian independence to date. Maintaining a critical stance and acknowledging the complexity of Central Asian realities, it examines how civil society has been shaped, hindered and enriched by internal and external forces, both contemporary and historical. Combining findings from empirical case studies with analysis of relevant literature, this book is both an investigation into the specificities of Central Asian civil societies and a broader examination of the emergence of civil society in 'transition' countries.

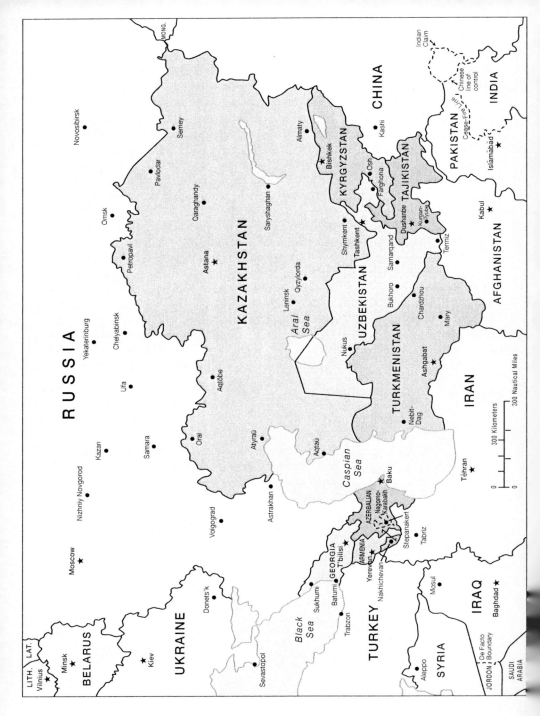

CHAPTER 1

Civil Society and the Central Asian Context: An Introduction to the Debates

There is such an intensity of debate about the term 'civil society' and its variety of meanings and interpretations that some scholars, criticising its overuse, have begun to question its validity.[1] However, proponents of the concept acknowledge this from the outset – later making an argument for the continued application of the term by pointing out its use as a conceptual tool. This chapter will begin with a brief background to the history behind the idea of civil society and will then examine the way in which the term is currently employed and understood by different development actors. This will be illustrated with reference to some of the academic literature on the theory of civil society. The aim of this section is to provide the reader with an introduction to the trends that influence development agencies working in Central Asia. The chapter will then detail a selection of debates put forward by scholars of the region, who have responded to the way in which theories of civil society been applied to the history, culture and current situation of Central Asia. It ends by briefly summarising the subsequent chapters and setting out the aims of this publication.

---

[1] See for example Seligman (2002) and Chandoke (1995).

Conceptions of Civil Society

Background
As this section will show, the ways in which civil society manifests itself, and how it can be promoted, are hotly contested. However, a general idea of the concept is usefully summed up in the following definition:

> An intermediate realm situated between state and household, populated by organised groups or associations which are separate from the state, enjoy some autonomy in relations with the state, and are formed voluntarily by members of society to protect or extend their interests (Manor, Robinson and White 1999: 4).

The term 'civil society' has its roots in the intellectual currents of the eighteenth century in Western Europe that in turn drew upon conceptions of the role of the individual, the state and society set out by the Ancient Greeks. The catalyst for this enquiry into the notion of civil society in Enlightenment Europe was the impact of industrialisation and the growth of modern capitalism on society. With greater economic liberty, men (but not women) had, from around the twelfth century onwards, gradually been able to access new social freedom and break away from the dominance of the nobility, to form new voluntary groupings and to interact in a public sphere. In this way, society and economy grew to become separate from the state. In the eighteenth century this was visible in associations of merchants, skilled craftsmen and property owners, for example, and there was great concern to protect these associations from intrusions by the state. Intellectual debate centred on the problem of self-interest in a commercial society and resultant social disintegration, but also on the argument that capitalist development could foster a new ethical order concerned with the common good (Howell and Pearce 2001). Scholars of the post-Enlightenment age, including Smith, Locke, Ferguson and Hegel, were asserting the potential of institutionalised solidarities and liberties (Sajoo 2002). As well as promoting trust and cooperation, 'a highly articulated civil society with over-lapping memberships was seen as the foundation of a stable democratic polity, a defence against domination by any one group, and a barrier to anti-democratic forces' (Edwards 2004: 7).

Approaches to Civil Society
Two hundred years later, following on from the end of the Cold War, the rise of global institutions and new currents in development aid, the concept of civil society has again risen to the fore. However, understandings of the term 'civil society' can vary considerably. Approaches to civil society can be seen to fall into two broad categories. The first of these has been labelled 'neo-liberal' or 'mainstream'.

This approach involves an instrumental understanding of civil society. The focus of development agencies following this approach will tend to be on associational activity and the potential of organisations, particularly NGOs, to play a role in, for example, strengthening democracy, or delivering services. The second approach has been labelled 'alternative' (Howell and Pearce 2001). The approach takes a broader consideration of the role of civil society and of the types of organisation or institution that can be a part of it and can include 'traditional' or 'communal' civil society (discussed below). It views civil society as more than a collection of organisations that are a means to an end: it is a potential force for positive change through people's participation and empowerment.

The terms 'neo-liberal' and 'alternative' are used to describe two broad approaches to the understanding of and support for civil society. Both of these labels encompass a number of different viewpoints, but their general directions are set out below.

The Neo-Liberal or Mainstream Approach

The neo-liberal approach is generally seen to have grown out of disenchantment with the idea of the developmental state. In the South and more obviously in the former Communist world, the role of the state in development policies had been regarded as crucial. But while post-1991 the primacy of the market was being trumpeted, it was also clear to advocates of liberal economies that the market would not function properly in societies where corruption was rife and the rule of law not properly enforced. Within the neo-liberal approach, having in place a network of citizens' associations within a strong civil society was thought to be one way of ensuring that good governance was seen to prevail, but also a way in which society's most vulnerable sectors could be protected. Along with its problem-solving properties, fostering civil society was seen by some policy makers in the West as a further way to roll back the functions of the state. However, this approach can also include a sense of the need to develop 'socially responsible' capitalism and for civil society groups to work in partnership with not just the market but also the state. Here the aim is not rolling back the state, but curbing the excesses of capitalism and working together to negotiate and arbitrate the development of an economy which is beneficial to all and does not result in the exclusion of the poor.

Along with smoothing the way for the functioning of the market, a vibrant civil society has come to be regarded by many Western donors as the key to promoting democracy. A key factor behind this policy direction is the work of Robert Putnam on social capital. In his understanding of social capital, networks of civic engagement amongst individuals generate trust and as a consequence facilitate collective action (Putnam 1995). This in turn contributes towards a thriving economy. These conclusions are based on an assessment of the importance of associational life in northern Italy compared with a dearth of similar activity in the South of the country (Putnam 1993). Putnam's work has become extremely popular with policy makers involved in international development, particularly those in the US. Various studies based on Putnam's theories, and on the 're-discovered' works of de Tocqueville (1994) on the nature of democracy in nineteenth-century America, have suggested that active associational forms and the consequent development of civic engagement contribute to the deepening of democracy as well as to economic development. Putnam himself asserts the relevance of this research for the building of social capital through civil society organisations in the developing world. For Howell and Pearce (2001) this mainstream approach is, in essence, one in which civil society is seen as an enabling tool for a Western agenda of liberal democracy and economics.

The Alternative Approach

By contrast, within the alternative conception of civil society, new actors, including women, marginalised people, some Northern NGOs, Southern organisations, grass-roots social movements and anti-globalisation campaigners are reinterpreting the term and, drawing on ideals of mutual support and solidarity and acknowledging power differentials within civil society itself, are using the concept to press for social justice. In a type of paradox, within the 'alternative' conception of civil society, the term is used to denote a sphere where the tenets of the neo-liberal approach are attacked (Howell and Pearce 2001). There is no single vision within the alternative approach, and it can include ideas of 'traditional' or 'communal' civil society, but the common thread that links these actors 'is the use of the concept of civil society to legitimize their right to resist the prevailing development paradigm' (Howell and Pearce 2001: 36).

We would argue that this alternative approach encompasses the idea that civil society is more than a collection of organisations undertaking disparate activities, and that interaction between different actors within civil society, and with the state, can create a space in which citizens are empowered to express their needs and outline their priorities. There is a growing body of literature on the idea of the public sphere, linked to a vision of civil society that is less concerned with the creation of associations, and concentrates more on the idea of civil society as an arena for critical debate amongst a range of different groups who come to have a real influence on decision taking and policy making. Sajoo, drawing on the work of Habermas, argues that the public sphere harbours, but is not identical to, organisations, institutions and social practices:

> Nebulous as this may appear, it is none the less the locus of citizen experience, interpretation and expression of opinion that is also the life-blood of civil society as a modern construct (Sajoo 2002: 5).

Chambers and Kymlicka (2002: 8) also give prominence to the public sphere, positing their interpretation of civil society as the 'site of progressive politics', through which 'a culture of inequality can be dismantled'. Finally, Edwards (2004) criticises the fact that civil society has been conflated with 'civility' and polite discussion, and privileges a space in which critical debate can take place, so as to find new meanings and new policy directions.

Civil Society Participation

For Edwards, one of the key roles of civil society is to promote, through the public sphere, a return to dialogic or participatory politics, not to limit democracy to periodic elections. The way in which civil society can promote broader democratic practices has been discussed by Gaventa (2003). He argues that participation has to be re-conceptualised as a 'right of citizenship', and that this participation goes beyond standard involvement such as voting in elections, to encompass the search for 'more direct mechanisms of ensuring citizen voice in the decision making process' (Gaventa 2003: 5). He recognises the tension between the need for representative working institutions of the state, and the demands of a mobilised civil society, but argues that 'The solution [to this tension] is not found in the separation of the civil society and good governance agendas, but in their interface' (ibid).

Spaces for participation are not neutral, however, and both Gaventa's work and that of Cornwall on which it is based (Cornwall 2002) stress the shifting nature of power within and between three types of space. These are: 1) closed spaces (where decision-making is made by élites without participation or consultation); 2) invited spaces (where citizens are invited to participate through pre-determined channels); 3) claimed/created spaces (which can be carved out by groups in civil society who mobilise in order to express their demands). Nor are these spaces static: they can be shaped and limited by internal and external power holders. For these authors, ensuring a 'level playing field' and achieving goals of participatory development must involve an analysis of power relations surrounding and operating within these spaces for participation.[2] They also note that the local, national and global 'places' of participation are in a dynamic relationship with one another. However, overall, they see these public spaces as creating 'enormous opportunities for re-defining and deepening meanings of democracy, for linking civil society and government reforms in new ways, for extending the rights of inclusive citizenship' (Gaventa 2003: 12).

---

[2] Case study material presented later on in this volume will show how often problematic issues of power dynamics have been underplayed by donors working in the Central Asian region.

Operationalising Civil Society

The analysts of the concept of civil society referenced in the preceding section are, in general, highly critical of normative approaches to civil society promotion taken by development agencies working in the developing or transition world. There has been a tendency to privilege local organisations that reflect Western assumptions as to the nature of civil society. Rejecting preconceived notions of what civil societies should look like, the authors examined here outline a more neutral public space or arena where a nation's different groupings and networks can discuss the direction they think their own development should take. But to what extent is this a non-normative idea? And how can it be put into practice?

One of the key problems in discussing issues of civil society, which is identified by all these scholars, is that the concept refers at the same time to something that exists, now, empirically, and to some future, ideal state. In many standard definitions, such as that provided at the start of this chapter, 'civil society' is described as existing between or beyond the state, the market and the family. Whilst this definition acknowledges that there is something 'out there' taking up this role, it is not a normative vision, as it carefully avoids specifying what kind of space this should be. This is the basis of INTRAC's definition, although INTRAC goes further and attaches values to the idea of civil society: ideally whatever is in this space should be concerned with social justice.[3] However, within the commentary of those examining the deficiencies of actually existing civil society, there is always an implication of the characteristics they believe it should be exhibiting instead. This trap becomes even more dangerous for those who would take on the role of civil society strengthening. However flexible one may wish to be to the needs of different groups with different agendas, those responsible for interventions must always make decisions as to the most appropriate recipients of information, training or grants: i.e. who is 'in' and who is 'out'.[4]

Clearly then, the way in which development agencies understand the idea of civil society will have an impact upon their approach to their work in practice. The following section examines some of the response by scholars of contemporary Central Asia to the approaches of Western donors' civil society strengthening projects in the region. The first of these relates to post-war political reconstruction in Tajikistan, the second to the position of 'traditional society' in relation to civil society, the third to the relation of Islam to these questions.

---

[3] Therefore, groups sometimes categorised as 'negative civil society' or 'uncivil society', such as the Mafia or terrorist organisations, would not be included.

[4] Furthermore, these interventions themselves are based on European or North American ideas of management, organisational development, networking, campaigning or service delivery.

Civil Society Promotion in Central Asia

In Central Asia, the principal source of external development aid is the United States Government, which channels funds for the region through USAID, and its primary focus is democracy promotion and market liberalisation. The main vehicle of civil society development is the NGO sector, whose progress is charted in USAID's regular 'Sustainability Index' reports. The approach of the US within the region is guided by the neo-liberal conceptualisation of civil society discussed above.

Since external donor agencies began work on civil society strengthening projects in the Central Asian region in the early 1990s, there has been growing criticism of the way in which Western 'blueprints' are being imposed upon Central Asian reality. This has included a response from the academic community, both inside and outside of the region, about the impacts of these efforts to promote particular forms of associational life. Akiner (2002) is especially critical of this approach in her overview of the potential for civil society emergence in Tajikistan. Considering the fragmentation of society, corruption and clientelism in politics, the weakness of the state and extremely high levels of poverty, Akiner believes conditions in Tajikistan are far from conducive to the emergence of civil society. Perhaps most damning of all, she writes there is 'scarcely a trace of an "emerging public" that seeks to influence official policy and shape civic life' (Akiner 2002: 183). Whilst there had been a type of Tajik Spring between 1989 and 1991, with greater public engagement in debate about the future of the nation, this, she argues, has been crushed by the events of the 1990s – most importantly, the civil war. She observes that Western-style NGOs and nascent political parties are in general irrelevant to the population as a whole and suffer from a lack of credibility. Akiner is highly critical of dominant Western conceptions of civil society, which she describes as a 'rag bag'; nonetheless she addresses each of its components in turn in order to conclude:

> Only the most superficial similarities to any Western theoretical postulates are to be found, hence this is surely an inappropriate analytical category ... To insist upon the application of such a framework leads to distortion and self-delusion (Akiner 2002: 185).

Akiner does not, however, see models of civil society developed by Muslim thinkers as significantly more useful than Western ones, considering the extremely limited knowledge of Islam of the majority of the population after 60 years of Soviet rule. For Akiner, it would be more appropriate to look for signs of the re-emergence of social and ethical responsibility. She would also see hope in spontaneous grass-roots initiatives and in manifestations of community empowerment (as

13

instanced in the work of the Aga Khan Foundation) which 'would permit genuine societal healing and recovery to take place' (Akiner 2002: 185). As she sees it, however, attempts of external donors to create civil society have limited meaning for Tajiks, and have done little to address the symptoms of social disintegration in the country.

Olivier Roy, another expert on society in the region, although critical of the concept, does not go so far as to question its validity entirely. He does, however, take issue with the very narrow definition of civil society often employed by external donors. Particularly in the early years of intervention, there was an implicit understanding that civil society would be manifested by NGO-type organisations. In a region where associations had been controlled through the Communist party, these were non-existent. However, as Roy argues, it was a mistake to interpret a lack of autonomous, voluntary bodies as synonymous with a lack of civil society. His own work analyses the former state and collective farms, where he notes dense networks of patronage and family ties that predated the Soviet era and continued to function even after the Soviet system of collective agriculture was forced upon them. Indeed, Roy argues, the very complementarity of these two modes of social organisation helped the traditional networks to thrive. Unlike Akiner, rather than reject Western ideas of civil society as inappropriate, he warns those working in Central Asia that, 'the concept of civil society should not ignore a traditional ... social fabric' (Roy 1999: 110).

Developing his arguments in a later article, Roy posits 'traditional society' based on kinship and patronage that allow people to resist the encroachment of the state as a conceptualisation of Central Asian civil society that is clearly set apart from the 'notion of networks of free citizens – professional associations, unions, political parties, public interest groups – that create political space as a prerequisite for building democracy and the rule of law' (Roy 2002: 123). The latter he asserts is pursued by external aid agencies and their 'indigenous subsidiaries' (externally funded NGOs) in the region, and is regarded by local people as:

> an abstract and idealised paradigm that stems from modern Western experiences, which have resulted from historical processes that spanned centuries (ibid: 124).

The criticism here is that external donors are attempting to impose this civil society blueprint in a matter of years. The author notes that those who rely entirely on Western ideas of political and economic freedom tend to believe that civil society in Central Asia will have to be created from scratch,

> either because there is nothing of value today upon which to build (the entire Soviet legacy being cast as negative) – or because there is no such thing as a

traditional society in Central Asia, owing to the onslaught of the Soviet system on previous social structures (ibid: 125).

Whilst such views already seem extreme and many donors do now acknowledge 'indigenous' forms of social organisation, there are still examples of research undertaken by USAID-funded international NGOs working in Central Asia that set out to 'prove' that citizens are not involved in any type of publicly orientated associational activity.[5] In summary, Roy argues that the efforts of external donors to promote civil society will ultimately fail in Central Asia, if they continue to work only with a small cadre of educated NGO workers who are isolated from the rest of their compatriots.

In her analysis of civil society in Tajikistan and Uzbekistan, Freizer (2004) also takes up the discussion of traditional networks and kinship groups, and argues for a reconceptualisation of civil society that will encompass these types of institutions and practices. This leads her to put forward the idea of a 'communal' civil society that reflects patterns of social relations in the region better than neo-liberal, Western models. The communal understanding of civil society has more to do with interactions within communities, than with state–society relations. Whilst acknowledging the arguments of Gellner (1994) that a civil society based on kinship can promote one group at the expense of another, Freizer argues that 'in Tajikistan and Uzbekistan kinship served as an important mobilizing factor through which individuals were able to express and defend their common interests'. She goes on to explain the importance of institutions such as the *mahalla* and *avlod* in providing social protection to members and resolving community problems.

A further key area of debate revolves around the promotion of Western ideas of civil society in a region where the main religion is Islam. Whilst it is generally accepted that Islam, in Central Asia, is very different from the more fundamental forms found in countries further South and West, the debate about civil society in the Muslim world is still relevant here. During the Soviet period, Islamic traditions were periodically fostered, then opposed and finally accommodated in a reduced and modified form. This has had an impact on the practice and influence of Islam today, as has the more recent emergence of some radical Islamic political groups across the region and the role of Islamic opposition in the Tajik Civil War.

Islam itself promotes certain organisational and associational forms, and there are also important Muslim traditions of philanthropy and charitable donations. Some commentators believe, however, that the hierarchical structure of Islamic societies, particularly in non-secular states and prevailing authoritarian tendencies, precludes the development of any true civil society (Kramer 2002). Others from

---

[5] For more detail see Earle's discussion of CHF's Community Development Assessment in Earle 2004a.

within the Muslim world reject outright the values associated with Western ideas of civil society (Mardin 1995) and promote a 'religious civil society' in which citizens would return to the true tenets of Islam. But these scholars are also divided as to the model of Islamic civil society upon which they would base this return (Arkoun 2002). Further, whilst some analysts believe that Western notions of civil society fit with the fundamental basis of Islam (Hanafi 2002), this is contradicted by those who state that non-voluntary membership of a certain group as a result of inherited identity cannot be equated with the associational activity of civil society (Edwards 2004: 30).

The paragraphs above lay out three important characteristics of Central Asian society that problematise the imposition of 'Western-style' ideas of civil society. First, the authoritarian nature of government (and in Tajikistan the legacy of civil war) which hinders involvement in the public sphere; second, the existence of a complex web of social relations based upon kinship and patronage which Western formulations are likely to overlook; and third, the potential clash between Western and Islamic values as to the nature of a good society. A fourth set of characteristics relates to the region's Soviet heritage and the transition towards capitalism which followed it. As will be shown in later chapters, a major influence on the development of civil society in the countries of Central Asia is their common history as part of the Soviet Union. From the 1920s onwards, throughout Central Asia and the rest of the former Soviet Union, a vertical structure of administration was developed and a process of centralised economic planning evolved. The tribes in northern Central Asia were forcibly settled during the 1920s, and collective or state farms established. This rapid process of modernisation, accompanied by the introduction – over a period of time – of universal education, a comprehensive health service and guaranteed employment resulted in new organisational forms, the influence of which is still felt today across the region.

Civil Society in Transition

As the discussion of the last section has suggested, much of the work of international development agencies in the Central Asian states during the 1990s drew heavily on the neo-liberal understanding of the nature and role of civil society. We would argue that the approach taken during this time, particularly by USAID-funded agencies, privileged the promotion of Western-style NGOs and, as a result, failed to give adequate attention to the cultural and institutional legacy of Soviet and pre-Soviet eras, that is crucial to the evolution of civil society in the region. Furthermore, the critical importance of the public sphere and the potential for citizens' participation in decision-making processes that affect their lives was overlooked in the drive to foster the growth of NGOs and associations.

Many of the economic reforms carried out in countries of the Former Soviet Union after independence, supposedly to lead from a centrally planned authoritarian state to a market economy with a democratic form of governance, were implemented in a flurry of donor optimism. Most early civil society support programmes were similarly over-optimistic. Funded by the USA or by the large multi-lateral donors, they were directed at giving support to pressure groups emerging around specific issues, such as the environment or open media. As will be shown, the availability of funds for such groups encouraged more, similar groups, to emerge. Most of these early groups were urban-based, very often set up and staffed by well-educated professionals – many of whom had suddenly found themselves unemployed or underemployed. Some were organisations which had existed during Soviet times and which now re-invented themselves in order to operate within the new environment. However, funding for civil society groups tended to favour groups that met Western expectations. Being largely urban-based, and staffed by 'experts' in a particular field, few of these groups had much contact with the poor. The result: by the end of the 1990s many NGOs with which organisations like INTRAC worked in Central Asia seemed to have very little contact with their so-called target groups.

The example of Central Asia illustrates the criticism that has been levelled against Putnam's enthusiasm for associational groups, and his argument that high levels of such activity automatically lead to the deepening of democracy. His theory has been loudly criticised by a number of scholars for a blinkered approach that fails to look at external influences and structural factors that affect levels of association, plus issues of inequality within civil society itself that impact upon whether or not people are able to use social assets to improve their situation. It also assumes that the social capital created as a result of associational activity will necessarily be used for the benefit of wider society, while empirical studies have shown that this is not necessarily the case. Furthermore, it ignores the crucial question of what type of association should be included in civil society, what these organisations should set out to achieve and how they can contribute to development.

Rather than stress a civil society strengthening agenda, other agencies, such as UNDP and the World Bank, put more emphasis on combating poverty in their approach to their work in the region, although they have also expressed their commitment to the potential of civil society. For these agencies, the engagement of civil society is key to goals of poverty reduction and greater equality. Their work on both poverty and civil society issues can be seen in community-level programming such as the World Bank's Community Driven Development and the village level components of UNDP's Social Governance Programme (discussed in Chapter 7). However, as this book will show, these institutions can have a tendency to stress the instrumental role and function of civil society groups. Western-style organisations have appeared or have been created that are able to function as vehicles for funding for poverty reduction, conflict prevention and public education. In many cases, and certainly in the early years of development interventions, existing organisations were overlooked and the potential for achieving empowerment or voice through membership of these organisations was not prioritised.

Since the late 1990s, donors have broadened their understanding of civil society, to incorporate different sorts of actors and groupings, including traditional local institutions and practices. However, this book will argue that efforts to empower populations through community mobilisation and involvement in civil society organisations are still limited. It should be acknowledged that debates on civil society participation within the public sphere are fairly new, particularly to Central Asia. Even so, there are examples of positive steps towards the consolidation of civil society as an arena for critical debate and the discussion of alternative development routes.

Whilst the notion of civil society, and the need to strengthen it, has been adopted by both the large multi-lateral / bi-lateral donors and by international development NGOs, it is important to stress here that not all agencies take an instrumental, neo-liberal approach to this type of work. Traditionally, certain INGOs have worked with associations and groups in order to promote more equitable forms of development. There are also more radical groups at work in the region who have an 'alternative' vision of the role and nature of civil society. However, we would argue that their influence and outreach is minimal compared to the interventions of the US Government and the multi-lateral institutions that follow a narrow and simplistic interpretation of civil society and promote the formation of Western-style associations.

Considering these problems of definition, and of transferability, should the concept of civil society be abandoned in Central Asia altogether? We would argue that for those concerned with development, the concept of civil society can be a useful tool for thinking about the potential for participatory democracy, poverty reduction and greater social justice. In particular, the idea of the public sphere could be key to both formulating and achieving these developmental aims. In countries where poverty and social inequality are increasing, it is not just the forms in which people come together to address their problems that is important, but what actually goes on within these associations. Civil society organisations in Central Asia need to become articulators of people's needs and interests and to make an impact beyond their immediate constituency, to voice the interests and concerns of their members and supporters, within the public sphere.

Outline and Aim of this Book

This book will argue that in order to understand fully how civil society is developing currently in Central Asia, it is crucial to have a broad conception of society, social relations, institutions and practices that have been influential historically. We argue that far from being a 'blank slate' at the time of independence, Central Asia has a rich and complex social fabric that has been built up through centuries of interaction between different ethnic groups. Whilst many external agencies have pushed the neo-liberal agenda in terms of civil society promotion, this book will show how an appreciation of the alternative vision of civil society can aid a more in-depth understanding of the development of the sector.

The idea behind the original research project upon which this book is based was to take a broader view, both of the constituent elements of civil society in Central Asia and of its role, and to gather empirical data that would provide an insight into the complexities and dynamics of civil society emergence in the region. The nuances of the research reports are discussed in **Chapter 2**. Throughout the book, we stress the importance of the need to understand the way in which the region's specific cultures and contexts will impact upon civil society emergence and **Chapter 3** provides a brief introduction and analysis of each country in turn. Above all, this book attempts to redress the balance of external agencies' focus on the non-governmental sector by examining in detail the different influences that the authors believe have shaped the civil society sector as it is evolving in the region. As a result, this publication, while it charts the emergence of Western-style organisations, also gives equal weight to pre-Soviet and Soviet practices and institutions and provides empirical evidence of their continued importance and influence. **Chapter 4** examines some of the institutions and practices that shaped and organised Central Asian societies prior to colonisation by the Russian empire. It provides empirical case study material of how these continue to be important for civil society promotion today and the challenges that 'tradition' can face for those who would promote participatory democracy and gender equality. **Chapter 5** examines Soviet era institutions and again shows how their historical influence and continued familiarity makes them an important element of post-independent Central Asian civil society. **Chapters 6** and **7** discuss new developments since independence, charting the emergence of and support for NGO-type organisations during the 1990s and the newer focus of external donors on community-based organisations. **Chapter 8** looks at civil society relations with government and the state, and uses the analytical framework on ideas of public space set out by Gaventa and discussed above to review examples of civil society–state collaboration and confrontation. The book ends with a conclusion that sums up the lessons learnt from the research process and from INTRAC's experience of capacity building for civil society strengthening in the Central Asian region.

CHAPTER 2

The Research Reports

INTRAC's Involvement in Central Asia

The first chapter of this volume set out some of the arguments against the promotion of civil society that follows narrow, Western understandings of the concept and uses simplistic formulae for putting this into practice. However, it should be acknowledged that this is an easy trap to fall into. INTRAC's own understanding of civil society and its work in the region has changed and matured considerably over the past decade.

INTRAC's involvement in Central Asia began in 1994 with an invitation from UNV/UNDP to design a community-based poverty alleviation programme for Kyrgyzstan. As a result of this process, INTRAC came to the conclusion that there were very few viable structures through which international agencies could work. This was at variance with the assumption of the multi-lateral agencies that, with the collapse of the old state structures, local NGOs would be automatically able to provide a new safety net for vulnerable populations. INTRAC believed that this situation could not be rectified without considerable input to the nascent NGO sector.

As a direct result of this initial involvement, between 1994 and 1997, INTRAC worked with NGOSOs and NGOs in Kazakhstan and Kyrgyzstan to provide capacity building in organisational development, strategic planning, small enterprise development, PRA and other institutional support. It also fostered the early development of co-ordination bodies, bringing together representatives of the sector from across the region. However, an internal review of the work after two years showed that organisational development and capacity building would only allow limited development of the NGO sector while the environment remained unsupportive (Pratt and Goodhand 1996). So INTRAC decided to become more deeply involved in institutional development of the sector as a whole, rather than capacity building of individual organisations.

Between 1997 and 2001 INTRAC's focus shifted to a programme that undertook multiple strategic approaches to assist with the institutional development of civil society in Kyrgyzstan, Kazakhstan, Tajikistan and Uzbekistan. This still maintained a focus on NGOs and set as its aim a contribution to the process of democratic transition through support for the emergence of a vibrant, effective and independent non-governmental sector in the region. This programme evolved into a second phase from 2001 onwards, which encompassed a greater number of actors within civil society and increased its focus on grass-roots organisations, traditional institutions and community development. As the current phase draws to a close, INTRAC is looking to work more closely with civil society organisations that engage with government and with policy processes at all levels, so as to bring the demands of their stakeholders into the wider public sphere.

The Research Project

The decision to undertake the research upon which this book is based came about as a result of the realisation within INTRAC that a broader understanding of the nature and potential of the civil society sector in Central Asia was needed. The aim of the research was to take a step back from programme work, and the concerns of donors and NGOs, so as to engage in a reflection of what was actually happening in the region with regards to the wider civil society sector.

Studies which aim to describe or measure the level of development of civil society can adopt either a normative approach, or an empirical one. Most analyses and classifications of civil society groups in Central Asia and other parts of the world tend to adopt a normative view about what constitutes civil society. For instance, the Comparative Non-profit Sector Project at the Johns Hopkins University Centre for Civil Society Studies 'undertakes studies of civil society using five basic criteria to evaluate possible civil organisations: formally constituted; private; non profit-distributing; self governing; voluntary'. The aim of the Centre is to generate data on the nature and level of civil society in different countries across the world, to compare this data and test theories about the differences identified.[1] This focus reflects much of the recent theoretical work on civil society that has emerged from the United States, and its particular ideological take on what constitutes a healthy civil society.

---

[1] www.jhu.edu/~cnp accessed June 2004.

The generally accepted, normative, view of civil society organisations that is reflected in much of the research in the region was discussed in the previous chapter. To recap: there is a space referred to as civil society which is located between the state and the market, and which is important in a democracy in that it can counter both the powers of the state and the market and can hold them accountable for their policies and activities. This view holds that civil society needs to be independent and separate from the state and the market and that it should consist of a plurality of groups that represent the interests of their membership in public debate. By implication, there are certain groups in civil society which are considered more civil than others and which development practitioners will identify as being appropriate to work with. Research work that takes this approach would most likely set out to locate groups that fit these criteria and identify what types of body are 'missing'. This type of investigation is therefore both influenced by, and reinforces a certain perception of civil society, its component parts and its role.

A different approach to research on civil society would involve undertaking a more empirical style investigation in order to determine what types of associational form exist or are emerging or re-emerging in a given country. This approach should tend towards 'thick description' and should avoid judgement about what civil society should look like. It is of course practically impossible to take a non-normative approach to research of this kind, as some boundaries have to be placed around the conceptualisation of civil society. However, this approach would recognise the validity and importance of a much broader set of associations, including those, for example, that might represent the interests of just one particular group of people. Whilst the research might then make some judgement about whether these groups' aims or ways of working accord with an understanding of civil society based upon the goals of social justice, the starting point of an empirical study would be to observe, at a basic level, how the different groups function. This approach would recognise that some of these may work with the state and/or market; i.e. that there may not be clear boundaries between the state, market and civil society, so strictly defined by some theorists.

This latter approach may concentrate more on interpreting the notion of civil society as the existence of a public space, and the recognition of the importance of this space as an intermediate area between the state and the market, where people can meet, discuss and engage in public initiatives. This interpretation is more focused on the emergence of associational activity, and what those involved in activities actually do, and less concerned with organisational form or the strict boundaries between these associations and the state or market. As Manor et al. (1999) have noted,

The idea of civil society in liberal democratic discourse is linked to certain intrinsic characteristics, notably voluntary participation, and separation and autonomy from the state. Social organisations in the real world only embody these characteristics to varying degrees: the boundaries between state and civil society are often blurred, the two organisational spheres may overlap and individuals may play roles in both sectors. ... In brief, the extent to which a specific civic organisation embodies the defining qualities of 'civil society' – separation, autonomy and voluntariness – is a question of degree rather than either or (Manor et al. 1999: 5–6).

Developing their argument, these commentators note that the nature of civil society can be expected to vary considerably between countries, and that groups of civil society actors are likely to have diverse ethical and political characteristics. They conclude that it would be wrong to assume that 'civil society is virtuous by definition, or that it contains an intrinsic potential for contributing to better governance' (ibid: 7).

INTRAC's aim was to unravel and expose the nuances of civil society development in Central Asia, along the lines set out by Manor et al. above. It was therefore planned that INTRAC would take an empirical approach to the research and would thereby contribute to a greater understanding of the dynamics and emergence of the civil society sector in Central Asia. The intended empirical nature of the project was reflected in the use of the term 'mapping': to record types of associations that could be seen to be emerging and functioning, rather than search for institutions that fitted the criteria of some previously formulated ideal.

The other aim of the research project was to build the capacity of local research institutes and NGOs in social research and analysis. This constituted a particular challenge: to encourage the adoption of qualitative social research methodologies and to promote a flexible attitude to the type of institutions, organisations and practices that could be considered to be part of an emerging civil society. As the research project progressed, it became clear that the mainstream concept of civil society outlined above, that privileges the idea of voluntary Western-style organisations in the model of NGOs, had become fairly standardised. This normative approach has dominated the literature and classification systems of many of the international organisations funding development work in Central Asia, and has been widely accepted as a definition of 'civil society'. This emerged most clearly in the contributions of local NGOs who were involved in the participatory components of the research methodology. It should be emphasised that the ideas and debates on civil society introduced to the Former Soviet Union in the 1990s were very new, and very enthusiastically received. The INTRAC research reports give a very useful insight into how these understandings of civil society have been adopted locally. The reports also provide an introduction to pre-Soviet and Soviet period associations and practices and give rich detail of the organisational forms that have recently appeared in Central Asia.

The Research Reports

As part of this investigation into civil society development in Central Asia, four studies were undertaken by groups of local researchers in Kazakhstan, Kyrgyzstan, Tajikistan and Uzbekistan. At the time the research project was conceived, INTRAC felt that the political situation in Turkmenistan would preclude participatory research and the undertaking of a mapping of civil society development in the country. Since that time INTRAC has built up a network of partners and associates in the country. This publication is thus able to draw upon reports and situational analyses written up by INTRAC's Central Asia Programme staff after visits to Turkmenistan.

All the local studies involved literature reviews, and then data collection through questionnaires, visits to key organisations, interviews and focus groups on particular topics. In both Kyrgyzstan and Kazakhstan, conferences were organised to share and discuss the findings of the studies. In Uzbekistan, extended round-table meetings were held in Tashkent and Nukus (capital of the Karakalpak autonomous republic). These findings, and the discussions they provoked, provide some of the basic material that makes up this book. However, much of the literature accessed by researchers on civil society developments has a rather narrow interpretation of the concept of civil society since it was produced in the early phase of international donor interest in strengthening civil society in these countries. As these ideas were so new, this first phase was characterised by the seeking out, funding and training of independent, pluralist-type interest groups.[2] This focus has had an impact on the way in which the researchers in INTRAC's study gathered and analysed their material. In general, they saw it as their task to focus on NGOs. They clearly regarded the ideas, effects and formations from the Soviet period as highly significant, but were unsure how to place or judge them; and they gave relatively little space to pre-Soviet forms of civil society. The research studies had an important impact on INTRAC's work in the region and are best read in conjunction with the learning generated by eight years of its programme work in Central Asia, and with information and views from other pieces of research and consultancy within the umbrella of INTRAC's DFID-funded Central Asia Programme (ICAP).

In Kazakhstan, Kyrgyzstan and Uzbekistan, a sample of civil society organisations was taken from the data on public associations held in the record offices of the Ministry of Justice or the Department of Statistics. This was supplemented from records on civil society groups held by some of the larger NGO support

---

[2] The extent to which this narrow view of civil society is now being revised will be examined in subsequent chapters.

organisations, to ensure that some non-registered groups were included. Questionnaires, designed in each case by the local researchers – and therefore different according to country – were sent out to a sample of organisations. Whilst a standardised methodology employed across the four countries would have facilitated comparison of data, in order to develop local research capacity the research teams were encouraged to devise their own locally appropriate data collection methods. In Kyrgyzstan and Uzbekistan, visits were made to other *oblast* (regional) centres, where interviews were conducted with a selection of organisations. Focus groups were organised to discuss issues around the meaning of civil society and its development in the country[3] and workshops were also held to feed back preliminary results to facilitators and research participants. In Tajikistan, interviews were held with key respondents in the sector, and in-depth case studies were produced of the development of civil society groups in three *oblasts* of the country.

The questionnaires posed quite general questions about the nature of civil society organisations, asking the respondents to name organisations they knew about and what areas of work these organisations were involved in, for example. The Kazakh questionnaire was sent out to students at the research institute where the study was being undertaken, a selection of residents in Almaty (the major city and former capital of Kazakhstan), and a selection of NGOs both in Almaty and in the regions. The response rate from the regions was very low. The questionnaire in Kyrgyzstan was targeted at staff of NGOs and other civil society organisations. It asked questions about the mission of the organisations, its areas of activity, financial sustainability, relationships with both private and public sectors, in addition to asking general questions about what was understood by the term 'civil society'.

Whilst the Kazakh and Kyrgyz studies concentrated on NGO-type organisations that the researchers identified as being part of the civil society sector, the Uzbek researchers took a broader view. This was perhaps due to the fact that the NGO sector is much newer and smaller in Uzbekistan than in its neighbouring states. This study took the Ministry of Justice's classification of organisations as its starting point (discussed in more detail below) and then selected organisations from each category across the country.[4] Questionnaires were sent out and inter-

---

[3] The Kazakh and Kyrgyz researchers spent time trying to find a 'universal definition of civil society', and, finding this difficult, decided – as part of the studies – to ask people their views. This was done by questionnaire in Kazakhstan, and by interviewing random people in the street in Kyrgyzstan.

[4] One settlement was selected in each of the following five regions of Uzbekistan, (two from the Southern region): Aral Sea Region; Nukus city; Tashkent Region, Tashkent; Ferghana Valley Region, Kokand; Central Region, Samarkand; Southern Region, Termez and Karshi.

views conducted with these selected groups. The questionnaire had 82 questions, 63 of which were 'various indicators and judgements about the status of the third sector in the country'. (Abdullaev et al. 2003: 7). These general questions were structured around the Civil Society Index (CSI), an analytical framework which attempts to measure the level of development of civil society by structuring a series of questions around four dimensions of civil society.[5] These are explained in more detail below.

In Tajikistan, as in Kazakhstan and Kyrgyzstan, the study focused mainly on the developing NGO sector, with some reference to the old-style public associations, particularly those that have adapted themselves to the new environment. It was less systematic in its attempts to get a broad cross-section of opinions from representative organisations, concentrating instead on key informants and specialists.

Thus, the studies conducted specifically as part of this project were very different in their approaches, this reflecting local experience, expertise and priorities for research skills development. The following sections examine each of the four reports in turn and look at some of the issues raised by the different approaches to the research process and the understanding of 'civil society'. A deeper analysis of findings and presentation of case study material will inform subsequent chapters of this book.

The Kyrgyzstan Mapping Report

The research work that fed into this report was undertaken by a consortium of Kyrgyz NGOs. Perhaps as a result, in its mapping of the civil society sector in the country, it gives an emphasis to organisations that have emerged since independence that call themselves NGOs. In the initial stages of the research, questionnaires on the issue of civil society were sent, in the main, to the staff of other NGOs, who were contacted through the use of databases drawn up by national and international NGOs. The majority of case studies are also drawn from the work of NGOs and the term is sometimes used interchangeably with 'CSO' (civil society organisation). Indeed, the authors state that NGOs and community-based organisations (CBOs) are the 'main elements of civil society in Kyrgyzstan' (Baimatov et al. 2002: 39). The report has a strong emphasis on what it calls 'institutionalised activities', by which it means the projects and programmes of NGOs. This is reflected in the definition of civil society used:

---

[5] This index was developed by CIVICUS (the World Alliance for Citizen Participation) and has been piloted in 13 countries. Since the Uzbek study, the methodology has been modified.

> Civil society refers to those organizations that exist between the level of the
> family and the state and which enjoy a degree of autonomy from the state and
> the market (Baimatov et al. 2003: 31).

The use of the word 'organizations' in this definition is particularly telling, rather
than a reference to a more general 'space' between the state and market. The
authors do not expand upon this definition themselves, but do include quotations
from a number of NGO staff who responded to their questionnaire.
Overwhelmingly, these responses refer to associational life set apart from the state
and market. The implication is that these organisations exist in order to contribute
to a pluralistic society and that the term 'civil society' is equivalent to 'organisations', preferably non-governmental ones. This we can infer from the researchers'
statement that, amongst members of the public interviewed in the street,

> The level of understanding of the concept of the Civil Society is quite low. The
> survey showed that the phenomenon of NGOs or other elements of Civil
> Society like professional associations and other groupings of concerned/inter-
> est citizens ... were not familiar to over half the people surveyed (ibid: 35).

The authors do not specify clearly what they believe the overall goal of civil society to be, although they do comment on 'uncivic' society, and argue that certain
types of organisation should be excluded from definitions of civil society. One of
the questions put to NGO staff members in the questionnaire was, 'What is civil
society?' A number of responses are recorded in the report, but only a couple of
these make reference to the idea that civil society organisations can be vehicles for
representation of people's interests or the expression of their ideas and opinions.
Whilst other NGO respondents may well have echoed these interpretations, the
emphasis given by the authors of the report is to those who referred to civil society as plurality of organisational forms. Interestingly, members of the public interviewed on the street brought up issues relating to Edwards' (2004) idea of the
'good society' and the public sphere in that they referred to free debate of issues
pertinent to the country as a whole, the expression of the interests of the people,
protection of human rights, fulfilment of rights enshrined in the constitution, and
the ideal of a peaceful, non-militarised society.

A number of passages in the report (Baimatov et al. 2002) provide evidence to
back up Olivier Roy's (Roy 2002) criticism of the tendency to impose Western
norms on Central Asian reality. For example, the authors state that 'Civil society
was born in Kyrgyzstan following independence' and that 'The Soviet system
denied the very idea of participatory civil society and stifled any conditions for its
emergence'. Furthermore, the authors regard traditional and clan-based society as
backward and an impediment to 'the formation of prerequisites for a modern and

pluralistic civil society'.[6] Finally, they affirm that an indicator for the development of the sector in Kyrgyzstan can be seen in 'the growing sense of common social identity among NGO and CBO members' and the fact that they are able to use concepts such as 'participatory development' and 'monitoring and evaluation'. This echoes Roy's argument that there is a tendency for those in the sector to exclude outsiders, with their use of 'development speak' and donor terminology.

Further evidence of a normative driven approach to the research can be found in the authors' preliminary conclusions, in which they set out a definition of CSOs elaborated by Alan Fowler (1997) in order to measure Kyrgyz organisations against it:

> Fowler notes three sets of purposes [of CSOS]: 1) to protect and regulate the lives and actions of citizens, that is to manage how society is defended as well as how it functions and progresses; 2) to ensure people livelihoods as well as creating and accumulating wealth; and 3) to pursue personal or social interests, beliefs and personal concerns. In the Kyrgyz Republic, Civil Society Organisations took not only the third role but [are] also playing the second role too (Baimatov et al. 2002: 26).

This is a reflection of Akiner's (2002) complaint: that so often attempts are made to make local contexts fit externally developed criteria of civil society, rather than critique the applicability of Western models for non-Western countries and generate new understandings of how civil societies might evolve. Interesting examples are given of Soviet era associations and their subsequent development, but without a discussion of what this implies for our understanding of civil society in the pre-independence period. By contrast, much less is said about pre-Soviet forms of social organisation and mutual help, despite the implications that these will have for contemporary development of civil society.

However, a more nuanced understanding of the value of organisations within civil society does emerge in the rest of the text, belying the simplistic definition of the term presented to the reader. Before any definition is given, in the opening sections of the report, much is made of the role that civil society has been playing in the Kyrgyz Republic since independence in social and political life. The political arena is given particular emphasis. Indeed, according to the authors, the political system in the country includes NGOs and CBOs as well as political parties. In response to claims that political life in the country is restricted and characterised by passive attitudes, the authors point out that CSOs have been emerging and have

---

[6] Interestingly, later on in the report in their discussion of NGOs, the authors briefly mention both Soviet and traditional forms of mutual aid and community mutual assistance and acknowledge their value.

been involved in national election processes. This they see as a contribution towards the growth of democracy:

> It is an absolutely new tradition, for example, to involve CSOs into discussion of significant political and economic programmes. New participatory approaches are becoming part of the political culture, thus making for a more profitable political environment for all players (Baimatov et al. 2002: 14).

The report does not provide much detail of the way in which civil society organisations have been involved in political decision-making, although there is discussion of their role in the consultation phase of the Comprehensive Development Framework, and on lobbying during the elaboration of a law that would regulate activities of NGOs. However, they believe that the role of civil society is 'soaring' and that, in particular, NGOs and CBOs are playing a 'significant role in domestic affairs' (ibid: 39).

The conclusions reached by the authors may be queried by other less enthusiastic observers of the Kyrgyz reality. However, it is clear from the authors' emphasis that they believe interaction with government and above all, recognition by the authorities, to be key indicators of the emergence of civil society in the country. The question remains, however, as to what ends the authors believe this type of recognition could lead. It could simply be for recognition in itself, and the creation of a pluralistic society made up of a varied group of organisations. Or, recognition of the sector could help to ensure an environment that facilitates the establishment of more such organisations. Or, this recognition could be an attempt to value the aims of all civil society's constituent parts and be the catalyst for a 'public sphere' in which the aims of these organisations could be articulated in order to establish developmental goals and policy directions for the country and its disadvantaged populations.

In sum, the Kyrgyz report is somewhat limited by the definition of civil society the authors impose upon themselves, and their decision to focus upon formally recognised institutions. So, whilst they mention other associational forms within civil society, such as *aksakals'* councils and a variety of traditional practices, these are excluded from further analysis. Instead, NGOs are privileged. In hindsight it is easy to criticise this approach as normative and incomplete, but it is illustrative of the focus of many in the sector working in Central Asia. Furthermore, this focus has generated a great deal of rich case study material documenting the formation and activities of a large number of new organisations that have emerged since independence. It gives the reader a picture of the types of social problems Central Asian people are most concerned about and wish to address, as well as identifying the initiatives that have been attractive to external donors.

The Kazakh Mapping Report

This report was drawn up by staff members of KIMEP, the Kazakhstan Institute of Management, Economics and Strategic Research under the President of the Republic of Kazakhstan. Although this is nominally a government body, judging by the content of the report, it appears that the Institute is able to be critical of the political climate and of the President himself in the presentation of its research findings.

In their methodology section early on in the report, the researchers set out the questions to be answered in the process of the research. The first of these was, 'Does civil society exist in Kazakhstan?' This could potentially have provoked a very interesting and broad investigation into the ways in which people in Kazakhstan mobilise around their interests and interact with each other and in the wider public sphere. It would also have allowed for a discussion of the extent to which different understandings of civil society were applicable to the Kazakh context. However, this type of broad investigation was precluded by the other research questions listed that instantly evoked the 'three sector model', with references to relationships with the state and business. The researchers' survey questionnaire was further weighted towards this type of model in its request for the identification of 'organisations, agencies and institutions that constitute civil society'.

However, compared with the Kyrgyz report, the Kazakh mapping does claim to set out with wider aims in its investigation of the development of civil society in the country. For example, the importance of identifying 'interaction patterns, links and cooperation between civil society organizations and government, business, as well as donor organizations' is acknowledged. The researchers also set out their aim to examine issues of internal sustainability and management of organisations within civil society as well as their interaction with target groups, as an indicator of the development of the sector (reflecting, perhaps, the business studies background of the researchers).

Interestingly, in the section on the existence of civil society in the context of Kazakhstan, the researchers state,

To commonly apply Western definitions of Civil Society to Kazakhstan forces the scholar to the sole conclusion that Civil Society does not exist (Dissenova et al. 2002: 21).

This, they argue, citing works by Kangas (1995) and Carley (1995), is because of the historical legacies that have shaped Kazakh society: the Soviet system and the continued importance of tribalism and ethnic loyalties. Kangas argues that both of these influences 'repudiated a civil society'. For these two writers, the current political climate in the country is a further hindrance to the development of civil

31

society, in that it is riddled with corruption and clientelism running along ethnic lines, and ruled over by an authoritarian President who continues to strengthen his hold on power.

However, passages in the rest of the report suggest that the researchers are not in full agreement with the argument of these writers that the legacy of Soviet and pre-Soviet times excludes the potential development of civil society. Indeed, the report contains some interesting discussion of what they call the 'NGO prototype' that emerged during *perestroika*, and of earlier awakenings of political consciousness and muted forms of resistance towards the Soviet system. As for traditional forms of social organisation, it also asks,

> Do tribalism and ethnic loyalties need to be destroyed? Could they in them-selves constitute a basic foundation for the formation of a unique Kazakh Civil Society? (Dissenova et al. 2002: 21).

The contradictions within the text, as to the possibility of building up a democrat-ic, just society through associations of citizens under an authoritarian government and in a clan-based social system, serve to highlight the difficulties inherent in working with civil society in contemporary Kazakhstan and the region as a whole. For whilst they state that the Government has done little to assist the sector, the researchers also note that,

> The major source and initiator of transformations is state power, and it guar-antees the sovereignty and safety of the society. Non-governmental institutions have to accommodate themselves to the dominating role of the state. It is important to find effective means of interaction between the state and the non-governmental organisations (Dissenova et al. 2002: 22).

They go on to argue, echoing some of the neo-liberal arguments examined in Chapter 1, that democracy can be promoted by the strength of civil society, thus implicitly rejecting the statements of Kangas and Carley, and indeed Akiner (2002), that democracy is a prerequisite for a flourishing civil society.

The problematic relationship between authoritarian state and a newly emerging civil society is one that reappears throughout the report. Overall, however, the impression that the reader receives is that the authors support the idea of civil soci-ety as service provider and problem solver. The chapter of the report on the con-text of Kazakhstan enumerates many of the problems the country faces that have been growing since independence, in health care, education, crime, drug abuse, poverty, freedom of speech and the building of national identity. At the end of each section, the power of NGOs to address each of these issues is evoked. The idea of the NGO as problem solver is further developed in the examination of civil society and state relations. Above all, the researchers speak of co-operation. According to them,

> The progress in co-operation is always notable in a few cases when an NGO manages to take on and fulfil some functions of the related government bodies (Dissenova et al. 2002: 34).

Co-operation then is understood in terms of contracting of service provision to the NGO sector. Within this type of relationship, the idea of civil society as a potential challenge to the dominance of the state is removed. Indeed, it is noted that none of the responses to the original questionnaires on the nature of civil society posed civil society in opposition to the centralised, authoritarian Government. The researchers do not question why these organisations would enter into this type of compliant relationship or what benefits they might accrue.

But despite the position laid out above, the report, in a somewhat contradictory manner, also measures the maturity of the sector by its new ability to lobby at government level. This is seen as evidence of the progress of NGOs and a number of successes are noted with regards to legislation concerning the sector itself and to the activities of environmental and women's NGOs that have advocacy campaigns.

This ambiguity is also reflected in the report's examination of civil society and business sector relations. Whilst the activities of oil companies are seen to be detrimental to the development of civil society, in that they are more concerned with maintaining political stability in the country than supporting organisations to promote change, later on in the report the researchers stress the importance of establishing joint projects between the two sectors. Power relations and their potential impact are glossed over, as they are, most notably of all, in the discussion of NGO relations with their donors, which are described as 'positive partnership links'. The issue of partnerships and state-society linkages has been acknowledged as a crucial precondition for effective development.

The discussion of the report here has focused on NGOs, and indeed, despite the evocation of the potential for a unique Kazakh civil society, by page 7 of the report, the term CSO has been replaced by NGO. The researchers claim, in the section devoted to the concept of civil society in Kazakhstan, that they will use the 'most general definition of the term' civil society in order to examine a broad range of organisational forms, including 'informal and perhaps illegal organisations that permeate the substructure of Kazakh society', that might be overlooked by a more rigid definition of the term. Indeed, the report gives space for an explanation of the recent development of political parties and of the problems facing the trade union federations. It also provides a short discussion of religious organisations, including foreign-based religious activity in Kazakhstan, and the Government response to this. However, in spite of the outright rejection of Western definitions of civil society noted above, the report in fact devotes the majority of its pages to discussion of NGOs. The interesting points raised about tribalism and ethnicity are not developed into an analysis of how they impact upon the ways in which the people of Kazakhstan tend to associate or voice their demands in the public sphere. Nor is there any investigation of other informal organisational forms. Similarly, although the researchers note the emergence of more autonomous people's associations towards the end of the Soviet period, the progression and the impact of these on current trends in civil society are not discussed.

In sum, the report provides useful background information on a number of new NGOs as well as some insight into the development of political parties, and the concerns of representatives of the 'official religions'. What it fails to do is to examine how these bodies might be vehicles for the interests and demands of the Kazakh people. The researchers appear caught between the strong critiques of the political system by American scholars, focused on the need for democracy, transparency and the rule of law, and the empirical reality that some form of non-governmental sector has been emerging, albeit one that has a problematic and shifting relationship with the state. Whilst at times contradictory, the ambiguity of the report serves to stress, for the reader, the difficulty of applying Western understandings of civil society in a country that has both an authoritarian state and a severely weakened institutional structure.

The Tajik Mapping Report

The data for this report was principally collected by a Tajik academic. Fieldwork findings are presented alongside references to secondary literature. This literature, in the main, is analysis by local academics and commentators of contemporary Tajik society. However, the report is supported by other documents that detail findings from the researcher's fieldwork visits to rural areas of the country.

Much of the report is quite neutral in its discussion of the types of organisation at work in the country. However, the conclusion of the report advocates an entirely new paradigm for civil society in Tajikistan, calling for a break with tradition:

> Civil society in Tajikistan needs cultural change, but cultural changes cannot be [achieved] via traditional communities due to breakdown [caused by] civil war and the diminished education of women (Boboroyov and Heap 2003a: 43).

The passage continues by calling for civil society within the country to be based on 'imagined communities' – recalling Edwards' elaboration of an 'ideal civil society'. The researcher's stance is clarified in an accompanying report (Boboyorov 2003) in which he displays his opposition to the identification of traditional bodies and institutions as part of civil society. He criticises international NGOs for working with local self-governance bodies (the *mahalla* committees, discussed below), since, he argues, these are simultaneously rooted in conservative tradition and too closely related to the central authorities. Promotion of these bodies will serve to maintain traditional power relations and could even extend the power of the state further into the lives of individuals. Similarly, efforts in rural areas to encourage farmer co-operatives, he believes, will strengthen traditional institutions.[7] He regards both the focus on the collective and engagement with traditional, conservative bodies as exclusive to the freedom of the individual.

Perhaps as a result of this rejection of the traditional, the Tajik report is based principally upon discussion of the NGO sector. There is very little analysis of other types of civic association or traditional practices, although there are references to a process of negotiation in the northern region between imams and local government to ease tensions caused by the practice of Islam in the area. The report does refer briefly to traditional practices and forms of social organisation that continued into the Soviet era and, as in the Kazakh report, there is some discussion of Soviet 'proto-NGOs'. However, there is no analysis of the impact of transition upon these bodies, and how or if these activities have continued in independent Tajikistan. On the whole, the picture provided by the research findings is that civil society is made up of an incipient NGO sector, but that the value of this sector has yet to be properly understood and valued by the Tajik people and Government.

There are a number of references in the text to the business activities of Tajik NGOs, and the fact that some small and medium-sized enterprises have been classified as NGOs. These entities are presented in a somewhat negative light in the report, and are said to be creating 'confusion' about the scope and role of civil society. This appears to reflect Western norms of civil society that stress its 'non-profit' nature and separation from the private sector, although the report puts the blame for the situation with American and European donors eager to install a free market economy, who 'showed little concern for "politically correct" and strictly defined NGOs' (Boboroyov and Heap 2003a: 16). Considering the levels of poverty and unemployment within the country, it is not surprising that the income-earning potential of new types of associational activity has been grasped by the impoverished population. Rather than dismissing these manifestations of entrepreneurialism, the report could have examined the way in which types of associations that respond to the economic needs of the population are developing.

---

[7] This highlights the fact that power hierarchies within traditional institutions should not be overlooked by external donors wishing to engage with them. This issue is further analysed in Chapter 3.

The value of NGOs is presented somewhat ambiguously in the report. NGOs are considered as a positive aspect of transition early on in the text:

> They [NGOs] bring the voices of different communities and groups to the attention of the public and offer people a way of participating in civil society (Boboroyov and Heap 2003a: 14).

The rapid emergence of NGOs since the ceasefire is also seen to be an indicator of the growth of civil society and they are described as a 'vibrant new social and economic sector of activity'. And yet, at the same time, their utility is also questioned. Many registered NGOs are inactive, and those that are functioning are badly managed, following donor agendas, dependent upon external funds and led by urban élites who fail to understand the needs of poorer sectors of society. The report notes that many women are not aware that organisations exist to assist them and that recognition of the value of NGOs varies considerably across regions of the country.

The report's assessment of the relationship between NGOs and the Government is also ambivalent. On the one hand, the growing recognition by the Government of the sector is documented. But there is also a noted lack of trust on the part of the authorities towards these new organisations, as they are associated with the type of activity during *perestroika* that challenged the governing élite and demanded the rapid implementation of radical changes to the system. According to the Tajik researcher, this lack of trust and perception that NGOs may be a threat are manifested in certain types of legislation that can make it difficult for organisations to register and operate. On the other hand, the report notes that NGOs are accepted by the authorities principally for their potential role as service deliverers. The report notes that civil war and economic crisis have opened up space for the creation of NGOs as they can find a role for themselves in plugging gaps in services:

> The inability of government to effectively tackle many of the social and economic problems that afflict the country has provided a significant space of [*sic*] NGO development (Boboroyov and Heap 2003a: 29).

Even this type of service delivery activity can be considered a threat, however, and Government officials favour NGOs that work on welfare for vulnerable sectors of the population.

The Tajik researcher does consider the potential role for NGOs in advocacy activity, and asks 'Can NGOs be the vanguard of the institutional change needed to develop civil society?' No direct response is provided to this question. It is noted that opportunities for advocacy remain limited, although examples are given of successful advocacy initiatives in the field of gender legislation.

Reflecting the researcher's adherence to a Western model of civil society that puts up strict boundaries between the 'three sectors', the report glosses over a Government-founded institution, The Movement for National Unity and Revival of Tajikistan. This is reported by Akiner (2002) to have 1.5 million members (a quarter of the Tajik population). Similarly, there is criticism in the report of former civil servants who have become involved in the NGO sector whilst retaining their connections to past positions of responsibility:

> This means the civil society sector is intimately connected with the former public sectors, and with personalities in government in ways that make it extremely difficult to separate personalities from positions (Boboroyov and Heap 2003a: 24).

Whilst this type of relationship goes against the separation of civil society from state as advocated by the normative, 'neo-liberal' approach, in practice these networks will exist in any society. In a country shot through with traditions of kinship ties and led by strong personalities, it is particularly unrealistic to imagine that these types of social interaction can be done away with. It is also possible that these links between civil society and civil servants could lead to a form of 'internal advocacy' where the voices of poorer sectors are heard at higher levels through channels not otherwise available to them.

To conclude, the concept of civil society that the researcher has used to structure the mapping of Tajikistan is not clearly stated in the report. The lack of a clearcut definition is perhaps a reflection of the relative novelty of the work in Tajikistan of the international non-governmental sector and international agencies compared to other countries in the Central Asian region. The outbreak of civil war in 1992 and the problematic security situation that continued even after fighting ceased in 1996 and peace was negotiated in 1997 meant that many agencies were only initiating their activities in Tajikistan at the end of the 1990s; this despite the very high levels of poverty in the country which had been further exacerbated by conflict. The impact of civil war on society and social cohesion and the importance of clan-based factionalism in the conflict has also perhaps led commentators and practitioners alike to exclude traditional forms of associational activity from potential realisations of a civil society.

The Uzbek Mapping Report

The report on the emergence of civil society in Uzbekistan is based on a very different methodological approach as compared to the other country studies. Undertaken by a private institute for social science research, it follows a framework designed by CIVICUS[8] and measures the development of civil society according to four distinct dimensions: structure, space, values and impact. 'Structure' refers to the size of civil society and its component parts. 'Space' equates to the legal, political and socio-cultural space in which civil society operates. 'Values' refers to the underlying values of civil society organisations. 'Impact' denotes the contribution of civil society to social, economic and political problem-solving. The Uzbek study cites the CIVICUS explanation of the measurement process: 'Indicators are developed for each of the parameters. Some of the indicators are universal, while application of others assumes specific social and cultural context. Each indicator is formulated as a positive statement. Respondents evaluate each indicator according to a seven point scale, where 1 means the lowest level of development, and 7 the highest one' (Abdullaev et al. 2003: 6).

The use of this methodology meant that it was the function of the research team to decide *a priori* which types of organisation in Uzbekistan would be categorised as civil society. The report identified the following groups: NGOs, political parties, religious organisations, professional societies and *mahalla* committees. *Mahalla* committees are local self-governing bodies based on the pre-Soviet *mahalla*: an institution that was originally found in the larger and longest settled urban areas of the Ferghana Valley. They were renamed *mahalla* committees during the Soviet era and incorporated into the system of government. Since independence they have been strengthened, particularly in Uzbekistan, where they are now found throughout the country and are responsible for distributing targeted social benefits to the population.[9] The inclusion of the *mahalla* committees as a component of civil society is particularly interesting; their links to the state have brought accusations of co-optation from some quarters. However, their status and role in society remains somewhat ambiguous. The issue is further complicated by the fact that reference to 'the *mahalla*' can signify a geographical area, a community group with strong social bonds or the self-governing body.[10] The report does not draw attention to the ambiguities of the status of the *mahalla* as a civil society organisation but the researchers do point out that,

---

[8] According to its website, CIVICUS is 'an international alliance established in 1993 to nurture the foundation, growth and protection of citizen action throughout the world, especially in areas where participatory democracy and citizens' freedom of association are threatened'. www.civicus.org

[9] In Uzbekistan, the self-governing bodies are now officially known as *mahallas*, but the Soviet term *mahalla* committee remains in common parlance.

[10] In order to avoid confusion, throughout this publication, these self-governing bodies will be referred to as the '*mahalla* committee' while the term '*mahalla*' will be used to denote the community or geographical area.

leaders of Mahalla [Committees] did not mind participating ... but their answers show a low awareness of the situation in the third sector, as compared to the NGOs.

The inclusion of political parties and religious organisations is also problematic. The report notes of the former:

All political parties of Uzbekistan in their program documents state an unreserved support to the President Islam Karimov's policy (Abdullaev et al. 2003: 28).

It also explains that religious organisations must adhere to a policy of non-interference in political matters. The ability of either type of organisation to contribute significantly to government policy within the 'impact' dimension of the framework is not questioned by the researchers.

Whilst the types of organisation examined by the researchers are given equal analysis, numbers of interviewees in each type of organisation vary considerably. The researchers noted that, despite their best efforts, it was not easy to get interviews with members of political parties, religious organisations and trade unions. When it comes to an analysis of the data, significantly greater weight is given to the examination of 'structure' and 'space', than to 'values' and 'impact'. This suggests, as with the other reports, a preoccupation with form over content; with how many organisations exist as opposed to what they actually do and achieve.

The section of the report on the concept of civil society in Uzbekistan asserts that 'elements of civil society can grow ripe for a prolonged period of time in the ... absence of political democracy' (35). This is a particularly important statement to make, considering the authoritarian nature of Government in Uzbekistan and the difficulties this causes for the work of civil society activists. Indeed, the researchers go on to remark that 'non-governmental organisations' are often perceived as 'anti-governmental' by the authorities and that:

The Government is deeply suspicious of any organisation which it does not control and thus on the one hand it severely limits the volume of new registrations under the Ministry of Justice's all-encompassing framework and on the other hand it ensures that only those organisations which are politically bland, non-threatening or possibly useful to its own objectives, can obtain registration (37).

Despite these limitations on freedom of association, increasing religious intolerance on the part of Government and consolidation of presidential power, 'scores' for each of the dimensions of civil society given by respondents in the research process are surprisingly high. This presumably is a reflection of the fact that civil society actors were asked to evaluate their own performance against the criteria set by the researchers. Their responses were not triangulated with other data, although respondents were asked about Uzbek citizens' perceptions of their work. In some cases, if participants were to give low scores to particular questions, it would suggest an element of doubt in the validity of their own work and role of their institution. For example, closer examination of the figures show NGOs giving very low scores to the politico-legal environment within the 'space' dimension, compared to *mahalla* committees who were scoring it very highly. This again raises questions as to the position of the body within Uzbek society.

Of particular note is the score for impact, which was high, even though a much lower score was given for the space dimension in which this impact can be made. But despite this high score for impact, the impression of NGOs, professional associations and trade unions given by the report is of a group of institutions that are somewhat inward-looking. Their focus does not appear to be on seeking space for themselves within the wider public sphere. When NGOs have been involved in lobbying, for example, this has been for legislation concerning their own status, rather than the interests of their members or target groups. Further, these are very much the 'invited' spaces, as elaborated by Gaventa in Chapter 1.[11] While examples were given of NGOs that had attempted to monitor the activities of the state, more detailed information as to what they had achieved through this endeavour is not supplied. Where NGOs and other associations gave high scores within the 'impact' dimension, this was in response to their ability to provide services.

Overall, the report generated a large amount of statistical data on perceptions of civil society in Uzbekistan that has been disaggregated by type of organisation and provides useful information on processes of establishing an organisation and the legal environment. It raises some important questions on the nature of civil society in Uzbekistan, particularly with regards to the role of the *mahalla/mahalla* committee, which has been taken up in subsequent INTRAC research.[12] Data from less structured interviews included in the report also point to a problematic relationship between international donors and the civil society sector. However, many of the questions need further investigation. The idea of 'values' is, critically, left without adequate investigation. For whilst civil society organisations will use the rhetoric of their value base, referring to the concepts of social justice and human rights, the report does not attempt to gauge how these terms are understood

---

[11] The idea that the civil society sector might carve out a space for itself had not been entertained by the researchers who devised the questionnaire. Respondents were only asked about instances where they had been invited to participate.

[12] See for example Earle 2004a.

by respondents, nor how these are played out in organisational activities or goals. Furthermore, the high score for values jars somewhat with the primary motivating factors for working for civil society organisations elaborated under the 'structure' dimension, which respondents noted as salaries and prestige.

Conclusion

The manner in which the data was collected for these four reports varies considerably, reflecting the different experiences and backgrounds of local researchers and their priorities for their own skills development. The way in which the data is presented and analysed also differs, but there are a number of underlying themes that cut across the four separate reports. All four texts articulate a wish to reject rigidly normative, Western models of civil society and express the need for a conceptual compromise that will take the historical reality of each Central Asian state into account. Contextually specific factors that will impact upon civil society development are noted by all of the researchers, notably the legacy of the Soviet era, 'proto-NGOs' that evolved during *perestroika*, pre-Soviet forms of social organisation, the economic constraints of the independent era, limited democratic reforms and space for public discussion and social systems premised upon strong family ties and regional associations.

However, despite assertions of the need for a new model and a recognition of specific aspects of Central Asian societies that will impact upon the growth of civil society, further analysis of these themes is not well developed in any of the four reports. Essentially, the researchers in each country focus on the evolving NGO sector and the general impression given is that their understanding of civil society is premised on the ideal of a pluralistic society that can contribute to a functioning democracy and liberal economy. As such, the content of the reports tends to reflect the priorities of external, particularly US, donor agencies. To reiterate, this is not surprising, considering the levels of funding that have been channelled into the region from these agencies, and the same agencies' emphasis on training workshops to improve awareness and understanding of the third sector.

The reports are full of rich and detailed description of the work of key NGOs in each country. This publication will draw upon these case studies and organisation profiles in later chapters. The country reports' identification of other types of civil society organisation and areas of activity also provided a catalyst for further research and investigation which was later carried out by INTRAC (see Earle 2004a).

CHAPTER 3

The Context for Civil Society Development in the Central Asian States

The first two chapters of this volume discussed the main theoretical conceptions of civil society and how these have influenced INTRAC's research process in Central Asia. This chapter seeks to add some of the contextual detail to the discussion of civil society development by looking at the historical influences that have shaped society in the region, as well as the impact of the transition period on social organisation and well-being.

All five countries share similar ancient histories. The present day Kazakhs, Kyrgyz, Turkmen and Uzbeks are of Turkic origin and are descended from the roaming tribes of the steppes. The Tajiks are related to the Persian inhabitants of the southern area between the two great rivers, the Amu Darya and the Syr Darya (the ancient Oxus and Jaxartes). The Arab influence was also felt in these areas after the seventh century, although direct rule by the Arabs did not last long. After the destruction of the area by the invading Mongols in the thirteenth century, Turkic influence grew amongst more static populations in the south of the region. In the late middle ages the people that are now called the Uzbeks established themselves permanently in this area, having travelled from the region now known as Siberia. Differences emerged in forms of social organisation between the nomads of the north and the newly settled areas of the south. Thus the Kazakhs in the steppes to the north, the Kyrgyz who were closely related to the Kazakhs but lived in the mountains, and the Turkmen based around the Karakum desert, continued to be organised according to tribe and clan lineages, although patterns of social organisation were not homogeneous amongst them and the extent to which populations were fully nomadic varied. In the settled areas of present day Uzbekistan and Tajikistan, different forms of association developed which were more appropriate for the needs of static populations. In these areas, populations were ruled from centres of power emanating in Khiva, Bukhara and Kokand.

The power of the local rulers (emirs and khans) of Central Asia was to be steadily weakened, however, as the Tsarist colonisation began. Territories were gradually annexed between 1731 and 1873 and by the late nineteenth century Europeans began to arrive to settle the Tsar's new lands of Turkestan. There had been resistance to the annexation, and resentment against the Russians continued in the early years of the twentieth century, leading to a revolt during World War One when the Tsar demanded men from Central Asia be 'requisitioned' into the Russian army. This revolt caused bloodshed on both sides, but was eventually harshly repressed. Resistance flared up again in the 1920s as a group, named by the Russians as the Basmachi, sought to create a pan-Turkic state. These rebels were also defeated by the Bolsheviks.

In the 1920s and 1930s life really began to change for the indigenous peoples of the region with the forced settlement of nomadic peoples into new collective farms that led to thousands of deaths and massive migration, particularly of Kazakh peoples (many of whom, unlike the semi-nomadic Kyrgyz, had no experience of settled existence) into China and Mongolia. This period also saw the Soviet drive for the emancipation of women. The campaign to throw off the veil was welcomed by many urban and educated women, but caused huge trauma in some families and communities – including both female suicides and 'honour' killings. By 1936 the five Soviet Socialist Republics had been carved out of the original area of Turkestan. Although designed to broadly reflect the distribution of nationalities, the new republican borders did not fully tally with ethnic or linguistic populations and left large enclaves of people outside their titular homelands. For the next seventy years, the region was ruled from Moscow.[1]

---

[1] The argument that everything was changed by the Soviet period was presented strongly in the first draft of the Kazakhstan mapping report. 'The impact of the Soviet regime in Kazakhstan was enormous. The result was that people here were left with a Soviet mentality. They cannot become nomad again, most of the population are atheists, half the population does not speak the native language or keep to the Kazakh cultural tradition. They are Russians *de facto* and Kazakhs *de jure*...' (Dissenova et al. 2002: 29).

However, whilst the experience of Soviet-style socialism in Central Asia lasted much longer than, for example, in the Eastern European countries, it could be argued that the 'sovietisation' of the region has been somewhat exaggerated by historians, particularly with regards to social organisation.[2] The distance of the Central Asian regions from the centre of power in Moscow and the way in which Soviet systems echoed some traditional institutions meant that Central Asian identity and the specifics of its society were never fully erased. The degree of sovietisation that took place is a moot point, however, and varies between rural and urban areas, and from country to country. Differing views on the issue are clearly seen in the country mapping reports.

With the break-up of the Soviet Union in 1991, independence was virtually thrust upon all five of the Central Asian republics. All of them suddenly faced the task of building nation states and constructing viable economies in new countries whose existing economies were structured around specialised production for the larger Soviet economy. The withdrawal of central subsidies from Moscow and changes to inter-republican trade arrangements led to a dramatic reduction in output across all five countries. As in other parts of the former Soviet Union (FSU), this sudden disruption to the forms of social and economic organisation led to huge and sudden reductions in economic production and a slide into acute poverty for populations who were used to having their basic needs met by the State.

Since 1991, economic and political developments have given rise to some marked differences in economic growth, stability and social development across the five countries. Whilst most countries in the FSU experienced output losses of more than 50 per cent between 1990 and 1995, after which growth resumed, the different rates of policy reform and different resource bases have resulted in varying degrees of economic independence and viability. Of the five Central Asian countries, only Uzbekistan has regained its 1990 level of GDP, largely due to its continued policy of state control over the economy. Kyrgyzstan and Tajikistan are still at less than 50 per cent of their 1990 GDP levels.

Nonetheless, there continue to be many contextual similarities in terms of civil society development across all five countries. These result from the similarities in some of the traditional practices and institutions prevalent throughout the region and especially from the common legislative, economic and administrative structures inherited from the Soviet period.

---

[2] The idea that Soviet power complemented local traditions is put forward in the Uzbek report. 'The Soviet totalitarian empire ... was a natural form of state organisation for traditional societies, based on the vertical distribution of power, privileges and sovereignty' (Abdullaev et al. 2003: 13).

Country Profiles

Kazakhstan, the northernmost of the five republics, is the ninth largest country in the world with a territory of 2.7 million square kilometres, equivalent to the total area of Western Europe. Despite this land mass, the population is relatively small, totalling around 16 million. The capital, since December 1997, is Astana, which has a population of around 400,000 people. The largest city and main business and cultural centre of the country is the former capital, Almaty, with a population of 1.3 million. Kazakhstan is rich in natural resources, and the presence of large gas and oil reserves in the Caspian Sea area has meant that it has attracted a great deal of foreign direct investment. Although it again suffered negative growth in 1998 as a result of the Russian fiscal crisis, it was experiencing growth rates of over 10 per cent per annum in the 2000–2002 period.

Despite this rapid economic growth, there are huge pockets of poverty, especially in the rural areas. In absolute numbers, Kazakhstan has at least as many, if not more, poor people as the smaller countries in Central Asia. UNDP's Human Development Report for 2000 states that 31.8 per cent of the population has an income below the poverty line. The majority of the poor live in rural areas (57 per cent) and the highest densities of poor people are in the south of the country and areas near to the Aral Sea. Whilst unemployment is officially 3.7 per cent of able-bodied people of employable age, it is estimated that the real rate is four times this figure.

Kyrgyzstan is a mountainous country located in the heart of Central Asia. With an area of 195,000 square kilometres, its territory is dominated by the Tian Shan mountain range. The population is around 5 million, mainly concentrated in relatively small areas in the north and south of the country which are less mountainous. About a fifth of the population lives in Bishkek, the capital. Traditionally the Kyrgyz were semi-nomadic pastoralists, herding sheep, horses and yaks, and Kyrgyzstan used to be the main supplier of wool to the Soviet Union. Cotton, wool and meat continue to be the main agricultural products and exports. Industrial exports include gold, mercury, uranium and electricity.

According to World Bank figures, 57 per cent of the population was living below the poverty line in 2001 and 17.8 per cent of the population is classified as extremely poor. Around 52 per cent of the labour force is involved in agricultural production. The estimated rate of unemployment is 7 per cent although the real rate is thought to be around 20 per cent, of whom 62 per cent are women.

Tajikistan, in the south-east of Central Asia, has a territory of 143,100 square kilometres, most of which is mountainous. It has an estimated population of 6 million, 73 per cent of which lives in rural areas.

Less than a year after independence in 1991, Tajikistan suffered a civil war between a Russian-backed Government and a mostly Islamic opposition. The civil war destroyed the economy almost completely and put a severe strain on financial resources. The war cost US$7 billion – estimated to be equivalent to 11 years of government expenditure (UNDP 2000: 4) and created more than one million refugees and internally displaced people. The war officially ended in 1996, but peace negotiations were not completed until 1997 when the United Tajik Opposition (UTO) was brought into the Government with 30 per cent of the seats in Parliament, and the post of Deputy Prime Minister.

Tajikistan is one of the 30 poorest nations in the world. World Bank figures for 2003 put 64 per cent of the population living below a poverty line set at US$2.15 per day at purchasing power parity. The Tajik PRSP (Poverty Reduction Strategy Paper) states that 60 per cent of the population consider themselves as poor (Government of Tajikistan 2002: 9). Writing in 2000, Falkingham remarked of Tajikistan that 'the picture that emerges is of a population facing severe economic, physical and psycho-social stress.' (Falkingham 2000: 222: n.4). According to ILO estimates, unemployment is around 30 per cent, although Tajiks themselves believe the number to be much higher (UNDP 2000: 19). The young are especially hard hit; 70 per cent were thought to be unemployed in 2000.

Turkmenistan, the westernmost of the Central Asian republics, has a land area of 143,100 square kilometres, and had an estimated population of 5.8 million in 2002. Forty-six per cent of the population lives in urban areas. With high fertility rates, the population is growing at around 3 per cent each year. As a result, 40 per cent of the population is under the age of 15, the average age is 23 and only 6 per cent of the population is over 60. Turkmenistan is the most ethnically homogeneous of all Central Asian countries with Turkmens constituting over 80 per cent of the population.

At the time of independence, Turkmenistan was one of the poorest of the Soviet republics. The Government has been slower to adopt economic reforms, and the state continues its leading role in the management of the economy and the provision of the population's basic needs (maintaining social allowances, low prices for foods and subsidised energy and transport). Although it is difficult to gauge current levels of poverty due to lack of data, the Asian Development Bank states that poverty incidence in Turkmenistan is perhaps the lowest among the transition countries of Central Asia (Asian Development Bank 2002). However, Turkmenistan has the highest levels of infant death and child mortality in Central Asia as a result of the collapse of medical services in rural areas.[3] As in the other

---

[3] EBRD data gives the 1990 figure of 45 deaths per 1000 live births, reducing to 27 per 1000 in 2003, and 43 per 1000 children under 5 in 2003 (World Bank (2003), 'Achieving the Human Development MDGs in CCA').

Central Asian countries, water and sanitation problems are very serious, since only 42 per cent of the rural population and 85 per cent of the urban population have access to safe drinking water (Eurasianet 2002). In addition, unemployment is growing, especially among young people.

Uzbekistan is the second largest of the Central Asian republics, located largely between the Amu Darya and Syr Darya rivers in the ancient area of Transoxiana. This is a dry, landlocked country of which 11 per cent consists of intensively cultivated, irrigated river valleys. The total population is around 25.5 million and over 60 per cent lives in these densely populated rural communities. Uzbekistan follows a policy of 'export development in primary industries and import replacement in the manufacturing sector' (Abdullaev et al. 2003: 15), and is now the world's second largest cotton exporter, a major producer of gold and oil, and a regionally significant producer of chemicals and machinery. Following independence in December 1991, the Government has continued its policy of support to the economy with subsidies and tight controls on production and prices. The state continues to be a dominating influence in the economy, with the agricultural sector accounting for 33 per cent of GDP, industry 24 per cent and services 43 per cent.

According to the World Bank's Living Standards Assessment 2003, an estimated 27.5 per cent of the population lives below the poverty line,[4] and approximately one third of all poor households can be classified as extremely poor. The Government, however, continues to deny the existence of poverty within the republic.

Table 1 Comparative data on population, income and poverty in the region[5]

Country	Population size 2002	Income per capita US $	% below national poverty line
Kazakhstan	14,794,830	1,510	35
Kyrgyzstan	5,003,890	290	56
Tajikistan	6,315,660	180	96
Turkmenistan	5,545,360	1,200	n.a.
Uzbekistan	25,391,440	450	28

[4] This poverty line is a food consumption poverty line based on 2100 calories per person per day. The figures are based on a household survey conducted in 2002.

[5] World Bank Development Indicators, and other World Bank estimates. National poverty lines are based on government estimates. Numbers living below the poverty line are based on the latest available World Bank figures.

Social Developments in the Period of Transition

As in the other countries of the FSU, economic activity declined severely in all countries of Central Asia following the break-up of the Soviet Union. The Soviet economy had operated as one large command economy, with production targets set centrally, and delivery and distribution of all output conducted by the State apparatus. The economies of the separate republics within the Union were by no means self-sufficient: just as individual towns could be centred on one major form of industry, so the separate republics concentrated largely on what was thought to be their comparative advantage. Thus, for example, in 1990 around 98 per cent of Kyrgyz exports went to trading partners within the Soviet Union. With the collapse of the Union, these markets were lost at a stroke.

The term 'transition' refers to the changeover from a command to market economy, and is a term used primarily by the international donor community and Western academics. In the immediate post-Soviet years, there was tremendous optimism on the part of these players that with the implementation of the necessary reforms (privatisation of production units and land, introduction of market prices, free trade), economic growth would take off with long-term benefits for all. All countries have, to varying degrees, introduced some reforms aimed at establishing a mixed market economy. Typically the reform package advocated by the multi-lateral donors includes institutional and legislative reform (including privatisation) and policy changes such as price reform, elimination/reduction in state subsidies and trade liberalisation.

Since independence, progress towards market reform in Central Asia has varied greatly from country to country. The Tajikistan Government has faced more basic economic problems, obliged to rebuild its economy almost from scratch after the devastation of the civil war. Some commentators believe that any changes made in the other Central Asian states have been motivated by political considerations, rather than economic rationality (Csaki and Tuck 2000). For example, the Kyrgyz Republic was the poorest state within the USSR, has few natural resources compared to its neighbours and little comparative advantage in agriculture considering its mountainous terrain and poor communications (Roy 2001). However, it is also the country that has progressed the furthest with privatisation. Many commentators have linked its good relations with the international financial institutions and the President's alleged commitment to democracy to its dire need for overseas aid (Olcott 2001; Roy 2001). Similarly, Kazakhstan has also taken significant steps towards privatisation, presumably in order to encourage foreign investment from energy corporations.

Uzbekistan and Turkmenistan have shown far less willingness to implement reforms, however, and a reluctance to privatise. The governments themselves explain this position as an attempt to maintain political stability in nascent, fragile states and avoid social fallout from abruptly implemented economic reforms. Certainly, as is noted above in the country profiles, greater social protection has been afforded to the populations of these countries. However, 'political stability' can also easily be interpreted as the desire of the political élite to maintain their power bases. Privatisation and the withdrawal of the state from systems of production that it entails would erode the power and control of the political élite both at national and local level. Uzbekistan, for example, continues to exert strong state control over the cotton sector, the 'white gold' that brings in foreign currency earnings.

After 13 years of independence for the region, and erratic progress towards a market economy, the end of the 'transition' is still not in sight.[6] Whilst some concessions to privatisation have been made, the countries of Central Asia are often perceived as becoming less democratic, rather than more pluralistic and open, as all five presidents consolidate their power.[7] Despite this, the Central Asian nations are all still classified as transition states. As the Tajik study noted, it is a term used by outsiders and not one readily understood by many people within the region.

Progress towards democratic and economic transition was problematised by the tendency of the World Bank to refer during the 1990s to the republics of the former Soviet Union and the countries of Central and Eastern Europe as 'transition countries' en masse and to assume that similar programmes of privatisation would be applicable to all of them. This glossed over significant characteristics of the different regions that included higher levels of dependency on the centralised economic system and much lower levels of familiarity with market mechanisms in Central Asia than in the European countries of the Soviet Bloc. The transition optimists also overestimated the willingness with which governments would relinquish control over production, particularly production linked to export earnings. Indeed, after ten years, the World Bank finally admitted that the process had proved to be anything but a 'smooth transition' and that experts had been surprised by the extent to which populations had been plunged into poverty (UNDP 1999).

---

[6] Lack of clarity about the direction of transition was summed up in the Tajik Mapping Report: 'The basic characteristic of the transition period in Tajikistan was uncertainty in ideological position, social policy and the perspectives for development' (Boboyorov and Heap 2003b: 12).

[7] Kyrgyzstan is regarded as the country in the region that has made most progress towards democratisation, followed by Kazakhstan and then Tajikistan. Turkmenistan is considered to have the most autocratic style of government, whilst Uzbekistan is also characterised by authoritarianism.

Land Reform

Central Asia has seen various degrees of privatisation of the land. This ranges from almost full privatisation in Kazakhstan and Kyrgyzstan, to continued state ownership of land in Tajikistan, Uzbekistan and Turkmenistan with arrangements for exploitation rights for private farmers. In Uzbekistan and Turkmenistan quotas are still in place for production of export crops, particularly cotton, including farms that have been restructured as 'joint stock companies'. Even in Kazakhstan and Kyrgyzstan, the privatisation of land was far from transparent and, as Roy points out, 'large estates [have been] created in favour of former *kolkhoz* apparatchiks (usually chairmen and their families)' (Roy 2002: 137). Former members of the collective are then either hired as wage labourers or reduced to the status of share-croppers.

Dependence on household plots for subsistence has increased since independence. Whilst many former *kolkhoz* workers were given land parcels after the restructuring of the farms, these have not led to the development of a strong peasant farm sector. This is, in part, because these plots are often too small and because agricultural inputs are very expensive. Also, agricultural workers who previously worked in specialised jobs in large-scale farms in the Soviet period are not necessarily able to adapt easily to running a small farm independently and without mechanised equipment. There has also been a lack of markets in which to sell products, and problems with transportation. As a result, analysts have noticed an unwillingness to leave the collective farms (Kudat et al. 2000) and in some areas, noticeably in Kazakhstan, the spontaneous formation of co-operatives amongst former *kolkhoz* workers. It was only after nearly a decade of independence that the World Bank acknowledged that the family farm was not necessarily the best model for the region and that alternative farm sizes and management systems might be more appropriate.

Patterns of Poverty

In Soviet times, the state provided employment for all able-bodied adults and assistance to those who were unable to work. If people were poor, this meant that they found themselves outside this system and were thus regarded as deviant in some way. The vast majority of the population enjoyed guaranteed employment and wide ranging subsidies on basic consumer goods and services provided through their place of work. The system of social protection consisted of pensions and social assistance programmes for those with special needs such as the disabled, orphans, or families with large numbers of children. In addition there was a system of privileges available to particular groups as a reward for their seniority or contribution to society, for example war veterans, teachers and miners. With the break-up of the Soviet Union and subsequent collapse of the Central Asian economies, the structures that guaranteed a certain standard of living also gave way. Even with the revival in economic production, the old systems are no longer viable mechanisms for guaranteed support for the population.

The nature of poverty in Central Asia is quite distinct from that of the developing world. As a UNDP study of Uzbekistan noted, the poor,

> tend to be 'human capital rich' as they receive at least nine years of education, and 'asset rich', with nine percent of them owning the house in which they live, eighty percent owning their land plots, and twelve percent owning a car. However, these assets, largely accumulated during the Soviet period, will eventually deteriorate if the low-income status of the poor persists, whilst past educational achievements may become progressively irrelevant to the needs of a new society (UNDP 2003: 5).

The growth of inequality and rapid deterioration in human development indicators have had a particularly harmful effect on society and individuals. It must be remembered that the countries of the former Soviet Union had high levels of human development and some of the lowest levels of inequality in the world. The Kyrgyz Republic is now one of the most unequal countries in the world: its Gini coefficient has nearly doubled since independence (World Bank 2000).

Results of the World Bank sponsored *Voices of the Poor* participatory research in the region show that poverty is very hard to accept for people who have lived under communist regimes (Narayan et al. 2000). The World Bank's research presents an overriding sense of injustice at growing poverty and inequality. Poorer people in the region are finding it increasingly difficult to access basic services that were once universally available, such as health and education, as funds dry up and public employees demand the payment of bribes. Rapid increases in unemployment levels are also particularly damaging to societies that had learnt to associate work in the formal sector as the key to social inclusion. Those that have retained their jobs often receive wages months in arrears, if at all, or are paid in kind (Earle 2002).

Poverty in the region also has specific urban and rural characteristics, and there is no simple urban/rural divide. One regional study summarises the issue as follows:

> The nature of poverty in the two kinds of locations [urban and rural] is different. In urban areas, the availability of food is undoubtedly the worst problem; poor urban households are food-poor. In rural areas, however, poor households are cash-poor. Buying bread, let alone clothing, winter heat, medicine, educa-

tional supplies, or transportation, may be out of the question. The rural poor are better off in terms of food, but the urban poor are better off in terms of everything else (Csaki and Tuck 2000: 15).

There are similarities in the patterns of poverty across all five countries. As in the rest of the former Soviet Union, there are particular groups of people who have been especially hard hit by the changes. These have been labelled the 'new poor' and include pensioners, the working poor, the long-term unemployed, young people in search of their first job, single-parent families, large families and significant numbers of internally displaced persons, particularly in Tajikistan.

Pensioners, who received generous provision in Soviet times, have found their benefits eaten away by the soaring inflation that affected all countries after independence. Today, pension payments across all five countries are minimal compared to living costs. Unemployment has increased across all five countries, although in all cases it is thought that the official figures under-represent the true situation. Unemployment is particularly high in rural areas where the re-organisation of the collective farms (*kolkhoz*) and state farms (*sovkhoz*) has resulted in loss of guaranteed employment. Women and young people in rural areas are particularly affected.

Utility and price subsidies were initially continued in all five countries, but have been reduced with privatisation of providers. Systems of assistance for the very poor who cannot afford to pay do exist, but reform of this system has generally led to a reduction in the categories of people who are entitled to assistance. In addition, all countries are now experiencing the collapse of social infrastructure since there has been limited maintenance of these structures since independence. Roads and forms of public transport have deteriorated, leaving many rural areas increasingly isolated. Water and sanitation provision is particularly problematic. In some areas, water is used despite high levels of bacterial and chemical contamination (Eurasianet 2002).

In rural areas where groups of small villages had together formed a collective farm, many of these villages now find themselves completely isolated, often without any form of support and minimal levels of contact with the former administrative centres. Cities and towns which were dependent on one large, but now defunct, enterprise (a case not uncommon in the planned Soviet economy), have been reduced to ghost towns. In all of Central Asia there are particularly high levels of youth unemployment. This is partly to do with the deterioration of the education system and especially the collapse of state provision for the institutes of higher education and accompanying reduced access to higher education.

Increased dependency on drugs, particularly among the young unemployed, is apparent. An estimated 65 per cent of illegal drugs from Afghanistan goes through Central Asian countries to Russia. The Agency of the Republic of Kazakhstan on

Statistics states that, in 2001, the number of officially registered drug users in Kazakhstan was 33,100 – but it is thought the real number is four to five times this figure.[8] According to both the Tajik and Turkmen Ministries of Health, Tajikistan and Turkmenistan are facing increasing levels of heroin addiction.

Whilst figures are not generally available on the incidence of HIV/AIDS, all the evidence points to rapidly increasing numbers. Infection rates are likely to increase still further, with the existence high youth unemployment, widespread availability and use of drugs and high rates of temporary labour migration. Infection rates are particularly high in Kazakhstan.

The inability of the state to pay salaries on time and the reduced value of these salaries has also had a profound effect on health services. Many doctors, particularly ethnic Russians, have migrated. At the same time, the ability of poorer people to access healthcare has decreased as bribes or unofficial payments have become almost mandatory in the sector, and relatives must pay for and sometimes administer medication (Falkingham 2004). A reduction in living standards has seen a rise in rates of certain types of infection, such as tuberculosis.

Whilst education had been a priority during the Soviet era, the system is now suffering from a lack of investment and the low level of state salaries. Without resources for facilities many schools have had to close, and those that are left open are often barely surviving. Problems with the education system, and the difficulties involved in reforming the curriculum, have meant that education, especially in rural areas, is often seen as less important than it was in the past. In all countries, from very high school enrolment and completion rates in 1990, there is a noticeable drop-off rate, especially in rural areas and especially among girls of secondary school age.

Finally, all countries have suffered population losses as those groups which could emigrate have chosen to do so. This applies to the large numbers of Slavs (Russians, Ukrainians and so on) who lived in Central Asia, and other ethnic groups such as the Germans.[9] Both Kazakhstan and Kyrgyzstan have experienced a 10 per cent decline in population since 1990.[10] In addition, there has been a wave of people returning to settle in their new national homeland – Kazakhs returning from Mongolia, China, Afghanistan and other Central Asian republics, Turkmens returning to their homeland from war-torn Tajikistan and so on. However, the

---

[8] In 2001 the Kazakh Government allocated US$1 million to programmes combating drug trafficking, and another US$1 million for the establishment of drug rehabilitation centres.

[9] Germans settled in Russia in the time of Catherine the Great, and then were relocated to Central Asia during World War Two.

[10] Even in 2000, in Kazakhstan, around 135,000 people emigrated (Kazakhstanskaya Pravda 2001: 4).

general pattern resulting from these shifts is that the more educated are leaving and more socially vulnerable groups are returning.

One of the coping mechanisms in response to the economic crisis has been large-scale internal migration from the rural areas to urban centres. This is especially marked in Kazakhstan and Kyrgyzstan, where groups settle in newly built suburbs of the towns. In Kazakhstan large numbers have migrated from the environmentally unfavourable areas in Kyzyl-Orda and Semipalatinsk *oblasts*, which served as nuclear testing grounds for the Soviet Union. Since 1991 in Kyrgyzstan, around one million rural people have moved to urban areas from remote areas, particularly from Naryn *oblast* and the mountainous areas of Osh and Jalal-Abad. Seasonal internal migration is also notable; the summer months see families from southern Kyrgyzstan travelling to the fertile area of the Chui Valley around Bishkek (the capital), where they camp in makeshift tents and cultivate the land. External migration, especially of young men, has also increased. This is a particular problem in Tajikistan, where the lack of alternative employment opportunities has meant that every spring around one million leave for Russia and other FSU countries looking for seasonal work. Some estimate that around one sixth of the male working population has left for good (Whitlock 2002: 266).[11] Kyrgyzstan has decided to introduce the facility for dual citizenship for its citizens working in Russia, and has opened a consulate in Siberia to serve the needs of its citizens working there. The average migrant from Kyrgyzstan to Russia is educated, skilled and under 30. The case study below documents the work of two organisations in Kazakhstan that emerged in response to the problems associated with the arrival of large numbers of migrants in Almaty, mainly as a result of growing poverty in rural areas.

Case Study – Baspana and Moldir, Kazakhstan

One of the first large NGOs in Kazakhstan, Baspana was founded by local activists in Almaty in May 1995 after a campaign of street protests and occupations of workers' hostels that had been threatened with privatisation or closure. Baspana means 'a shelter above your head' in Kazakh and the organisation focuses on improving the poor people's accommodation and lobbying in the interests of the homeless. Its target group is Kazakh migrants who flooded into Almaty during the 1990s from the impoverished rural areas of Kazakhstan following the closure of collective farms and the general crisis in agriculture. A smaller number of migrants were ethnic Kazakhs returning to their newly independent homeland from other parts of FSU, particularly Mongolia and China.

---

[11] The Russian Embassy in Dushanbe estimates the number at close to one million, with US$30–40 m sent home monthly to support families (International Crisis Group 2001: 22).

As well as taking over hostels, Baspana helped the homeless to build new peri-urban settlements around Almaty. Residents' committees were formed to manage building work and installation of basic services; later, using and adapting the experience of NGOs in South Asia, self-help groups were created to run micro-credit programmes both on a collective and individual basis. By the end of the 1990s, squatting on land or unused property became more difficult, as local government established greater control. Baspana successfully put forward its own candidates for election as deputies at the city level and, with their help, by the early 2000s had sufficient leverage on public investment in infrastructure and services (roads, electricity and water), social services and schools, to have significantly improved the lives of 50,000 city residents.

Baspana's focus shifted gradually from the construction of cheap housing to the promotion of local services, small business and other strategies to counteract unemployment. The organisation began to move from its roots as a social movement of the homeless to a mature NGO enabling a wide range of community and popular initiatives.

Another Almaty-based NGO working with hostel residents and marginal groups is Moldir. The organisation was set up in 1993 and has since built upon initial local-level success to develop a national profile. Originally called the Association of Single Parents, Moldir's objectives are 'to provide psychological, legal, social and information support to the most vulnerable families in Almaty, in order to encourage their civic spirit, better welfare and gender equality'.

Most of Moldir's programmes are related to problems faced by women, although it has recently broadened its activities to general issues of poverty. It provides legal advice surgeries, lobbies for the interests of single mothers and helps them to find employment and provides psychological support and charity. It has worked with the Social Protection Department in setting up self-help groups for single mothers in hostels and some of the new residential areas (that house immigrants) in Almaty. These groups operate a revolving credit scheme to assist group members in their everyday needs, including setting up small businesses. Moldir has also run training courses on issues such as healthy lifestyles, and has an information service which disseminates leaflets and booklets in Kazakh and Russian.

In 2000, Moldir was invited to join the Public Expert Council on Entrepreneurship under the auspices of the Almaty City Mayor. Through this forum, they have been able to promote the interests of women in business, for example pressing for a reduction in taxes and for simpler procedures in establishing a private company.

> The activities of Moldir are well known in Almaty and beyond. As a result it has come to act as a support organisation to smaller NGOs who want to acquaint themselves with the methods that it uses, particularly on promoting self-help groups and for advice on writing project proposals.

Politics and the Strengthening of Presidential Rule

Recent years have seen a move towards the establishment of presidential dynasties in all five countries of Central Asia. Four of the five presidents have been in power since independence, with the Tajik President installed in 1992, and in all cases constitutions have been modified in order to allow extended terms. The phenomenon of presidential rule in Central Asia clearly reflects both national and Soviet-era traditions, and also the exigencies of countries facing a very severe economic crisis. Tajikistan and Uzbekistan also face significant violence and security problems.

In Turkmenistan, President Saparmurat Niyazov has held office uninterrupted since 1985 when he was appointed head of the Turkmen Communist Party. In 1992 Niyazov was elected President unchallenged, obtaining 99.5 per cent of the vote, and in 1999 he was awarded this post for life although he has undertaken to step down by 2010. As the self-styled 'Turkmenbashi' or moral and spiritual leader of the Turkmens, pictures and statues of Niyazov are to be seen on buildings and placards across the country. A numbers of schools, factories, the country's main port, and some days of the week have been named after him and his mother. Niyazov's book *Rukhnama* on the culture, history and identity of the Turkmen people is compulsory reading for students at all levels of the education system. All this is part of an attempt to build a Turkmen nation in isolation from outside influences (Turkmenistan is the only country in Central Asia with an official policy of neutrality).[12] The country's valuable natural resources and exports (gas, cotton and so on) and small population are other factors in this strategy.

The President of Uzbekistan, Islam Karimov, was first secretary of the Uzbek Communist Party from 1989 and was elected President of Uzbekistan in December 1991. In 1995 Karimov extended his mandate until 2000, and in January 2000 he was re-elected with 92 per cent of the vote. Power is highly centralised in the hands of the President, and the Parliament (Oliy Majlis) is generally considered

---

[12] Niyazov is an orphan of the earthquake which flattened Ashgabat in 1948 and this, combined with national bitterness around the severity of Tsarist colonisation of Turkmenistan, may lie behind an approach which emphasises a complete rebuilding of the country and its institutions. INTRAC NGO Mapping Report, January 2003 and internal Political and Civil Society Report, December 2003 (by Charlie Buxton).

to be excluded from active government and strategic decision-making. Karimov's main policy direction has been to turn Uzbekistan into an independent regional power in line with its historic position as a centre of ancient civilisation, its economic potential based on cotton production and gold extraction, and the largest population among the five countries of Central Asia. Acts of terrorism in Uzbekistan in 1999 and 2004 have undoubtedly contributed to greater repression of human rights. The country now enjoys an important military/political relationship with the USA as part of the 'war on terror'.

In Kazakhstan, President Nursultan Nazarbaev has been President since his election in 1991. In 1995 a referendum established a continuation of his presidency until 2000. In 1999 further presidential elections were held, almost two years before their scheduled date, and the constitution was amended at the same time to extend the presidential term from five to seven years. Freedom House cites the Organisation for Security and Cooperation in Europe (OSCE), which monitored the elections and which refused to recognise the results, which it said 'fell far short' of being democratic.[13] Nazarbaev is currently the head of state, commander-in-chief of the armed forces and may veto laws passed by the Parliament. He is a staunch supporter of economic and political links with Russia and a prime force in the Commonwealth of Independent States (CIS). At the same time Kazakhstan's oil and gas resources have been opened up to Western companies. His policies have undoubtedly helped maintain the multi-ethnic fabric of the country. In 2003 Nazarbaev's elder daughter Dariga, already the owner and director of several business and media holdings, formed a new political party and there are signs that she is being groomed to bid for the presidency when her father retires.

Whilst the political history of post-independence Tajikistan has been dominated by the civil war and its aftermath, the dominant Peoples' Democratic Party is made up of former Communist Party members. The head of this party is President Imomali Rahmonov, a former collective farm director, who has been President since 1992. In 2003 a national referendum confirmed the extension of the President's mandate up until 2020. In Tajikistan's vulnerable and isolated situation, Rahmonov has attempted both to open up to international and Western aid programmes, and to maintain the benefits of Russian military assistance on the border with Afghanistan.

Of all the five republics, only Kyrgyzstan operates a more liberal form of government. Indeed during the 1990s the country gained the accolade as Central Asia's 'island of democracy'. President Askar Akaev, a former physics scientist, has been President since independence and was re-elected for the third time in 2001. Akaev is strongly associated with a policy of working with all the main

---

[13] Freedom House Overview of Kazakhstan 2002:
http://www.freedomhouse.org/research/freeworld/2002/countryratings/kazakhstan.htm

powers, and this has meant a sometimes difficult balancing act; for example the agreement to open US and Russian air bases some 30 kilometres apart, and the controversial decision in 2002 to hand back land to China to settle a long-running border dispute and open the way for Chinese investment in the country. Undoubtedly the President must take some credit for the maintenance of the freest media in Central Asia, albeit one not without problems. A referendum held in early 2004 resulted in changes that created a one-chamber Parliament and strengthened the role of Prime Minister, but still disappointed civil society groups who feared the prolongation of the Akaev dynasty. Shortly before this book went to press, Akaev was removed from office by a popular uprising after elections that were widely believed to be fraudulent. He fled to Russia from where he announced his formal resignation in early April 2005.

Political Parties and the Role of Parliaments

During the 1990s, the states of Central Asia began the complex process of creating a free and effective multi-party system. The results are mixed to date. On the one hand, political parties have proliferated in Kazakhstan and Kyrgyzstan from the early 1990s and, more recently, Tajikistan. On the other hand, in all countries the political parties have limited influence.

In Kazakhstan, new conditions for the registration of parties imposed during 2004 have restricted their number to less than ten. In Turkmenistan opposition parties are banned. In Uzbekistan, the growth of political opposition during *perestroika* in the late 1980s led eventually to the creation of two groupings. The first of these, Birlik, was a movement in support of democratic national identity that sponsored mass demonstrations and called for recognition of Uzbek as the state language. The second, breakaway group, called Erk, was distinctly more supportive of Government policies. However, by the mid-1990s all parties in open opposition to the Government were outlawed and their leaders exiled.

Not surprisingly given the problems faced by political parties, in all countries of the region the national parliament yields in importance to the president and his centralised executive power. However, it is possible to roughly identify in which instances the political space is opening up and where by contrast, more restrictions are being imposed.

In Tajikistan the dominant Peoples' Democratic Party includes many former members of the Communist Party. However, the Islamic Renaissance Party is guaranteed a proportion of the seats in Parliament, as part of the post-war settlement and is the only Islamic political party to have gained power in Central Asia. These parties are described in more detail in the case study below.

Case Study – Political Parties in Tajikistan

Difficult conditions within the country and complex security threats have not provided an enabling environment for opposition parties to emerge in the independent era. While more than 20 political parties had been established in 1992, this number has now decreased to 13. The party of the President, and that of the majority of government officials, is the People's Democratic Party. As a result, the PDP is the most powerful player in the *Majlis-i Oli* (national Parliament).

The Islamic Renaissance Party of Tajikistan was established in 1990 and was one of the first new political parties to emerge. It quickly became influential in the political life of the country. Different Islamic institutions supported its activities and goals at the local level and its influence at community level spread rapidly. Initially, the IRPT did not have much in common with the 'democratic opposition', but these actors buried their differences in order to oppose the Communist government. The civil war forced many leaders and members of the IRPT into exile abroad. As a result of a long dialogue between the Government of Tajikistan and United Tajik Opposition (UTO), in which the armed Islamists played a central role, the General Agreement on Peace and National Reconciliation was signed in June 1997. According to the Agreement, 30 per cent of parliamentary seats would be given over to the representatives of the UTO.

The Democratic Party of Tajikistan (DPT) was established in 1990, and was, in the early years of independence, one of the most influential opposition parties with political influence and support from people across Tajikistan. However, with the onset of the civil war, regionalist and localist groups became more prominent, and the DPT lost influence within the UTO. This was also due to the dominance of Islamists and separatist interests in the DPT itself. The leaders and many of the members of DPT went into exile abroad. Some have never returned home; others gathered in Almaty and re-established the Party independently before returning to Tajikistan (Boboroyov and Heap 2003b).

An example of a newer party, set up in early 2003, is the Social Democratic Party of Tajikistan (SDPT). Unlike the IRPT, it campaigned against the constitutional amendments contained in the national referendum in summer 2003, effectively winning leadership of the political opposition bloc (Davlatov 2003).

The other two countries with a relatively open party system, Kazakhstan and Kyrgyzstan, illustrate the complexities of pluralistic political development. Kyrgyzstan has a plethora of political parties, increasing to over 40 in the early 2000s. However, these often lack a clear platform and are organised around one individual, clan or regional grouping. Various experiments with proportional representation appear not to have solved the problem. A similar analysis is made by Akiner in relation to Tajikistan:

> The new parties are small, under-funded and for the most part dominated by a single individual; they also have a very narrow social base. They attract little support from the wider public (2002: 175).

Some commentators have gone so far as to state that NGOs in Kyrgyzstan play a more important role than political parties in public life (Bialeva 2004), since they have greater resources and a more active ongoing presence in the community. NGOs have also played a key role in efforts to improve the election systems (and monitor the elections themselves) in the region.

The countries have also tried out different parliamentary structures. Kyrgyzstan's move to a one-chamber parliament was mentioned above (it is also argued that this will be cheaper for a small, less wealthy country). By contrast, in December 2004, Uzbekistan voted in deputies for a new two-chamber parliament (as opposed to the previous one-chamber structure) which it was claimed would professionalise and strengthen the role of the institution.

In Kazakhstan, the tougher new regulations have forced the concentration of the electorate into supporting a smaller number of political parties, including Otan, the Agrarian Party, Asar, the Communist Party, Ak-Zhol and Democratic Choice. Kazakhstan is fast emerging as a modern country on a recognisable capitalist model. A recent report for INTRAC on the interface between political and civil society activity noted the emergence of 'power-élite groups' in which political parties, banks, large companies, media outlets and even NGOs are beginning to form together in blocs in a manner familiar in Western societies (Sakhanov 2004).[14]

While the consolidation of parties in Kazakhstan might give an opportunity to a more active parliament to assert its role *vis-à-vis* the executive power, events in early 2005 were more worrying. The opposition party Democratic Choice for Kazakhstan, two of whose leaders were imprisoned in 2003 (one was later

---

[14] However, the author carefully defines the term: 'Power-elite groups is a term expressing the transition position of a group of people who have concentrated in their hands control of the state's economic and administrative resources, but have not yet consolidated their position as a new Kazakhstan social elite in the minds of Kazakhstan society and not have yet won international recognition' (Sakhanov 2004: 4).

released), was finally banned on the grounds of being a threat to public order.

In Turkmenistan, a one-party state since independence, the ruling Democratic Party of Turkmenistan is headed by the President. Incipient opposition parties have been banned, and most of their leaders have fled abroad. The Ministry of Internal Affairs undertakes surveillance of those suspected of being involved in any type of unofficial political involvement. It justifies this activity by emphasising the need for vigilance in fighting crime and involvement in the narcotics trade. An attempted assassination of the President in November 2002 led to a security clampdown and further restrictions on political life and civil society activity. In autumn 2003, Turkmenistan's record in this area was criticised in resolutions passed by both the OSCE and the UN General Assembly.

In Uzbekistan only political parties which are supportive of the Government are allowed to operate. These include the Peoples' Democratic Party of Uzbekistan (the successor of the Communist Party) which Karimov headed until 1996, and the Fidokorlar (National Democratic Party) which he is now most closely associated with. In September 2003, the President proposed that there should be a party protecting the rights of entrepreneurs and business people. So a fifth party has been created, the Liberal Democratic Party. In 1997, new legislation was introduced to ban all political affiliations based on religious or ethnic grounds. All opposition groups in Uzbekistan now operate from exile. This is discussed further below.

Islamic Opposition

Whilst Islam is accorded religious, cultural and historical importance, there is a widespread fear of Islamic political parties, especially since the rise of fundamentalism in countries to the south. As stated above, Tajikistan is the only country where Islamic political parties are allowed to operate, and the power sharing arrangement seems to have brought a degree of stability to the country for the moment. Islam is less well-established in Kazakhstan[15] and Kyrgyzstan, except in southern Kyrgyzstan around Osh and Jalal Abad.

Uzbekistan has the largest Muslim population in Central Asia, incorporating, as it does, the ancient centres of learning of Khiva, Bukhara, Samarkand and the Ferghana valley centres of Kokand and Andijan. During the Soviet period, Islam was strictly regulated. In the period immediately prior to independence and since, Islam has been rediscovered, but it is still essentially regulated by the regime: sermons are edited and guidelines on spiritual and social issues are distributed. Since

---

[15] George (2001) notes that the current Islamic 'revival' in Kazakhstan is found among the more westernised middle classes, as part of reaffirmation of national identity.

independence, a loose network of independent clergy (imams), who are reluctant to comply with government guidelines, has emerged. The Mosques of these imams are not registered.[16] The All-Union (all FSU) Muslim organisation, the Islamic Renaissance Party (founded in Astrakhan in present-day Russia) opened its Uzbek chapter in 1992, until it was banned and its leader disappeared.

The Adolat (Justice) Islamic movement was established in Ferghana valley, around Namangan and Andijan, and took control of the area briefly in 1992 and imposed an Islamic order, with sharia courts and the abolition of alcohol. It was seen as representing a regionalist threat to the centre and was later banned. (Subsequently, a new pro-government political party with the same name was formed.) During the 1990s there were other attempts to ban Western forms of dress and prevent mixed gender meetings. The most extreme Islamic opposition movement is the Islamic Movement of Uzbekistan (IMU) supported by Saudi Wahabbism, which was founded in 1997 in Kabul and which has the explicit aim of ousting Karimov.

The international organisation, Hizb ut-Tahrir (the liberation party), based in London and which aims to revive the Caliphate and establish a transnational community of Muslims based on sharia law, is also banned in Uzbekistan. The movement relays its message through the distribution of leaflets. There have been numerous arrests in recent years of those suspected of belonging to Hizb ut-Tahrir along with allegations of torture at the hands of the authorities.

A modest revival of Islam has been noted in Turkmenistan since independence and the Government has incorporated some aspects of Muslim tradition into its efforts to define a Turkmen identity.[17] The state funds a Council on Religious Affairs, which has representatives from both the Muslim community and the Russian Orthodox church. This plays an intermediary role between the government bureaucracy and religious organisations.

The need to find a balance between the promotion of a national identity which refers back to the pre-Soviet times, and therefore must acknowledge the role of Islam, and the fear of a threat from politicised, fundamentalist Muslim groups is one that concerns all five nations. In Uzbekistan, the balance has tipped towards repression, and allegations of torture against those suspected of belonging to non-registered Islamic groups has brought international condemnation and threats of the withdrawal of aid. At the community level, a recent study found that the role

---

[16] Roy (2002: 133) says of these 'such endeavours to foster new types of grass-root communities ... have yet to succeed, but one should not underestimate the potential impact of the call to create a more equitable and just society through the application of Islamic laws and values'.

[17] Bureau of Democracy, Human Rights and Labor. US Department of State, March 2002, Country Reports on Human Rights Practices, Turkmenistan.

of religious groups is respected, but that these groups, because of their confessional and self-sufficient nature, stand somewhat apart from the rest of civil society (FACT 2003).

Local Government and Decentralisation

All five countries have inherited administrative structures from the Soviet Union, with decentralised levels of administration (Hokimats in Kazakhstan, Akimats in Kyrgyzstan, Khokimats in Uzbekistan, Khukumats in Tajikistan and Khakimlik in Turkmenistan) at *oblast* (provincial) and *raion* (district) level. Alongside these administrations, there are bodies of locally elected councillors (at *raion* and *oblast* level) who meet at least twice a year, and who exert some influence over their respective administrative bodies.

At *oblast* and *raion* levels, positions are all appointed, ensuring these provincial and district governors and mayors see their main responsibility and accountability as being to the President. Donors make a great play of this. However, as will be shown in the following chapters, there are many and increasing examples of enlightened officials at lower levels of the state apparatus working in innovative ways with local residents and groups.

The sub-district administrations in rural areas (which, in Soviet times, were attached to state farms, collective farms and enterprises) have now been re-organised into new local bodies and in all five countries laws on local self-administration have 'established the right to self-administration'. This re-organisation at local level seems to be evolving and is influenced by varying proposals for decentralisation. In some countries, the leadership at this level has been made into an elected post. These local levels of government (self-government bodies) are responsible for the maintenance of public buildings and infrastructure (schools, public baths, water supplies, local roads and so on), providing the community with necessary technical services, and collecting tax, user fees and rent payments.

In Kyrgyzstan, a new local level self-management body (to run alongside the state administrative body at village level) was established in 1996 and is known as the Ail Okmotu. In December 2001, new legislation declared that the head of the Ail Okmotu should be appointed by election.[18] Individuals are to be elected for a period of five years by a general meeting of the constituent village/s. In early 2005, it was announced that Kazakhstan will begin experimenting with elected local officials at the lower levels of government. The Tajik Government is also moving towards elections for officials at the Jamoat (*raion*) level.

---

[18] Although in practice those elected have to be approved by the local *Akim*.

In Uzbekistan, the local self-governing body is the *mahalla* committee. Each committee has the duty of recording births, marriages and deaths, and will also have a varying number of sub-committees, for example to organise ceremonial events, maintain public order, housing stock and finances and to deal with issues concerning women, youth and veterans. For more information on the debate about the *mahalla* committee's role in civil society, see the first case study in Chapter 8.

In all five countries, all local administrations receive the bulk of their revenue from state transfers. At all levels of local government (local, *raion* and *oblast*) the administrations have limited financial autonomy and are strongly dependent on the centre. National budget funds are redistributed among budgets of different levels according to long-established rules and procedures. The dependence of local levels of government upon the central bureaucracy is thus entrenched in the local budget structure. The local levels of administration have the responsibility for distributing funds, from the local Department of Social Protection to specified groups of populations in their territories (families with many children, female-headed households, pensioners, veterans and so on).

Local taxes form a very small share of self-government revenues. Local self-governing structures have the right to keep a percentage of the rates and taxes they collect in their locality (for electricity and so on) before passing the greater part to the district authorities; this constitutes a very small income. Whilst these bodies also have the right to raise revenue locally, and are being actively encouraged to do so, there seems to be limited opportunity for this. There are examples of these local government structures that have set up small income-generating enterprises (dairies, canteens, small shops) in order to increase their revenue and also to create employment.

National Poverty Reduction Programmes

As stated previously, in Soviet times the concept of poverty did not exist, and the term is still not in official use in either Turkmenistan or Uzbekistan. The prevalent, Soviet, approach had focused on ensuring the provision of basic products, consumer goods and services for the citizens. The World Bank study, 'Consultations with the Poor', conducted in Kyrgyzstan in 1996, was one of the first attempts to monitor poverty in the region.

Of the five countries, only Kyrgyzstan and Tajikistan are fully involved in the World Bank's programme of financing which requires the production of Poverty Reduction Strategy Papers.[19] In Kyrgyzstan, the final version of the PRSP was

---

[19] Uzbekistan has worked on an 'interim' poverty reduction strategy paper.

published in 2003, and in Tajikistan in 2002. Kyrgyzstan was one of the ten original pilot countries for the World Bank's new Comprehensive Development Framework (CDF) approach to channelling development assistance monies through the government budget. Kyrgyzstan hosted a relatively wide consultation process during 2001, involving regional governments and representatives of civil society and the private sector. Once production of Poverty Reduction Strategy Papers became a necessary mechanism for developing the CDF, Kyrgyzstan then drew on the material produced for the CDF in order to produce its Poverty Reduction Strategy (PRS). In Tajikistan the PRSP was developed by a Presidential Working Group led by the state adviser to the President on economic policy and consisting of scientists and government officials. Nine sector working groups were established consisting of representatives from Parliament, local authorities, higher educational establishments, the private sector, NGOs and other. Between March and June 2001, 56 seminars and round-table conferences were conducted to discuss the sector notes prepared for the PRSP. These involved more than 2,000 participants.

Kazakhstan, which is regarded as a middle-income country, has drawn up its own domestic poverty reduction strategy which relies almost exclusively on the anticipated spin-off effects from economic growth. In Uzbekistan, the Asian Development Bank has been working with the Centre for Economic Research in assisting the Government of Uzbekistan in the preparation of a National Comprehensive Mid-term Strategy for Improving the Living Standards of the People in Uzbekistan. The first draft of this was produced in late 2003. Turkmenistan still does not recognise poverty as a problem; however it has worked with UNDP in monitoring progress under the UN Millennium Development Goals.

However, these Poverty Reduction Programmes are very macro-level programmes, and the link with local level budgeting procedures is hard to ascertain. Those enlightened *oblasts* and more local governments, where they exist, have to operate within the traditional restrictive vertical budgetary-setting procedures. In addition, a report from the Overseas Development Institute's PRSP Monitoring and Synthesis Project noted that most PRSPs in the countries of the FSU that have produced them had given a higher priority to equitable growth, employment and social welfare than 'poverty reduction'. This study also noted the limited local ownership of the process, with involvement often limited to financial ministries and officials; limited linkages to other planning and budgetary processes; limited involvement of parliamentarians, limited participation characterised by low levels of trust between governments and citizens and the low levels of capacity of civil society organisations to engage.[20]

---

[20] Quoted in the Department for International Development's Regional Assistance Plan for Central Asia, South Caucasus & Moldova, June 2004 (http://www.dfid.gov.uk/pubs/files/rapcascm.pdf, accessed 2 June 2005).

Issues of civil society engagement in policy processes will be examined in further detail in Chapter 8.

Conclusion

Despite differences in certain areas, particularly in the potential for exploitation of natural resources and for economic growth, there are underlying similarities between the Central Asian states, particularly with regards to social organisation. The Soviet era left a clear mark on all five nations in terms of social organisation and political systems. Structures of government are similar, especially in the authority vested in the presidency and in the structures and processes of local government.

The collapse of the Soviet economic network and command system of production affected the region in its entirety. The effects of the 'transition' period have also manifested themselves in similar ways throughout the region, and patterns of social disintegration, unemployment and poverty can be identified across national frontiers. In general, independence brought with it, for the majority of the populations, radical and disturbing changes to the established way of life. Communities have become polarised, and established formal and informal networks have been weakened. It is against this backdrop that some alternative support mechanisms have emerged amongst poorer communities, and there is some evidence of the strengthening of pre-Soviet solidarity groupings. The next chapters will look in more detail at pre-Soviet and then Soviet forms of social organisation, and how organisational forms and practices continue to be important in contemporary Central Asia.

CHAPTER 4

Pre-Soviet Forms of Association

The Celebration of the Past

The post-independence period has been one of a national cultural-historical revival in all five countries of Central Asia. This is obvious even to visitors on a short stay in the region. In Kyrgyzstan, the oral epics of Manas have been studied and honoured, as have famous folk-singers or Manaschi.[1] In Kazakhstan, grand new monuments erected in different regions celebrate leaders from the three 'hordes'. Huge renovations have been carried out in the world-famous cultural-historical sites of Uzbekistan. In even the smallest villages around the region small silver-roofed mosques have sprung up – a huge investment of local as well as external resources. In Dushanbe, where the statue of Lenin once stood (site of some of the first clashes of the civil war) there is now an enormous monument to the Timurids, recalling the age when this was not a small isolated nation but a power that extended to the Black Sea and Indian Ocean. In Ashgabat, as well as the revolving statue of Turkmenbashi, there are monuments honouring Turkmen warriors from different centuries in the many new squares and parks of the capital.

None of this could be done without an engagement from the intelligentsia or 'cultural élites'. A recent study of such groups in Uzbekistan shows how they have been co-opted into the nation-building project (Adams 2004). Ideologically, the independence period has presented the educated classes of the region, on whom so much in political life and civil society depends, with a choice: join the state's celebration of traditional values, or try to press forward to (Western-style) modernity.

---

[1] Manas is an epic poem about a Kyrgyz warrior called Manas, which was recited and thus preserved by wandering bards called Manaschi.

Many NGOs are vehicles for individuals and groups pursuing the second option, and among those working in the civil society sector in the 1990s there was often an element of scepticism about the promotion of traditional forms of culture and association – as reflected in the mapping reports discussed in Chapter 2.

However, the attitude of international agencies themselves towards these elements of indigenous Central Asian society has not remained static since their initial engagement in the region. There is a newer focus on the community coming from external donors, and greater awareness of the need to engage with social systems already present, particularly in rural areas. This trend has only begun to gather momentum over the past four or five years. The misconception that civil society could start from a 'blank slate' was quite prevalent among donors during the 1990s. Even now, pre-Soviet traditions, institutions and practices are only classified as 'civil society' when they lend themselves to the aspirations and working practices of external donors. In contemporary discussions of civil society in Central Asia, there is often much criticism of agencies which duplicate structures that already exist in rural communities by creating 'initiative groups' to implement projects. As a result, a number of donors have started to work with particular aspects of what they now view as 'traditional' civil society: most notably the *aksakals*, the *mahalla*, black cashiers or *gaps* and *ashar*. These are the most visible aspects of traditional forms of social organisation and are useful for external donors, in that they can facilitate certain types of initiative: *aksakals* can give legitimacy to donor work in a particular area, if they are brought on-side; the *mahalla* has the potential to enshrine the tenets of participatory local democracy; *ashar* is a culturally recognised form of voluntary labour that can be used to mobilise communities for project implementation; and the black cash desks are similar to the ideas behind rotating micro-credit initiatives. These are the elements of pre-Soviet society that many donors have taken to working with in recent years. This chapter will briefly describe them and examine how they have been both adopted and used by external donors.

The question raised but not fully answered in INTRAC's country reports about how to define indigenous forms of social organisation reflects a general dilemma as to how to evaluate and classify these. Whilst more recently donors' incorporation of certain traditional aspects of Central Asian society into their work has perhaps brought these forms of organisation greater legitimacy, there is still debate in the literature and amongst practitioners as to whether these practices and institutions should be classified as a part of civil society.[2]

Historically, in Western Europe, emerging forms of association that were open for individuals to join according to their individual interests or motivations were seen as progressive elements of society. These contrasted in nature to organisational and asso-

---

[2] Babajanian et al. (2005) argue that traditional networks should be understood as elements of 'communal' civil society.

ciational forms that were based on kinship and other traditional structures, which could be seen (and experienced) as restrictive. This was the moment in which individuals were able to join other like-minded people in groups that were based around particular interests (merchants' guilds, for example) in order to support each other and perhaps work to promote the interests of the group. Solidarity groupings based on birth were left behind. This emergence of forms of association that could be both joined and left freely is seen as the key point in the development of civil society.

However, increasingly, analysts of civil society in non-Western contexts are advocating that definitions of the concept should take in the idea of traditional or 'communal' civil society. They argue that certain forms of traditional network or kinship structures are an intrinsic part of society that cannot be ignored or over-written and that including them within a definition of civil society makes more sense for certain non-Western contexts. Indeed, the literature about civil society development in other parts of the world frequently sees the existence of tradition-al and communal forms of social grouping as an indicator of real, 'locally grown', civil society. Furthermore, they constitute what are possibly more appropriate forms of association for these societies, as they are better suited to local context. They are seen by some as a local response to the homogenising effects of global capitalism and the neo-liberal assumption that one size fits all. They may provide more appropriate structures for citizens to have some influence on developments affecting their lives than structures imported from the West.

Certainly it is now hard to ignore traditional elements of Central Asian society, since in all five nations so much attention has been given by government to redis-covering and reclaiming pre-Soviet history and culture. However, it is important not to exaggerate the break with the Soviet period – which promoted important ele-ments of history and culture, and during which many traditional practices contin-ued.[3] Today, the nation-building projects of Central Asian governments are re-eval-uating the worth of the pre-Soviet era, and affording great value to that perceived as 'traditional'. This includes practices that would be considered unacceptable by foreign donors.[4] These will be discussed in the following section.

---

[3] One example is the female mullahs or 'otines' who maintained their roles as religious mentors for women (Fathi 1997). Another is the practice of polygamy (Akiner 1997). Many of these aspects of traditional society were outlawed by the Soviet system, but they continued on a small scale, were rarely documented and were purposively kept secret.

[4] Polygamy, as a traditional practice, has probably been afforded a further degree of legiti-macy by the serious debate held at government level in Kyrgyzstan and Tajikistan as to whether it should be legalised as an attempt to alleviate poverty for women, minimise prostitution and increase the ethnic titular population. In Tajikistan, it is considered by some to be a practical solution to the gender imbalance resulting from male deaths during the civil war (Tabyshalieva 2000).

Pre-Soviet Social Organisation

External observers often refer to the complex nature of Central Asian society, with vague mention of clans, tribes and kinship groups. As Roy has explained, gaining a clear understanding of what he calls, more generally, 'solidarity groupings' is fraught with difficulty. This is because identities that people of the region assign to themselves vary dramatically, and change according to circumstance. These can be regional or ethno-linguistic, refer to an ancient tribe, a city or a village or imply a type of 'aristocratic' religious ancestry.

Discussing tribalism, Roy explains that in the strict sense of 'lineage groups defined by a genealogy which organises them into a system, into circles or branches', it is relevant to Kazakhs, Kyrgyz and Turkmens, for whom 'tribal belonging is generally recognised and plays an important role in the functioning of the society and of political life, at least in rural areas' (Roy 2000: 23). He notes that tribes have never existed for Tajiks, and although among certain Uzbek groups there is a memory of tribalism, 'it is rarely relevant to explain political affiliations and is often discarded disdainfully by young generations' (Roy 2000). But he argues that tribal identity is a shifting notion that can be reinvented.

The existence of tribal identities is linked to the ways in which society had traditionally been organised. As was shown in Chapter 2, the Uzbeks began to distinguish themselves from other neighbouring groups when, from around the fourteenth century onwards, the Uzbek khans converted to Islam, and moved from their base in southern Siberia towards the plains of Transoxiania.[5] Of the Uzbeks, Melvin notes,

> Their previously nomadic lifestyle began to give way to a sedentary existence. Many Uzbeks settled in the cities and towns of the region and began to assimilate with the previous inhabitants of the region (Melvin 2000: 6).[6]

This may explain why memories of tribalism amongst Uzbeks are weaker than amongst the other Turkic Central Asian peoples who have a more recent history of nomadic existence.

---

[5] They were not the first to settle these areas, however. The plains were the site of some of the most famous Silk Road cities. These had existed at the time Alexander the Great was in the region. He passed through Marakanda, which was to become Samarkand, in approximately 330 BCE.

[6] Melvin continues: 'elite level bilingualism became an important part of the region's identity with the political life of the court conducted predominantly in a Turkic language (Chagatai), while high culture was largely the province of Persian'(2000: 6). Uzbek is a Turkic language, and Tajik a Persian one.

The Tajik way of life, however, was very different, since Tajiks were related to the ancient Persians and have been settled for over two thousand years. As Akiner (2002: 152) states, there were two main areas of Tajik settlement: on the plains (the Ferghana Valley and the basins of the Zarafshan, Syr Darya and Surkhandarya Rivers); and in the foothills and mountain valleys of present day Tajikistan.[7] As the Uzbeks moved from the tribal steppe lands in the north to the plains they began to take control of the settled areas. The Uzbeks settled and gradually adopted associational forms more appropriate to the administrative needs of settled areas.

For the rest of the Central Asian peoples, however, the nomadic or semi-nomadic lifestyle was the norm. In Kazakhstan, Kangas (1995: 273) states that during the pre-Soviet period traditional norms and values, based on clan and tribal loyalties, were passed from one generation to another over centuries. These norms dictated behaviour and communal interaction: 'Politics was the art of family ties and loyalties.' Narbekova states,

Ethnic identity ... is an important aspect of Kazakh national consciousness ... Although most Western scholars argue that tribalism is associated with political instability, it is largely responsible for the survival of Kazakh society through various periods of history (Narbekova 1999: 167).

Kazakh people were divided between three tribal and nomadic 'hordes': the Great, Middle and Little hordes, each of which had a regional base. The divisions between the three hordes of Kazakh people were supposedly abolished by the Tsarist Russians between 1822 and 1845.

The Kyrgyz moved into the area that is now Kyrgyzstan (and other surrounding areas) after the invasion of their lands further north by the Mongols. Like the Kazakhs, they were a nomadic people whose way of life was dictated by the seasons and the search for pastures for their horses and sheep. Anderson says of the Kyrgyz:

Communities were organised around kinship groups and every Kyrgyz was supposed to be able to trace their ancestors back at least seven generations ... As families grew, their auls (mobile villages) were split up as sons left home with flocks and spouse to seek fresh pastures elsewhere ... Each family belonged to a larger clan group, and each of these in turn was part of a wider tribal confederation. And though these were mostly nomadic peoples each of these communities had a territorial base, and each was dominated by an 'aristocracy' – defined largely in terms of the size of cattle holdings which in turn determined access to the most favourable pastures (Anderson 1999: 2).

---

[7] The plain dwellers were part of the urban-based civilisations of Transoxiana. The mountain dwellers were largely cut off from outside influences until the Soviet era.

However, the tribal confederations of the Kyrgyz were more numerous than those of the Kazakhs, and there were traditions within these which strike some modern analysts as representing democratic practices, including some forms of consensual decision-making, and a limited form of meritocracy when it came to choosing leaders.

In more settled rural areas, the story is somewhat different. For example, in Karakalpakstan, now the semi-autonomous republic in the far west of present day Uzbekistan, each tribe occupied a certain territory. Within the territory, clans built irrigation canals and used adjacent lands for growing crops and grazing. These lands were communally owned. Here,

> Karakalpak villages (auls) were located along their kin canals, diverted from the primary canal which was usually called after the kinship group which had constructed it. Water was used in turns. Each of the auls had their own outlet from a canal. The volume of water delivered to it was proportional to the number of workers assigned by the aul for the cleaning of the canal in the spring. Kindred groups (koshe) within the auls used communal lands, and regulated the ways of life (FACT 2003: 9).

Recent INTRAC research in Karakalpakstan would suggest that in some rural areas, villages still have names that refer to the dominant clan (which are used interchangeably with the names bestowed upon them by the local *kolkhoz*) and certain traditions surrounding marriage between or within clans are still adhered to.

As suggested above, rural settlements in Transoxiana were often centred around the irrigation channels constructed from the great river systems. Specific forms of association developed around these territorial areas. Similar patterns of communal forms of land use existed across almost all of what is now Uzbekistan prior to the shake-up of agriculture instigated by the Soviets.

> A rural community in irrigated farming areas usually owned grasslands and non-irrigated lands for summer crops. Communal areas under crops were distributed ... by lot. The right for an allotment remained for the period that it was cultivated. An abandoned plot may be used by other people (under a system of neighbourhood priority). Usually, communal lands were not sold, and only in the beginning of the twentieth century was this rule broken in some areas (FACT 2003: 8).

Social Groupings in Contemporary Central Asia

Awareness of tribal groupings and clan affiliations is still current among some Central Asian peoples. These were not entirely wiped out by seventy years of the Soviet system. The authors of the Kyrgyz mapping report argue that with independence, tribal and ethnic identities are becoming more important (Baimatov et al. 2002). Certainly for the Kazakhs and Kyrgyz, the nomadic way of life within which tribal identity was originally so important is no longer in evidence. Nonetheless it is supported by some aspects of life – at least symbolically – such as the summer migration of rural Kyrgyz families to the summer *jailoo* (pastures), or the transfer of large tracts of land sown to corn in the Soviet period back to grassland for herding and the re-establishment of pastimes like falconry.

But whilst tribes and clans are no longer independent institutions in Central Asia, there are arguments that they have become the basis for some political organisation, and that systems of patronage enable clan members in positions of power or authority to distribute benefits and other high-ranking positions to members of the same clan. The Kazakh report suggests that the process of rediscovery of Kazakh national heritage has given weight to the idea that tribes and clans are important and that there has been a certain 'rediscovery' of old tribal links. They go further, arguing that a type of Kazakh aristocracy continues to exist:

> Leaders associated with traditional clan based communities have emerged in every sphere of society, occupying high positions both in political and business structures (Dissenova et al. 2002: 16).

It is the view of the researchers writing the Kazakh report that these traditional relationships have, to some extent, filled the vacuum caused by the collapse of the Soviet system. Roy has pointed out, by contrast, that in some areas there is a high degree of continuity with Soviet times.

> The kolkhozes were usually established on the basis of local identity groups, whatever the anthropological nature of these groups (clans in tribal areas, extended families and mahalla in other areas, identity groups called *awlad*, *qawm*, etc) (Roy 1999: 112).

The families within these identity groups that took up leadership of the *kolkhoz* were not always the same élite that had been dominant in the years preceding the Bolshevik Revolution. But Roy's fieldwork in Tajikistan and Uzbekistan during the 1990s suggests not only that leadership of the *kolkhozes* during the Soviet era was held within the same family, but that with independence this pattern of leadership has not changed. Indeed, he believes that independence has accentuated the role of former *kolkhoz* leaders, who behaved more like local notables than *apparatchiks*.

> There was no turnover of kolkhoz leaders in Central Asia. The leading families were well-rooted in the local population (sometimes they had ties to an older leadership, tribal or religious; sometimes they were descended from the elites created by the Bolshevik Revolution). ... This importance of the 'dynasties' of kolkhoz leaders is expressed by the changing of names after independence – the Soviet name is often dropped in favour of that of the founding father or the chairman who shaped the kolkhoz's identity during the post-Stalin era (Roy 1999: 115).

Roy sees a similar type of 'window-dressing' in Kyrgyzstan and Kazakhstan where supposed privatisation of farms has done little to reshape local power structures in rural areas, which are still based on the domination of local notables. Furthermore, urban élites will often have strong links to rural areas.

The extent to which tribal and clan identities impact upon daily life in the independent era and how they might influence newer forms of associations is not clear. It is a subject, it would appear, that has yet to be researched in detail. Roy's work suggests that solidarity groupings are very important indeed. He argues that, above all, what matters is belonging to some kind of group, whatever it is based upon, since an individual's relationship to the state or access to resources will pass through the network to which he or she belongs. For Western observers, the existence of tribes is often assumed to mean factionalism, potential for conflict and entrenched forms of clientelism. This may go some way to explain the absence of exploratory research on the topic.

Other traditional Central Asian practices have a more visible impact on populations, particularly women. These include bride-stealing, the subjugation of the *kelin* or daughter-in-law (especially those who move to the home of their husband's family) and polygamy. The first of these, bride-stealing, is not a clear-cut issue. While it appears that the practice is on the increase, it is a term that can encompass many different arrangements, including consensual marriages between couples where family members might not approve of the union or as a ruse by the groom's family to avoid paying bride price. Some scholars in the region play down the statistics that show the increase in the practice, linking these to increased economic insecurity and the difficulty of paying for elaborate weddings. However, the research of Dr Russell Kleinbach[8] at the American University of Central Asia in Bishkek and video documentary evidence shows that the practice is often tanta-

---

[8] http://faculty.philau.edu/kleinbachr/ala_kachuu.htm (accessed 2 June 2005).

mount to abduction and rape. Furthermore, Handrahan's (2004) research has produced statistical evidence of the widespread occurrence of these kidnappings and the use of violence against women being kidnapped in this way.

Another aspect of traditional Central Asian culture are the *tois*. These are large-scale community celebrations held to celebrate marriages and circumcisions, as well as to mark funerals and significant dates of mourning after a death. Social pressure to host these occasions, the expectation of gifts and reciprocation in kind can be a significant financial burden for many. Families are often obliged to sell off assets in order to organise such events. These forms of reciprocal arrangement could well be seen as elements of a certain type of civil society. Although in times of economic difficulty people are often thought to rely more heavily on networks of mutual support, there is some evidence to suggest that poorer members of society are avoiding involvement in the *tois* (Kuehnast and Dudwick 2004). This will have an impact upon relationships within communities as social capital is diminished. Unlike in the West, there is no clear division between the public and the private spheres: births, deaths and marriages are community affairs, not family ones. It should be noted that the ways in which widespread poverty impacts upon forms of social support can vary greatly. Research in Tajikistan suggests that traditional mutual support and solidarity remain very strong and in some cases are the only means for poor households to survive.[9]

Finally, there is the role of Islam. Clearly, religion was very important in pre-Soviet times in the settled areas of Central Asia. It has often been reported that the settled peoples of the region identified themselves, not as Tajiks or Uzbeks, for example, but as Muslims. As in other Muslim countries, the mosque plays a potentially important role in terms of encouraging charitable giving and providing education. Adherence to Islam is certainly becoming more visible all around the region, but in general there is thought to be a very low level of understanding of the tenets and teachings of Islam. Unfortunately, little research has been done into the role of the mosque and religious associations in the development of civil society in Central Asia. This may well be due to the sensitive nature of the topic and the difficulties associated with doing research on it.

Engaging with 'Traditional' Forms of Social Organisation

INTRAC's new programme of civil society strengthening from 2001 made a conscious effort to understand and involve traditional forms of social or community organisation. This was in response to the realisation that previous work had

---

[9] E-mail communication with B. Babajanian, February 2005.

focused on NGOs and that the development community needed to build up knowledge about other players in civil society (Garbutt 2003).

In order to prepare a programme of support to community-based organisations (CBOs), INTRAC engaged local community development advisors in Kyrgyzstan, Kazakhstan and Uzbekistan and began a short research phase. The primary aim of this work was to further understanding of the dynamics of communities, particularly in rural areas (which had not enjoyed the same attention from donors in the 1990s). The secondary aim was to decide which of these institutions could become possible 'partners' in civil society strengthening and which practices could help promote social development work.

The research took a case study approach to an examination of community development. Three communities for study were selected in each country by the local researchers in consultation with ICAP partners – national NGOs, civil society support centres and NGO support organisations. The fieldwork trips were generally undertaken after a number of previous visits by the local researchers and other contact with partners at training events and workshops. The first day of each visit was often spent with local NGO or support centre staff to learn more about the area and the projects being implemented in order to reach consensus about which communities would be appropriate for study. The three local researchers spent approximately five days in each case study area in their designated countries, collecting data through semi-structured interviews, focus groups and occasional mini-surveys. Data from the case studies was then analysed and written up into an INTRAC publication (Earle et al. 2004). This paper covers the following themes: the individual and the community-based organisation; the resilience of Soviet institutions; pre-Soviet practices and forms of social organisation; perceptions of gender and 'women's role' and community engagement with local government. Subsequent sections of this volume draw on this recent work.

There are certain traditional forms of association that have become very popular with donors. These are generally derived from traditions amongst settled populations. For example, cities in the Ferghana Valley and on the plains in present-day Uzbekistan and Kyrgyzstan had common features of neighbourhood organisation. Towns and settlements were divided up into *mahalla* in Tashkent and the Ferghana Valley or *guzar* in the cities of Bukhara, Karshi, Shakhrisabz. Traditionally located around a mosque, and sharing certain common property resources, these neighbourhoods were based on democratic principles and mutual assistance where social pressure was exerted on residents to behave in socially acceptable ways, or face expulsion. As already noted, these institutions formed the basis for Soviet and independent era local self-government bodies, and the concept of *mahalla* as community and the influence it exerts on local populations is still very strong in some areas. They are considered one of the most important traditional civic institutions in Central Asia. Donors have taken to involving them in projects based around ideas of social partnership as representatives of the state, but also make reference to their tradition of mutual assistance.

Village Elders in Kyrgyzstan and Uzbekistan

Within the *mahallas*, various social practices were followed that were linked to Islam. Traditional forms of obligatory philanthropy existed, which included charitable giving and provision of food to poorer families at community celebrations without them having to contribute in kind. Local imams and elders, known as *aksakals* in Kyrgyzstan and Uzbekistan, played an important role in community life. *Aksakals* and elders are still very much a feature of life across the region, particularly in rural areas, although the religious connection between *aksakals* and the mosque is no longer so explicit. They are men who are generally held in high esteem by their communities and who are chosen by their peers to fulfil particular village functions. In some cases, one individual can be the unofficial 'chief' of a village. Duties include sitting on the *aksakals*' court, which deals with disputes between neighbours and between and within families, including discouraging divorce. They are also responsible for mobilising community members to participate in neighbourhood or village activities and for organising celebrations. Sievers (2003) notes that it was the responsibility of the *aksakals* in traditional urban Uzbek *mahallas* to encourage richer residents to distribute some of their wealth amongst poorer residents.

As has been noted above, donors' drive to work in rural villages is a relatively recent phenomenon. Wanting to ensure distance between their work and the apparatus of the state, and to ensure 'participation' in and 'ownership' of a project, donors have tended to negotiate access to communities through the *aksakals*. This is not just a mark of respect or an attempt to adhere to local custom. *Aksakals* are, in essence, 'gatekeepers', who can use their authority to arrange village meetings to discuss whether to co-operate with donors.

The term *aksakal* means, literally, 'white beard', and they are almost always male and a member of the older generation. Their role as adjudicator in domestic and community disputes and the respect they command locally suggests an ability to take an objective stance and to draw on years of experience when deciding what is best for their community. This is not always the case, however, as can be seen by the case study below.

Case Study – *Aksakals*

Research in south Kyrgyzstan showed how the desire of donors to reach local communities could put the *aksakal* in a strong position to consolidate his own power. In one village where research was undertaken, the *aksakal* had used his influence to dictate the direction of an irrigation system that was to be installed in a neighbouring village. This was to ensure that the houses of his two sons who were resident in the second village would be the principal beneficiaries of the water pipeline. These individuals were already relatively wealthy. Their gains from the project came at the expense of less well-off households in the village. During the research visit, a group of poorer women expressed their disappointment with the project: the location of their garden plots relative to the pipeline meant that there had not been noticeable improvements to their productivity. This project had been donor funded and standard participatory methods had been employed to assess needs and priorities within the village. However, the women pointed out that contradicting the *aksakal* so as to benefit from the project would not have been in their long-term interests. He is a respected man, in some way related to the majority of residents in the village. Furthermore, he gives charity to poorer residents after the harvest and can provide temporary paid employment to villagers at certain times in the agricultural calendar. It was further feared by this group of women that speaking out against his plans for village improvement would jeopardise their chances of inclusion in a micro-credit scheme soon to be introduced in the village, which it was thought he would be administrating.

Further investigation provided clarity on why the local American-funded support centre was keen to work with this particular *aksakal*. Since the village had been established in the late 1980s, he had often mobilised the population to improve local infrastructure, and had ideas for further development in the community. For donors in Central Asia, experience and motivation are often the key criteria that help shape decisions as to which villages in one particular area will be funded. However, this particular example shows how important it is to examine power relationships in villages and how these might affect the way that projects are designed and implemented.

Donors' aim is for project related decision-making processes to be democratic, but if the *aksakals* do not decide in favour, implementation of a project will be very difficult, even if local people are keen to be involved. *Aksakals'* influence is needed to call further meetings and organise contributions of labour or cash from villagers. Also, taking into consideration their weight of authority, villagers are unlikely to question or contradict such a decision. In sum, *aksakals* can make or break donor projects (Earle et al. 2003).

The example above also highlights the problem of gender relations in rural communities, and the extent to which women feel able to voice their priorities. Other analysts of the region have raised similar concerns about issues of authority in rural communities and how these can be concentrated in the elderly male figures of the *aksakals'* court and the *mahalla*.[10] Ilkhamov (2001) notes that the increasing levels of adherence to the tenets of Islam has meant a return to a greater emphasis on patriarchal values in poor rural areas of Central Asia. Kandiyoti (2002) sees a retrenchment of attitudes towards women, who, with the growth of subsistence agriculture, are being increasingly drawn back into the sphere of the household. She records a positive example, in Uzbekistan, of the *mahalla* committee finding in favour of a women claimant who wished to carry on working as a nurse while pregnant, against her father-in-law's wishes, but notes that a trend in the opposite direction is more likely.

> Women's committees still exist within *mahalla* committees ... There is some evidence that they are still used by women as a possible resource in cases of conflict, but this is taking place against a background of hardening attitudes regarding women's work and mobility (Kandiyoti 2002: 63).

She goes on to note that 'increasing social conservatism and the lack of alternative avenues to press their rights are likely to have disempowering consequences for women' (2000: 70). Certainly, the low status accorded to women, particularly the *kelin*, has the potential to limit women's access to a fair hearing from the *mahalla* committees or the *aksakals'* courts were they to enter into dispute with a male family member, for example. More research is needed into the role of the *aksakal* and the *aksakals'* court in rural areas to examine the extent to which elderly male villagers are open to the needs of the younger generation, particularly of women. Handrahan (2001) notes that in Kyrgyzstan, the unelected members of these courts have been given powers of judgement and punishment by the President and that they have the local police force under their control. She cites an Amnesty International report on allegations of illegal detention and punishments of whipping and stoning meted out by the *aksakals'* courts. Babajanian (2004), writing about the Tajik context, indicates that cultural and traditional norms can reinforce the exclusion of women and other social groups.

---

[10] The sentences on women passed by all male tribal councils in Pakistan have brought international condemnation.

> ## Case Study – the *Avlod* in Tajikistan
>
> The *avlod* is a traditional community institution found in Tajikistan that regulates relationships among community members who are joined by kinship bonds. The *avlod* can protect the interests of its community members and contribute to their well-being. For example, if a village resident expresses a wish to migrate to find work, this decision must be approved by the *avlod* elders or its head. Their involvement seeks to ensure that the potential migrant (generally male) and his family are supported by the rest of the community. As such, the *avlod* raises a contribution for the migrant's travel expenses and makes arrangements for the care of his family. However, as Babajanian (2004) points out, there are also negative consequences of the *avlod's* intervention in family affairs. He notes cases where the *avlod* has prevented wives of labour migrants from selling crops and managing household budgets during their husbands' absence. He also points out that kinship affiliation to *avlods* can divide communities and that members may promote their own interests at the expense of broader community needs.
>
> Source: Babajanian 2004.

There are also positive examples of attempts to adapt traditional structures to the needs of other groups, and it should be acknowledged that ensuring that traditional institutions are inclusive ones is not an easy task. In Tajikistan, the Aga Khan Foundation's Mountain Societies Development and Support Programme has established village organisations along the lines of traditional village groups. Their approach is considered an effective way of promoting community mobilisation (Babajanian 2004).[11] A Kyrgyz initiative documented by INTRAC in Talas *oblast* involved the formation of a community-based organisation determined to act to stem the flow of younger people leaving the village for urban centres. The leader and members of the group were themselves young, and initially faced opposition from the local authorities and the rest of the village. However, once the group proved itself by taking up initiatives that benefited the whole community (after it received funding from an American donor) the leader of this group was invited onto the *aksakals'* council as an equal partner. This does not appear to have been at the behest of the donor, rather that the skills and commitment of the group were acknowledged by the *aksakals'* council. 'Youth' *aksakals* are not prevalent in Central Asia, however. Nor is it common to find women in rural areas who command authority in the public sphere. As such, donors need to be aware that power relations and structural hierarchies are thoroughly entrenched in Central Asian rural society and that simplistic needs assessments and participatory tools will not

---

[11] The village organisations are discussed in more detail in Chapter 7.

necessarily uncover a wide range of contrasting viewpoints. This is also highlighted in the case study of the use of *ashar*.

Ashar

One of the key roles of the *aksakals*, for donors, is organising community voluntary labour. Voluntary labour by the community for the community has a long history in the region. The practice is known as *ashar* in Kyrgyzstan (it is most prevalent in the south of the country) and *assar* in Kazakhstan. In Uzbekistan and Tajikistan it is known as *hashar*. Writing about the Uzbek *mahalla*, Sievers describes the practice of *hashar* in the following way:

> Uzbeks have a well-developed practice of mutual assistance called *hashar* that transcends bilateral relations. Mahalla rais [chairmen] and members draw on hashar to motivate residents to, *inter alia*, maintain the cleanliness of streets and gutters and improve the look of their mahalla on the eve of celebrations and state holidays (Sievers 2003: 112).

It is not a phenomenon limited to urban areas, but its origins are not clear. It has been suggested by Horton (2002) that it was a nomadic tradition used to ensure the survival of tribe members who had been subject to some misfortune (loss of a yurt or death of horses and other livestock). However, research in Kyrgyzstan suggests that it is more prevalent in the traditionally settled areas of the south.

Preliminary investigations by INTRAC in one *raion* in south Kyrgyzstan found that the practice was principally used, during the Soviet period, to bring together extended family and other community members to help with the construction and repair of housing. Whilst those who contributed might not benefit directly, or even in the medium term, opting out of these village arrangements appears to have been uncommon. Involvement in collective works to maintain village or farm infrastructure was not, according to the respondents, the norm,[12] although the authorities would occasionally organise a *subbotnik*.[13]

INTRAC's research in south Kyrgyzstan suggests that community assistance to individuals or families in the form of housebuilding, for example, is now not so common, but that *ashar* that is used to repair or install shared community resources and

---

[12] The occurrence of 'community self-help' to repair village infrastructure prior to independence has been noted in more isolated areas of Tajikistan. Conversation with S. Freizer, October 2003.

[13] Organisation of unpaid labour groups on Saturdays in Soviet times, used typically in Central Asia for clearing irrigation ditches.

infrastructure, such as schools, bath houses, roads and irrigations systems is very much on the increase. This is, in large part, due to donor interest in the practice.

Case Study – *Ashar*

The majority of donors in the region who are engaged in development initiatives at the grass-roots level in Central Asia require a contribution to match or complement their own funds.[14] Rural areas of Central Asia tend to be cash poor; those employed by the state are very often only paid in kind. As a result, mobilisation of voluntary community labour is seen as the compromise solution. This community contribution is presented as *ashar*.

INTRAC undertook research in south Kyrgyzstan, in a *raion* where *ashar* had been promoted by the local staff of an American donor funded 'civil society support centre', who were disbursing small grants for infrastructure projects in local villages. Five villages were visited in which, over the past five years, *ashar* had been used to repair schools, renovate and extend irrigation systems, mend roads and bridges and prepare land for a school's vegetable garden. In terms of mobilising labour and raising awareness of the villagers' own capacity to improve their environment, the method seems to be having a considerable amount of success. Respondents noted frequently that '*ashar* persuades people of their own potential'. Whilst this may well be an imitation of 'donor-speak' there was some evidence to suggest that once villagers had completed one initiative, they would begin to plan another.

Some activities in the region had been undertaken without the push from donors – notably the building or repairing of mosques in the early years after independence. However, the more recent burst of this type of activity is probably linked to the availability of donor money. Village elders and leaders know that receipt of a grant is more likely if community *ashar* has already taken place. Thus in four out of the five villages visited, communities had at some point since independence contributed their labour to the improvement of infrastructure, without external assistance. They had then received funds from the American donor through the local support centre for further local works. The staff of the centre pointed to a domino effect in the *raion*, where these same communities would go on to carry out other non-funded projects, and villages neighbouring those that had received a grant would plan a project that addressed their own needs. In some cases, this involved a grant application, although examples were given of communities who had not been successful in their applications but had nevertheless found ways to implement their projects.

---

[14] This is thought to ensure local 'ownership' of a project and to improve the chances that project outputs will be maintained. This is donor policy in other regions of the world as well.

There is some evidence of the awareness-raising potential of *ashar* as a method. However, there are also limitations to its use, particularly when analysed within the framework of the 'participation' agenda. Donors may be able to report, quite truthfully, that projects achieved close to 'full participation' since, from our research, it would appear there is still considerable social pressure for everyone in a particular community to contribute to *ashar* in some way. But genuine participation means more than simple involvement. It means transfer of power and responsibilities to local residents and it implies handing over the design, as well as the implementation, of a project to those who will benefit from it. *Ashar*, in itself, is not a democratic practice. Traditionally, it is announced by the local *mahalla* or *ayil okmotu* (in Kyrgyzstan) or in the mosque after Friday prayers. It is traditionally a top-down directive, without space for discussion or negotiation. In one village in south Kyrgyzstan, where more in-depth research was undertaken, it became clear that decisions about when, where and why *ashar* should be carried out were left up to one powerful individual alone. Real participation of villagers in the stages leading up to *ashar* is therefore restricted. Women's potential input is further limited by their subordinate position in society. Speaking in public is discouraged and women in more conservative areas of Central Asia are not permitted inside the mosque: one Kyrgyz NGO worker joked, 'Women find out about *ashar* in the evenings'. Whilst the method clearly has some benefits, donors should be aware of the constraints attached to it. We would argue that, considering social obligations to contribute; the fact that it is announced by figures of authority; and the lack of community input into decision-making, it does not correlate with 'ideal' types of participation.

Gaps, Gashtak and Black Chest

Other forms of mutual help, with their roots in the pre-Soviet era, were what would now be called rotating savings groups, that centred around smaller family or neighbourhood groups. These would not necessarily be based on cash however, and could be more of an opportunity for a social gathering. Research findings on this type of associational form vary, but it is generally agreed that they continued to exist, even to flourish during the Soviet era. In Uzbek, these institutions are called *gaps* from the verb 'to talk', whilst in Tajik they are known as *gashtak* or 'taking in turn'. Traditionally, these were held amongst men, who would invite other group members to their homes or to a tea-house for a meal or entertainment.[15] Akiner has examined the *gashtak* in Tajikistan and notes that during the Soviet era it became

---

[15] Akiner also states that *gap* groups also existed among women, though were less common than male groups. She cites an example of a mixed group (2002: 171).

akin to a private dining club. Its members would be drawn from particular circles of professional colleagues, social acquaintances or neighbours ... . Less structured forms also existed, likewise centred around the communal consumption of food and drink (Akiner 2002: 171).

She continues:

Members of such circles acknowledged a social obligation to assist one another whenever possible. ... Not least these circles served as an independent channel for the dissemination and discussion of news and current affairs. The bonds created in such circles were often so powerful that they would be 'inherited' by the children of members who would regard each other as kin and rely on each other for help (2002).

Whilst perhaps traditionally an all-male pursuit, Kandiyoti writes on women's *gaps* in one province of the Ferghana valley in Uzbekistan; similar associational forms that function as a type of rotating savings system, doubling as an occasion for socialising (Kandiyoti 1998). The way in which these operate can vary, but in general, members take it in turns to prepare a meal for the rest of the group. The hostess then receives a pre-agreed financial contribution from each of her guests. These groups can have a redistributive function, in that poorer women might be invited to eat, but without the obligation to make contributions. Kandiyoti considers these to be an important way of providing large cash sums for special purchases and ceremonial expenses. She further notes that the order in which people come to be recipients can be altered if an individual or her family has a particular need. She records one innovative and somewhat controversial *gap* which is purely for *kelins*. These young women in the Ferghana Valley are often not permitted to join other women's *gaps*, and if they have come from outside the *mahalla*, do not know the other young women within it, as they have few opportunities to leave their husbands' family home and socialise.

Another type of activity that involves cash only, without the socialising aspect, is the 'black cashier' or 'black chest'. Kandiyoti's research in Uzbekistan suggests that the black chest was generally used by those on moderate wages during the Soviet era to save up for more expensive consumer goods. She believes that the inclusion of the cash and savings element into the *gaps* is something that has occurred post-independence as a response to the difficult economic situation. Traditionally money had been transferred in the *gaps*, but this usually went towards entertainment expenses, rather than serving as a livelihood strategy. The tradition of *Yntymak* has also been noted, where villagers contribute money for community celebrations, such as *navruz*[16] and for community/family occasions such as weddings and funerals.

---

[16] A national Islamic holiday across Central Asia that was originally a Zoroastrian festival. It marks the end of Winter.

Case Study – Credit Schemes

Rotating savings schemes are familiar to populations across the region. There has been a considerable interest on the part of external donors to promote micro-credit programmes in the region and some have attempted to use traditional savings groups as a base from which to build up larger crediting schemes. One example is that of the French-funded organisation ACTED, working in Tajikistan. These activities are documented in an assessment report produced by Soros and CGAP (The Consultative Group to Assist the Poor) on the micro-finance sector in Tajikistan. Many of the other initiatives documented in the report involve much larger credit transfers with complex rules and accounting systems. However, the ACTED programme takes the ROSCA, or rotating savings association approach, that enables the members to manage the credit structure themselves. Groups of 12 people (generally female heads of household), made up of two sub-groups, each contribute $4 to initial share capital. The difference between this and the traditional groups is that ACTED then contributes three times the capital put in by the members. Loans are then made to one member of each sub-group for a period of one month, after which two further members receive loans and so on, until the cycle is complete after six months. Members set their own interest rates. Results of this initiative appear to have been positive, and have led ACTED to provide further, larger loans to leaders of the groups who have shown good management skills and a commitment to their group. These loans are generally used for animal breeding or food trading. Other donors' micro-finance initiatives have also been based on providing loans to groups, rather than individuals, and are often geared towards women (Fichett and Owen 2002).

The idea of savings groups and mutual help has also been used to promote self-help groups. The organisation DCCA (Development Cooperation in Central Asia) has used this approach in Kazakhstan and Kyrgyzstan. Self-help groups, generally composed of women, are formed and receive credit in order to set up a savings and loans scheme such as that explained above. But as well as providing loans for individual members, the groups are intended to undertake other joint 'problem-solving' activities (DCCA 2003.)

The formation and support of self-help groups has become a popular strategy amongst NGOs in the region. The idea of traditional solidarity is promoted in this approach, as other members of the group are responsible for individuals who have taken loans and are expected to exert 'social pressure' to ensure that loans are repaid. In some cases, training workshops and exchange visits have been organised by organisations that have had success in this area, notably the urban women's support group in Kazakhstan, Moldir.

Newer micro-credit initiatives based on familiar solidarity groupings appear to be popular in the region, particularly amongst women's NGOs. However, it is likely that problems associated with micro-credit in other parts of the world, in terms of access to loans and credit, will also emerge as a problem in Central Asia. For example, it is often not the poorest people who are able or willing to be involved in these schemes.[17] Furthermore, INTRAC research in rural areas of Karakalpakstan showed that traditional savings associations (where donors were not involved) were becoming less workable. In areas where citizens were dependent for their survival on the state farm, or rather the subsistence plots it provided them, those who were 'employed' by the farm were generally not receiving any cash income at all. Their 'wages' were directed straight to their accounts at the farm shop. Only pensioners who were receiving monthly cash benefits (when not delayed) were able to put money into traditional rotating savings groups. The problems of age and gender surface here again: whether or not young women would be permitted by their family and in-laws to become involved in newer micro-credit schemes is not clear. The emphasis on small business start-up might also be problematic as it is not always socially acceptable for women to be engaged in trade, and in conservative areas, women are not permitted to work outside the home without their husbands' consent (Ikramova and McConnell 1999).

Conclusion

Traditional forms of association, especially the strong extended family linkages, are very important today, and are, for many, the main safety net that remains for them. These types of grouping have also been extended into a strong sense of regionalism, which was (inadvertently) fostered during Soviet times. Whilst an understanding of 'communal' civil society will include these types of traditional and modified solidarity groupings, practitioners working in the area of social development have tended to be less interested in groups based on systems of patronage and fealty, and more interested in forms that put forward a communal and equitable approach to solving community problems. However, in the real world, it may not be so easy to distinguish between the two, and it may be more realistic to accept the importance of patronage networks for the majority of the population.

---

[17] Nonetheless, a report for UNDP on the progress of the Poverty Reduction Strategy in Kyrgyzstan, in Autumn 2004, showed that self-help groups were reaching the poor significantly more than, for example, credit unions (20 per cent of members compared to 6 per cent), while small and medium enterprise support measures were significantly weaker than either. Source: CASE consultants for UNDP Kyrgyzstan, September 2004.

The drive to engage with community-based organisations since the end of the 1990s has seen donors taking a new interest in certain aspects of traditional Central Asian society. But this is not a wholesale drive to support communal civil society – donor focus is clearly on elements of pre-Soviet practices and institutions that fit most closely with Western models of civil society and that can be harnessed to promote social development goals.

As noted in this chapter, donor agencies have been keen to co-operate with local elders or *aksakals*, and to promote the use of *ashar*, or *hashar*. But whilst that which is considered conducive to development has been heavily promoted, aspects of traditional society that might have a harmful impact on certain sectors of society, particularly women, have not been given much consideration. Roy notes that

> The official policy of indigenisation is strengthening the role of traditional social fabric – the informal networks of solidarity based on clans, extended families and neighbourhoods – and the emphases of the patriarchal system and the social control of male elders (quoted in Kudat et al. 2000: 11 n.13).

He believes that this could impact negatively upon women's rights. Handrahan puts forward a similar argument on the potentially harmful impacts of 'traditional' civil society. Writing on Kyrgyzstan, her conclusions are relevant for other previously nomadic societies:

> Tribalism is ... equated with civil society in Kyrgyz understanding, leading to the argument that the origins of the tribal Kyrgyz had roots in democratic principles. ... Historically, nomadic society relied on co-operation and individualism; however, the roots of the Kyrgyz nomadic tradition have been completely erased and Russified. Therefore, a resurgence of tribal norms in modern life results in patriarchal and often barbaric rule by terror, resplendent with human rights violations rather than civil society and progressive stability (Handrahan 2001: 477).

She further notes that the patriarchal nature of tribalism excludes women as 'channels of non-descent', who are deemed not important.

There has been a lack of donor engagement with some of these sensitive gender issues. Part of the problem is that many practices that can impact negatively on women's rights are viewed as 'traditional' and as a result have been caught up in the veneration of all that is pre-Soviet. Furthermore, perceptions of Soviet-style equality, in conjunction with strongly held ideas about Central Asian womanhood and social hierarchies, make the role of women and women's status a particularly difficult topic for discussion. For donors to state reservations about customary practices and attitudes would constitute a criticism of 'tradition'. This is problematic at a time when tradition is being given huge prominence by governments in the region as they seek to establish a firm national identity.

The use of certain seemingly benign aspects of traditional society has facilitated donor access to communities in both urban and rural areas. However, unless donors examine their engagement with 'traditional' civil society and find ways to make it more inclusive, their projects will potentially do more harm than good, by giving greater legitimacy to patriarchal, hierarchical and undemocratic practices.

The example of the youth *aksakals* shows how traditional institutions can be adapted to find a more equitable way of solving community problems. It is an interesting initiative as it takes a form of authority that is understood by all, but opens up opportunities for different types of people to input into community decision-making and arbitration. Similarly, the *gaps* for the *kelins* investigated by Kandiyoti in one village of the Ferghana Valley in Uzbekistan show an attempt to adapt traditional practice so as to provide a social space for an excluded group, bringing women both cash benefits and increased social status. These are perhaps lessons for donors who wish to work with *aksakals* and to use *ashar* to consider how more meaningful levels of participation and involvement can be promoted within these familiar structures to bring wider benefits to marginalised groups.

CHAPTER 5

Soviet Forms of Social Organisation

This chapter examines the different types of association that were established during the Soviet period. These institutions and the function they played have relevance for the way in which civil society has emerged since independence in Central Asia. Firstly this is because the memory of these Soviet era organisations and their work colours local perceptions as to the current nature of civil society. Although they were government controlled, these associations had a significant impact upon the way in which individuals interacted with each other in society – a function mirrored by NGOs today. Secondly, many of these associations continue to exist, although they may have transformed themselves in some way. To varying degrees, these associations continue to have resonance and a measure of legitimacy in the eyes of the populations of Central Asia. The chapter goes on to examine how these organisations have adapted to the changing environment in the region and analyses some of the challenges they face.

From the 1930s public associations were increasingly guided by the Communist Party and operated within official ideology. Some public organisations were direct subsidiaries of government structures, financed by the State, and established at the suggestion of either the State or the Party.[1] Public associations often served as a channel to provide for 'extra-curricula' activities for different groups within the population (different age groups, interest groups or those linked by profession), and had a mass membership often counted in millions. Some of the most influential Soviet public organisations and activities are described in the following sections.

---

[1] Thus it was impossible for a private individual to establish an organisation.

Public Organisations

The Pioneers' League was set up in May 1922 at the second conference of the Leninist Young Communist League of Russia. It was to be a 'mass, voluntary community organisation' of children and teenagers (from 10–15 years). As the Kazakh mapping report notes, 'At the end of the 1930s almost every school in the USSR had a pioneer organisation within which different occupational entities such as biological, military, sport, medical, art and hobby clubs were organised' (Dissenova et al. 2002: 17). By end of the 1970s there were 23 million members of the Pioneers' League across the Soviet Union.

On leaving the Pioneers' League, ambitious young people would join the Leninist Young Communist League, more commonly known as the *Komsomol*. Originally founded in 1918, at the height of revolutionary fervour, this mass organisation of young people had been involved in major policy reforms such as the collectivisation of agriculture and the implementation of the first Five Year Plans. The Kazakh study states that every year four million young people joined the *Komsomol*, and by the end of 1978 it had over 28 million members across the Soviet Union (Dissenova et al. 2002: 17).

Apart from young people, bodies existed to respond to the particular needs of other sections of society, such as pensioners, veterans and women. Indeed, the women's councils were an integral part of the Soviet system of social organisation that operated as branches of the Soviet Women's Committee, organised hierarchically from republic level down through the *oblasts*, *raions*, towns and villages. These committees worked under the guidance of the Party to foster civic activity and ensure the communist future of the constituent republics. They were principally involved in moral education and organisation of cultural events, as well as ensuring adequate working conditions and living standards for women, and encouraging women to become involved in the Supreme Soviet (parliament) and government structures, to fulfil quotas.

Public associations also existed to serve the professional interests of specific groups of people. These associations included many whose purpose was broadly philanthropic, although the ethos of such organisations was more of a technical, task-oriented nature. Thus the 'Professional Associations', often called 'Scientific and Technical Associations'[2] in Soviet times, were developed for most major professions and specialisms, including the productive sectors. Like all other public associations, these bodies were supported by the State, issued bulletins and newsletters, organised workshops and conferences, and could employ specialists to conduct pieces of research or produce scientific papers for example. There were

---

[2] Or *zhanyie* (knowledge) societies.

Scientific Associations of teachers, surgeons, architects, miners, inventors and innovators, to name but a few. Similarly, for those involved in the arts, there were Cultural Associations which provided support and a place for professional development. It was regarded as an honour to be invited to become a member, for instance, of the Union of Writers, or the Union of Composers.

Associations existed to provide support for other interest groups, such as the Sports Association, the Nature Protection Societies, and for broadly philanthropic activities such as the Association of Invalids, the Association for the Deaf and Blind. As with the other public associations, all these organisations were supported by the State.

Trade Unions

The trade unions were not a strong force in the USSR until the mid 1930s. After the Revolution, trade unions in different industries had operated separately from each other and had continued to be relatively independent from the State. By the beginning of the 1940s, the process of centralisation of all trade unions was underway, until they were united under one strong vertical organisational structure. Their role as conduits for decisions made by the Party and policy implementation became increasingly important. By this time, they had lost their initial mission of protecting workers' rights, and had become cogs in the large machine of organising social and economic life. Trade union officials were subject to double accountability, to their superiors in the Central Council of the Trade Unions, and to the Communist Party structures. The function of the trade unions increasingly became focused around the distribution of social services, overseeing the payment of pensions and benefits from the social insurance fund, including sickness, maternity and disability benefits. They were responsible for the construction and maintenance of holiday centres (sanatoria) and distributed free holidays to their members, and arranged for children of members to attend Pioneer camps (Dissenova et al 2002: 18).

Foundations

In Soviet times, the term *fond* in Russian, or foundation, could mean an organisation which held collections of books, films, historical documents or artefacts. In addition, Public Union Foundations were widespread and implemented public activities. Examples include the Peace Foundation which collected resources from local groups of the population to send to poorer countries, and the Committee for Solidarity with Asia, which undertook similar activities. The Red Cross, which was managed from

Moscow, had branches throughout all the Soviet republics, and collected (semi-compulsory) contributions for its work which was based in the Ministry of Health. Most people were 'members' of the Red Cross, through their place of work or class at school, and members were expected to contribute funds to its operations by buying stamps for their membership cards. These contributions paid for the network of visiting nurses who provided home care to those categories of the population who required it. The Red Cross societies also undertook other social support activities, including humanitarian assistance following natural disasters.

Co-operatives

Consumers' co-operatives existed in every region and district (*oblast* and *raion*) of the Soviet Union, although these were very different from the organisations of the same name in the West. These organisations were designed to protect the rights of their client enterprises and shops, rather than individual consumers. At the local level they served a vital purpose in ensuring the supply of basic goods and services to the population and local enterprise, since the formal distribution structures were often inefficient and delays and shortages were very frequent. Regional (*oblast*) levels of the consumer union had the opportunity and duty to trade with other parts of the Soviet Union (including the Baltic and Caucasus countries which were renowned for good quality products) to ensure supplies.

The Kyrgyzstan mapping report recounts how, during the first period of the five-year plans, when pressure was on to promote productive activity, workmen's co-operatives or *artel* businesses were encouraged around the country to counter the fall in production which had accompanied the chaos following the *basmachi* uprising and the first years of enforced collectivisation. These *artel* businesses, entirely owned by the Soviet authorities, consisted of organisations which recruited qualified workers for specific activities. Thus *artels* developed in sectors such as mining, fur processing, fisheries, poultry, timber, construction, civil works and storage of grain. They operated under the slogan, 'The young and independent Soviet state (Kyrgyzstan) must learn to sell and buy!'[3] The *artels* provided accommodation, food, insurance and salaries. 'The widespread growth of these organisations can be attributed to rapid and extensive national campaigns for the exploration and extraction of mineral resources, development of virgin and unused lands, and construction of heavy industrial facilities and cities' (Baimatov et al. 2002: 43).[4] However, *artels*

[3] This is similar to the temporary Soviet policy, in the early 1920s, of encouraging rich peasants (kulaks) to increase production of desperately needed grain.

[4] The Kyrgyz study goes on to suggest that the incorporation of Kyrgyzstan into the rouble area in post-war years, encouraged the growth of *artels* and attracted more people to join them.

gradually declined from the 1950s onwards, as more large-scale enterprises were established and infrastructure improved – only to make a reappearance in a new (or larger) small business function in the first years of *perestroika*.

Subbotniki

Activity in Soviet public or collective life was characterised by a kind of 'obligatory volunteerism'. A vivid example of this is the near-universal practice of *subbotniki* whereby people would provide labour on their days off (from *subbota*, Saturday). Introduced in the 1920s, this was an important mechanism for organising communal work through the local Party (or associated Public Organisation – such as Komsomol) for tasks in local communities or institutions such as schools, or the workplace. The idea of *subbotniki* penetrated down to the level of neighbourhoods and communities where it was often driven by local residents. In some cases it could take on a social welfare function, akin to the traditional practice of *hashar* or *ashar*, as discussed in Chapter 4.

The Legacy of Soviet Public Organisations in Contemporary Central Asia

Legislation

The discussion of public associations in the Soviet era presented above is relevant in a multitude of ways to the discussion of civil society in Central Asia today. For some commentators, including the authors of the Kazakh report, these were the prototype for today's NGOs. They are the base upon which newer forms of organisation can emerge in the independence era.

In terms of legislation, the link between the two periods is very clear. The first Soviet Law on Public Associations, 'On Public Organisations and Unions', was passed in 1930 (Ponomarev 1994). All subsequent legislation, including the legislation currently in force in the five independent republics, is based on this concept of Public Organisation. Thus the Kazakh law on Public Associations of 1996 is a hybrid of the old Soviet law and the more progressive Kazakh Civil Code, which broadens the forms of public association. However, in all countries, national and local associations still have to be registered with the Ministries of Justice, and the same, rather restrictive legislation (about permitted geographical areas of activity, types of funding allowed, for example), which was developed in an era when the purpose of legislation was to control the activities of public organisations, still applies. This legislation thus governs the registration and regulation of the whole range of 'public' organisations, from political parties, to trade unions, to non-governmental organisations, and the same rules apply to all these forms of organisation, regardless of their purpose. In recent years there has been a great deal of work, largely on the part of NGOs, to lobby for changes to this legislative base.[5] Modifications have been introduced to take account of new types of organisations like NGOs, and of key issues like taxation and registration procedures and costs; but these modifications do not alter the basic structure of the legislation.

Many of the Soviet-type public associations still exist in all countries, although in modified form. Whilst State funding has at the least declined, and more often ceased altogether, a number of them have been revived in order to serve a new function or to transform themselves into a different type of organisation. The availability of funding from international donors since the mid 1990s has had some part in this.

Public Associations

The former Soviet public associations can be identified in contemporary Central Asian in a number of guises. Many continue to function more or less as they used to, although perhaps with a change of name. This is particularly noticeable in Uzbekistan and Turkmenistan, where this form of association is still predominant. Other, new, associations have been created along similar lines as the old ones. These associations, along with Foundations and Public Organisations do still have a powerful resonance in the region, and – to varying degrees – have a strong sense of legitimacy. Furthermore, the predominance of this organisational form colours people's and groups' expectations of what a public association or organisation should look like. As a result, there is not generally an expectation amongst the wider population that these groups or associations should be independent from the State, nor that they would necessarily want to be totally separate from the State. The State is still perceived as having the responsibility and power to deliver on social issues and consequently to support groups of citizens who are involved in the public sphere for these ends.

A case study from Soghd *oblast* documented in the annexes to the Tajik mapping report notes that many Soviet era membership groups, such as those representing professional groups and intellectuals or peasant and labour unions, continue to exist and retain their members, who work in both State as well as private institutions. These associations have in theory become independent and address a number of issues, including business promotion, agriculture, poverty and social protection. However, their activities are still very much influenced by the government's policies on professional and labour issues (Boboyorov and Heap 2003c).

---

[5] The International Centre for Not-for-Profit Law (ICNL) has worked with groups in all countries to develop and lobby for more appropriate forms of legislation for the NGO sector.

This same study also describes the activities of what are referred to as Charitable Foundations, organisations linked to the government that provide social and cultural services in the post-independence era. There are about ten such bodies in the country, some of which do little more than support programmes of the State bodies, organising cultural and social events. According to the authors of the report, most of these foundations have cultural or historical agendas, and are fairly passive, have very limited resources, and tend to react to initiatives of the government. However, the more developed of these have begun to work in the area of social entrepreneurship programmes, particularly in the agricultural sector. An example is the Farmers' Development Fund based in Khujand, which works with communities, peasant farms and associations to provide training and micro-credit programmes.

In Uzbekistan, the close links between Soviet era associations and the present government remain. An INTRAC mapping report from 1998 notes a number of examples of these old-style Public Associations active in the country, including the Committee of Women of the Republic of Uzbekistan, the Association of Scientific Women, the Association of Disabled People of Uzbekistan, the Public Youth Movement Kamolot, the Veterans' Foundation Nuroniy, the Fund known as *Soglom Avlod Uchun* (for a healthy generation) whose patron is the President, the *Umid* (hope) Fund which supports gifted youth to study abroad and ECOSAN, an organisation dealing with environmental issues.

In Turkmenistan, the government-oriented NGOs (sometimes called GONGOs) play an important role in the absence of a more autonomous civil society sector. They include the Women's Union and Youth Union. INTRAC's 2002 NGO Mapping Report in Turkmenistan identified that the Soviet system is still in place, whereby the deputy *hakim* for social affairs in *velayats* (provinces) is a woman and often the leader of the local branch of the Women's Union. Due to the difficulty in registering independent NGOs in Turkmenistan, many local groups register under the umbrella of the GONGOs and the latter can play a key role in building bridges between NGOs and government (Buxton and Musabaeva 2002: 23–4). The following case study is an example of a Soviet-style organisation that is finding a way to provide services to its members, despite the difficult political situation.

Case Study – The Turkmenistan Union of Entrepreneurs

This organisation was set up in 1993 and entered a new phase of heightened activity after 2002, when it was revitalised with new staff and management. The Union is led by a successful businessman, whose own company, and those of six other members, sponsor its activities. It has also recently received a grant from the OSCE. The Union now has 160 members who are all involved in trade, production or agriculture, and the organisation exists to defend its

---

members' interests. In practice this ranges from supporting members in court cases involving leases and other disputes, to lobbying the President and the government on relevant legal issues. The President of the Republic is also the honorary president of the Union, which was set up, according to its members, in order to take on the State's role of providing support to entrepreneurs. It has rented office space, within which a library and computer resource centre is situated. The Union plans to open similar centres in each of the *velayats* (*oblasts*).

In the countries in the region which have undergone a greater degree of democratic reform, the difficulty is of a different order: how public associations with previously close, influential links with the State can find a place for themselves within civil society. For example, an INTRAC report from Kazakhstan describes the National Association of Farmers, which is an organisation with 70,000 members whom it seeks to represent in areas such as social protection, farming infrastructure, business and marketing advice and the introduction of new credit schemes. In practice, the report notes:

The National Association of Farmers sees its role as assisting President Nazarbayev in implementing his agricultural policy. However, the reality of the situation clearly indicates that in Kazakhstan farmers are leaving the land. The Association feels that, in its role as an NGO, it should lobby the government to legislatively tie the farmers to the land, since farmers' migration occurs as a result of farmers' misunderstanding of their role in the economy (Padamsey 2000: 13).

According to the author, this state of affairs is an indication that the Association does not fully understand who it is really accountable to, and what its own role is in civil society.

Another more positive example from Kazakhstan is of the Pensioners' Public Movement, a national association that has transformed itself into a powerful pressure group. Originally established in 1992 in seven cities of the country, from 1997 onwards the Movement began to receive grants from international private foundations and European and American INGOs. It now has branches in 23 cities. As well as providing support to individuals, providing advice on pensions and access to benefits and taking cases to court if necessary, it also lobbies government on the needs of the older people more generally, and on flaws in pension legislation.

The pensioners' movement has benefited from external assistance, but the difficulty in accessing funding is one of the reasons why some formerly Soviet public associations do not sever their relations with government entirely. In

Kyrgyzstan, some of the old-style public organisations, especially the professional associations, have made the decision to turn themselves into co-operatives. For instance, the Association of Veterinary Services in Kyrgyzstan has transformed itself into a co-operative, and has achieved this without external assistance. The Association consists of 30 professional members who used to work as vets and cattle breeders. It has plans to set up vet stations in all villages and a network of pharmacies. In this way, it is replicating structures that used to exist but which collapsed after the break-up of the Soviet Union. Another interesting example given in the Kyrgyz report is the Soviet-era Geographical Society of the Kyrgyz SSR, which promoted tourist, scientific and regional study activities, which is seen by the authors of the report to have been the precursor of the newly emerging tourist industry in the country (Baimatov et al. 2002: 63).

Women's Councils

Reorganising hierarchical Soviet structures in the independence era is a challenging task, and it seems that while some formerly Soviet organisations have managed a successful transition, others have found it harder to find a place for themselves in the new society. The ability to become established as fully independent and functioning bodies seems to vary considerably from country to country and between different sectors. The Women's Councils across Central Asia are a particularly interesting area for study. Many of these Councils, at village, *raion*, *oblast* and national level continue to function and some have overhauled themselves to become active in new areas of work like micro-credit provision, or other forms of support and information provision – for instance in raising awareness about domestic violence. However, the dilemma of finding independence from state structures and accessing funding remains. Furthermore, whilst these organisations can build on their target group's familiarity with their Soviet era activities, finding a balance between these and newer initiatives can be problematic, as the following example shows.

Case Study – Village-Level Women's Council

INTRAC undertook research on a village-level women's council in south Kazakhstan, located on the rural outskirts of a large city. The legacy of the Soviet era Women's Council was clearly seen in the hierarchical structure that remained, with links between the village council and offices at *raion* and *oblast* levels. Research findings showed a reluctance amongst leaders of the village council to alter their approach to their target group, and their work continued to reflect that of the Soviet era organisation. During Soviet times, the role of these bodies had been to monitor the living standards of women and their families and ensure they were receiving the correct state benefits.

They also organised community and educational events and in some cases distributed charity.

Currently, the council still provides information on living standards to the local authorities and organises community events. It no longer receives funds from the state to do this and has had to find resources elsewhere. The emphasis on welfare and charity within the organisation is another Soviet feature still in evidence. Whilst the leaders of the village council stated that they had recently set up a 'self-help' group for 60 vulnerable women, in reality, these women are recipients of charitable aid, raised by a core of eight 'activists' within the council. Alongside this focus on charity, however, the women's councils at the *raion* and *oblast* level have started to promote the idea of women in business and of micro-credit. The village-level council has also sent women to training sessions on these issues and the leaders spoke of 'women's right' to engage in business. However, this attempt to encourage women's participation in the market economy contrasts strongly with other council activities, that include the production of a booklet glorifying the *oblast's* 'heroine mothers' (women who have had more than ten children) and support for the preservation of traditional gender roles. There did not appear to be any recognition amongst the council leadership of the potential difficulties local women would have, being both entrepreneurs and models of Central Asian womanhood. This is an example of an organisation adopting new ideas and discourses whilst simultaneously retaining a Soviet era 'mindset'.

The leaders of the village-level council are now attempting to register their organisation as an NGO. Although they already claim to be an independent body, they stated that registration was the only way that they would be truly free from the influence and intervention of the Government authorities at *raion* level.

This is not to say, however, that the former Women's Councils are necessarily weak organisations. At the national level, in Uzbekistan, it would appear that they are able to wield a degree of influence over the work of other actors in the sector. This is apparent from the example of the Business Women's Association (BWA) in Uzbekistan. (This body is discussed in more detail in Chapter 6.) Whilst some of its original branches were set up shortly after independence, these did not have a great deal of success in the first four or five years of independence. The Business Women's Associations in Kokand, Samarkand and Tashkent had established themselves independently of government, but when these separate organisations sought to unite in the mid 1990s and extend coverage of the network to all regions of the country, they found that this was very difficult without support from the government authorities at *oblast* level (*Hokimiyats*) and indeed, the Women's Council.

Eventually, coverage of the whole country by the BWA was assured, but the newer organisations were created from the centre and chairwomen were selected with the support of the Women's Council. As a result, in some areas, the branches of the BWA are thought, erroneously, to be part of the local-level substructure of the Women's Council. Legally they are independent, but even representatives of the branch in Bukhara in an interview with an INTRAC researcher in 2002 noted that the organisation often feels like a 'branch of the city mayor's office'.

Red Cross and Red Crescent Society

The Red Cross and Red Crescent societies, in all five countries, illustrate how public associations from the Soviet era have managed to adapt quite successfully to the new political and economic situation of independence. With the degeneration of public enterprises, and the collapse of Soviet structures, the former principal method of funding through membership fees is no longer viable. In recent years, the greater part of the humanitarian work of these societies has been funded from the International Federation of the Red Cross, and from the National Societies in the West. They are also, increasingly, seeking funding from other donors, and adapting their ways of working accordingly. More strategically they are trying to find a new, or 'niche' role for themselves, so as to complement the role and activities of the state. In tuberculosis control, for instance, the state provides curative care, whilst Red Crescent societies provide home care and work with vulnerable groups. In all five states, the Red Crescent societies retain their comprehensive structures, covering all of the country and, because of their history, well-known public profile and respected work in times of need, these organisations are still regarded as respectable charitable bodies. In recent years, income from membership fees has started to rise again, although it is nowhere near the levels raised in Soviet times.

Trade Unions

Whilst the original structures of trade unions still largely persist, membership of these once powerful organisations has declined, largely as a result of the collapse or drastic reduction of employment in state-run enterprises. The Kazakh report states that traditional trade unions have not tended to find a role for themselves in the private sector, since new enterprises and companies tend to be fairly small. Generally speaking, these traditional trade union structures are trying to establish a new niche for themselves. As well as problems with financing, the Kazakh researchers also refer to general mistrust amongst the population towards the unions, which they do not see as capable of improving working conditions or defending the interests of workers. This lack of trust is perhaps a reflection of their role during the Soviet era during which the unions acted as organs of the State, delivering social insurance, rather than actively defending the rights of workers in a more antagonistic relationship with the State, as seen in other parts of the world. In all five republics, organisations founded in the Soviet era continue to act as confederations of trade unions. Their loyalty tends to be towards the State. As the Tajik report notes, the emphasis of the national Confederation of Trade Unions is on maintaining stability and on co-operation with the State. Despite these problems, trade unions were identified by participants of the research as a component part of civil society.

The case of Kazakhstan shows the variations between the successor of the Soviet era umbrella trade union body, and a newer organisation representing 'free' trade unions. The Kazakh report identifies two umbrella bodies that unite all the trade unions of Kazakhstan. One of these is a direct successor to the Soviet era body. The other has its roots in the first independent trade union in Kazakhstan that emerged during *perestroika*. The former, the Federation of Trade Unions, inherited Soviet era rehabilitation centres, sanatoria and tourist hotels, from which it continues to draw revenue. This body works closely with the Kazakh Government in a commission on social partnership and regulation of socio-economic and labour relations. There is even a group within the national Parliament made up of MPs elected from trade unions and their sympathisers, which acts to influence particular relevant legislation. Trade union members are also elected to local government structures.

According to the Kazakh report, the Federation has more than two million members. The newer Confederation of Free Trade Unions has approximately 800,000 members. The two umbrella bodies do not co-operate, however, and the Confederation has a different approach towards relations with Government and has criticised the older body for failing to confront the authorities with strikes and protests. The Confederation has attempted to introduce draft laws into Parliament to reform the social protection system in the context of changing patterns of ownership and labour relations. These were not, however, supported by the Government, although it has had more success with new laws on social partnerships. Alongside lobbying activity, since it was established in 1991 the Confederation has introduced a training programme for leaders and activists, which operates at provincial and national level, and has set up resources centres to deliver these activities. Topics covered include the basics of the market economy, types of trade union activity, relations with employers as well as with local and national authorities, and influencing of public opinion on the work of the new trade unions. The Kazakh report, although stressing the limitations on union action and the financial problems of both bodies, notes that the establishment of free trade unions implies that people are beginning to recognise the potential for these newer bodies to do more to protect their interests against the State and employers.

In meetings with INTRAC, the leader of the Confederation commented that while the NGO sector has been funded actively by international donors, citizens are still passive, and important rights at the workplace have been taken away. The Confederation itself works 'more like an advocacy NGO' since the huge changes in the ownership and structure of the economy mean that there is no effective framework yet for union–employer bargaining.[6]

In Kyrgyzstan, the work of trade unions is severely curtailed by the collapse of national industry, but despite economic downturn, the report notes that those who receive wages continue to pay their 1 per cent membership fees. The authors suggest that this might be out of habit, but do note that members are entitled to benefits such as contributions towards medical care and legal protection in case of industrial dispute. The Kyrgyz report also notes that the unions have managed to preserve their unity since independence, and the 26 sectors of union activity that existed prior to the break-up of the Soviet Union continue in place. However, the report states that unions in the country are undergoing a process of transition, characterised by the term 'survival strategy'. Whilst once a central, powerful and proactive force, trade unions are now looking to strengthen their function as bodies that protect the workforce. New unions are emerging, but these are geared more towards workers outside heavy industry. The report notes that the biggest problem facing the unions is the need for re-qualification of labour in the new economy.

The umbrella body in Kyrgyzstan, the Federation of Trade Unions, was established in 1990, and works independently from the State. The constitution of 1993 divested unions of the right to put forward legislative initiatives. However, the report notes that they continue to do so, and that laws that contradict this position have since been passed. Union influence is limited, however, since, unlike in Kazakhstan, there is no allowance for tripartism, in which unions negotiate with employers and the Government and unions' understanding of social partnership is weak. As Smith has observed,

Trade Unions will lose many of their nominal membership of one million over the next few years and will need to re-focus on recruiting and servicing workers in smaller private enterprises; advocacy for all working people, not just those in work; facilitating the social economy; and creating real partnership with other stakeholders (Smith 1999: 14).

In Uzbekistan, where more of the traditional structures of employment are maintained, there are no new trade unions, and those that exist must be formally linked to the Trade Union Federation. This organisation works closely with the Government and regulates the activities of the country's trade unions. A law passed in 1992 stipulates that trade unions are voluntary public organisations that express

---

[6] For further discussion see the report of INTRAC's first regional conference (Garbutt and Heap 2003).

and protect the social and economic rights and interests of workers. The law ensures the independence of the unions from the state infrastructure. In reality, trade unions that do exist are mainly those working within the public sector, in schools and factories. Whilst in theory trade unions can exist in private businesses, there is resistance to this, as their presence would force the employer to provide social support to employees. Trade unions in Uzbekistan are primarily concerned with ensuring social protection to workers in the form of sick pay, holidays and child care. In theory they could involve themselves in lobbying work and organise industrial action. However, the potential for this type of action is severely curtailed by the political climate and financial constraints.

The Uzbek mapping report states that since independence, greater emphasis has been put on trade unions to act as individual actors within a system, rather than focusing all responsibility for workers' issues on the central bodies. Support for trade unions has been voiced by the President, who has been reported as setting great store by the potential of the trade unions:

> The trade unions, with their millions of members, do great work to defend the social, economic, spiritual and intellectual rights of their members, to guarantee the harmony of interests in society. ... I am sure that the stable and fruitful relations between our state, workers and trade unions will result in the development of society on the basis of principles of social partnership (Uzbek President Karimov speaking in 2000, quoted in Abdullaev et al. 2003: 15).

But whilst the principle of social partnership as the way to protect trade union members has been adopted, the Uzbek report notes 'the republican trade unions still pay insufficient attention to the implementation of social partnership policy; not all its opportunities and mechanisms ... are used.' The report concludes that the trade unions retain the 'birthmarks' of the Soviet past both in the principles of the organisations and their activity.

Not surprisingly, in Turkmenistan, the Government-controlled Colleagues Union is the only trade union permitted. In Tajikistan, similarly, all unions are under the control of the State, and workers within State enterprises belong to the Confederation of Trade Unions, a Soviet era umbrella organisation of 20 separate labour unions, which controls access to pension funds, health care, housing, day care and other social services. The confederation claims a membership of 1.5 million workers. The separate, but also state-controlled, Trade Unions of Private Enterprise, includes registered unions in small and meduim enterprises. Despite their lack of independence, the Tajik report remains optimistic about the ability of professional unions to confront Government, noting that some independent sources of financing during the Soviet era allowed these bodies to mobilise members over certain issues. However, in an interview in 2003, a representative from the

Federation of Trade Unions of Tajikistan, quoted in the Tajik report, noted: 'For Tajikistan there is no need for meetings and other protests and demonstrations of the workers. The position of the Federation of Trade Unions is to support the state; it works for adopting laws and works with the professional environments to observe them.'

This suggests that opportunities to defend workers' rights may be limited, and the activities of unions curtailed by more than just funding constraints.

The Re-emergence of *Artels* and Co-operatives

Artels, groups of workers within one specialty, had been encouraged in the early Soviet years, as noted above. Similar organisational forms re-emerged in the 1980s at the time when the Soviet economy began to face serious structural difficulties. During the period of *perestroika*, co-operatives, as *artels* had been, were encouraged in order to revitalise the economy. The first co-operatives to appear at this time dealt mainly with marketing of goods at lower prices, storage of food, and some agricultural production and livestock breeding. The Kyrgyz study notes that towards the end of the 1980s the co-operative movement began to grow in an unprecedented manner, which led to the adoption of several laws on co-operative activity. Since independence, these forms have essentially developed into privately run, autonomous small and medium business enterprises. However, in some cases the language of co-operation (rather than that of the profit motive) persists.

In an interview in 2001, a representative of the Regional Union of Co-operatives of Talas *oblast* noted,

> The (regional) Union focuses on the encouragement and effective institutional development of the co-operative movement in the region. It builds relations with other *oblast* (regional) co-operatives, commercial outlets and small businesses, to co-ordinate the co-operative policies and activities of member co-operatives and provides training.

This Union hopes to develop into a financially self-sufficient organisation. At present, it obtains its funding from its joining and membership fees and raises some income from services and entrepreneurial activities.

One organisation that received support from the Union was the Jon Aryk Agricultural, Sheep and Goat Breeding Cooperative. It was formed in response to the massive decline in livestock numbers that occurred shortly after independence as veterinary services declined and financial support for livestock herding from the State disappeared. According to the Kyrgyz report, these new co-operatives have fully replaced former Government-owned enterprises. However, Jon Aryk is an example of a highly entrepreneurial institution, in that it has worked with a range of different actors, including the Union of Co-operatives in Talas, the Ministry of Agriculture and Water and international funding institutions, in order to secure a range of benefits for its members. Its main activities centre on logistical and organisation support for smaller livestock breeding businesses, as well as protecting their interests and effectively marketing their products. The co-operative also hopes to build a strong research capacity for agricultural and livestock development.

Conclusion

The former public associations, trade unions and co-operatives are a visible legacy of the Soviet era that play a part in today's civil society in Central Asia. There are a number of Public Associations that were founded in the Soviet era and supported by the government that have managed to continue working in the newly independent states of the region. Their position with regards to the State and to civil society is not an easy one, however. This could be described as a 'catch 22' situation. In some ways, maintaining ties to the State and marketing an organisation as the successor of a Soviet institution is an attractive strategy. This would build on the fact that the organisation is known by its target group and already has a public face. It is also a way of ensuring an easier working environment and access to some continued, if drastically reduced, State funding. Influence over government decision-making on relevant social policies may also be more achievable. Certainly, in the context of a repressive regime, an organisation may be able to achieve much more for its members by working within the system than outside it. However, as governments in the region continue to cut back on the provision and maintenance of State infrastructure, so the public's trust in its institutions continues to wane. It also leaves these organisations open to accusations (and not always inaccurate ones) that they serve simply as a pawn of the government.

On the other hand those organisations that attempt to sever links with the State altogether instantly have problems with funding, which may prevent them from functioning at all. Thus, while the newer Confederation of Free Trade Unions in Kazakhstan may wish to get its message across to the Government by holding strikes, it does not have sufficient resources to organise or maintain industrial action. The example of the Village Women's Council in south Kazakhstan shows an organisation that has raised funds from sources other than Government, but continues to be dependent upon the local authorities in order to operate.

For some of the former associations and co-operatives, converting to work as a type of business enterprise serves as the solution to the problem. Finally, the Red Crescent seems to be an example of an organisation that has managed to find a niche for itself working alongside government in areas where it can complement state policies, but diversifying its funding base to ensure its independence.

CHAPTER 6

New Developments Since Independence: The Emergence of NGOs

This chapter examines the growth of the so-called non-governmental organisation (NGO) sector in the five countries. The term NGO was originally introduced by the donor community, and particularly promoted by agencies from the United States, as these actors looked to fund this type of organisation as part of their civil society strengthening strategy. The focus of these agencies, when they first became involved in the region in the early 1990s, was largely democracy promotion. As noted in the first chapter of this publication, support for a pluralistic civil society was seen to go hand in hand with economic liberalisation and the emergence of democratic governance. Since civil society, in the mainstream definition of the term, is clearly set apart from the State, the use of the term 'non-governmental' was an important statement. However, this term sits uncomfortably in the region. Indeed, in many parts of the former Soviet Union, the term non-commercial organisation (NKO in Russian) is preferred. In Uzbekistan, actors in the sector have coined the acronym NNO (which stands for non-governmental and non-commercial organisation). Certainly, in Tajikistan and Turkmenistan, the term 'non-governmental' can be understood as 'anti-governmental', and may have further hampered the development of the sector.

This chapter seeks to give a brief overview of the development of the NGO sector, and donor funding of NGOs, across the region, identifying what the authors believe to be the key trends, and illustrating these with a selection of case studies.

There are inevitably omissions, and many organisations that are doing influential and successful work have not been mentioned. However, a full description of NGO emergence and development is beyond the scope of this chapter.

The Variety of Organisations Classified as 'NGOs'

With the advent of independence, and the arrival of donor-funded programmes, increased attention was accorded to organisations which could be classified as non-governmental. As shown below, some pressure groups or interest groups showing similarities to organisational forms understood as elements of civil society in the West did exist – especially groups involved in ecology and environmental issues. In addition, many other new organisations sprang up after independence, both in response to the sudden increase in external funding available, and as an attempt to address the needs of populations that found themselves suddenly and unexpectedly impoverished. Many of these organisations focused on specific social groups, such as women and young people, and had a humanitarian focus. These organisations could register and define and label themselves as NGOs, or they could form around an 'initiative group', which by definition was not registered, but which constituted a group of people organising themselves to tackle a particular problem or issue. Generally when initiative groups did register themselves, which they often had to do in order to receive funding, they then became NGOs.

Although donors may have had a specific idea about the type of organisations classified under this moniker, the term has come to cover a variety of institutional forms. As shown in the preceding chapter, some public associations and foundations continued to operate after independence, or re-emerged and re-invented themselves during the 1990s and have called themselves NGOs. As a result, it is possible to find, under the heading of NGO, some organisations that would not normally be regarded as part of the NGO or third sector in other countries. For example, there are professional associations, like the Association of Paediatricians in Bukhara, which is increasingly operating like a private consultancy business, giving advice to government and other agencies. In the last chapter we showed how some of the old nature lovers associations have turned themselves into tourist operators. In a similar way, some new public associations, foundations and charities, very much in the old Soviet style, have been set up, very often by well connected individuals (like the wives of prominent politicians). The governments themselves have created a number of organisations to work on specific issues, and these have come to be known, somewhat pejoratively, as GONGOs (Government Organised NGOs).

Stages in the Development of the NGO Sector

The research studies from the five Central Asian countries attempted to identify specific stages in the emergence of the new NGO sector. Much of the research concentrated on the NGO form, since most of the literature about civil society in Central Asia tends to equate civil society with NGOs. However, we suggest that it is perhaps more appropriate to include some of the other types of public association in our discussion about civil society.

Kazakhstan

In the Kazakh studies, the first stage of NGO development is identified by the emergence of organisations that acted as pressure groups and focused on specific issues at the start of *perestroika*, and is seen to continue until the creation of a more enabling legal environment for civil society activity and the advent of significant external donor funding. Thus, the Kazakh mapping report notes,

> The first stage was from 1985 to 1994. ... In 1985 the first non-governmental organisations began to emerge gradually. The most common were environmental associations and historical societies (Dissenova et al. 2002: 24).

The emergence of societies based around environmental issues can be related to a growing awareness of the severity of environmental degradation that had been caused largely by Soviet policies. This had included nuclear testing, heavy industry, intensive agriculture and mono-cropping. One of the most popular movements was the Nevada-Semipalatinsk public movement whose main goal was the closure of the Semipalatinsk nuclear testing ground. This movement brought together broad sections of society: grass-roots activists, environmentalists, politicians and popular public figures.[1] The late 1980s were also a time of increasing interest in the rediscovery of national culture and identity and an increasing national consciousness. As a response to this, historic and educational societies appeared, such as Adilet, Memorial and Zheltoksan. It was through these organisations that some people in Kazakhstan began to find a voice. For the first time in many years people

---

[1] This movement was headed by Olzhas Suleimenov, a well-known Kazakh writer and strong charismatic leader. At one stage it looked as though Suleimenov would become a serious contender for the post of President, but he was sent to Italy as Kazakh Ambassador before the elections. The Kazakh research states that, when Suleimenov left, the movement continued for a while but did not have a 'lasting impact on the democratisation process. Nevertheless the organisation laid the foundation for numerous environmental movements and achieved its goal in that the testing ground was closed' (Dissenova et al. 2002: 24).

gained an opportunity to express their opinion openly about the political regime and unite in public organisations (Franz et al. 2002).

According to the Kazakh researchers, the second stage in the development of NGOs in Kazakhstan occurred after independence, and was characterised by the arrival of international donor agencies, including international NGOs, who were interested in the promotion of civil society. This was often on the model of their Eastern European programmes. This period, from 1994–97, saw a huge increase in the number of Kazakh organisations.[2] Support to these new organisations came in the form of grants, seminars, training and round-table discussions from external donors. At the same time, the Central Asian Sustainable Development Information Network (CASDIN) was also established to serve the needs of these new organisations. Many of these new NGOs focused on the growing problems arising from the transition process (including the collapse of the economy and of social and industrial infrastructure). Especially notable was the increase in women's NGOs, reflecting the fact that many women were having to bear the brunt of economic collapse and the reduction in social care and benefit systems. Also, many educated women now found themselves unemployed or underemployed, and were able to put their energies into organising NGOs.

The third stage identified by the Kazakh researchers began in 1998 and continues to the present day. This phase is characterised, according to the report, by a certain level of NGO maturity, with organisations able to undertake advocacy and lobbying roles, and also to enter into relationships with the state. The report identifies two NGOs (Baspana and Moldir) that, in different ways, represent and support poor and vulnerable groups in the city of Almaty.

Kyrgyzstan

The Kyrgyz mapping study identifies the first phase of NGO development as occurring between 1991 and 1997. This saw the first 'mass political movements' that emerged around the time of independence along with the growth in political parties and citizens' initiative groups. During this period, around 1993 and 1994, national NGOs were established, and international organisations such as the Kyrgyz American Human Rights Committee Ukuk, UNDP, Counterpart Consortium, INTRAC and the Soros Foundation began working in the country. The research study states:

1995 saw donors suggest new programmes and projects, the birth of NGOs. The first Volunteer conference was held in Bishkek, a gathering of around 70

---

[2] Statistics on the number of NGOs in the Central Asian states vary wildly. This is because many more NGOs have registered than are actually actively working. See below for more discussion.

organisations from across Kyrgyzstan. In 1996 a conference led to the establishment of the Women's Forum, and in 1997 a group of NGOs began to lobby government to improve the legislation concerning the registration of NGOs (Baimatov et al. 2002: 20).

The second phase, beginning in 1998, was characterised by the realisation on the part of NGOs that they needed to become involved in advocacy and lobbying both with Government and political parties. Centre Interbilim and others began to launch campaigns on topical issues – for example, the chemical pollution of Issyk-Kul Lake after an accidental release of cyanide by the multi-national gold-mining company Kumtor into a local river. The work of Centre Interbilim is presented in the case study below.

The view of the Kyrgyz researchers on the development of NGOs encouraged debate amongst workshop participants brought together to discuss the findings of the research in the country. Some saw the current phase (at the time the report was written) of NGO development as one characterised by a climate in which only the 'fittest' organisations were surviving. Others identified a set of more proactive NGOs emerging between 1995 and 2000, after the initial proliferation of organisations that had appeared as a response to external funding. A number of participants believed that since 2000 there had been increasing co-operation between NGOs and Government.

Case Study – Centre Interbilim

Established in early 1994 in Kyrgyzstan, Centre Interbilim (CIB) is widely regarded as the most developed and well-established NGO in the country that performs a variety of roles in the civil society sector. It was specifically established with a mission to strengthen and encourage the growth of NGOs as well as to help create a more favourable environment for the new sector as a whole. At the time, this two-level approach was considered very innovative. Initially, CIB provided NGOs with access to computers and gave advice on the 'new' phenomenon of NGOs. There was clearly a demand for its services, and CIB began to hold seminars and workshops and to provide advice in the regions beyond Bishkek. In 1995 it opened an office in Osh to extend its work to the southern regions and in 1996 it played the lead role in establishing the NGO Forum to improve the legal context and rights of national NGOs. Following this, CIB went on to take up a national advocacy role, focusing on electoral issues, individual human rights cases, legislation and environmental degradation. It further initiated a national NGO group to work on issues that affected civil society as a whole.

By 1998 it had covered sufficient ground to take on capacity building of local NGOs through information provision, counselling and training. CIB also created and became involved in networks of likeminded NGOs in order to address a range of issues relevant to NGOs and civil society. Tapping the combined influence of these networks, CIB initiated lobbying and advocacy initiatives at national and regional levels, benefiting the civil society and NGO sector.

In recent years CIB's target group of NGOs has matured and now functions as its partner: in order to reach a wider range and volume of NGOs, CIB has developed the 'cluster group' approach to capacity building, whereby about 20 small NGOs in a particular geographic location agree to work with CIB as a group, receiving training en masse and helping each other when necessary.

A report by Sinclair (2004) notes that the organisation's comprehensive approach to training and sensitisation of local NGOs combined with its national role as advocate and lobbyist has given it an almost iconic image in the country. He concludes that outside the NGO sector, CIB is widely respected by politicians, media organisations, academics, businessmen and donors who see the value in defending civil society against an increasingly autocratic government.

Tajikistan

The pattern identified in pre-war Tajikistan is similar to developments identified in the Kazakh report. The first phase began before independence, during the period of *perestroika*, and centred on the emergence of specific interest and campaigning groups. In the late 1980s, some of the existing public professional associations (war veterans, union of scientists), together with some new informal associations of intellectuals, developed 'semi official parallel structures to allow for voice of dissent to address certain issues'. The first informal debating circles were initiated by a group of intellectuals at the end of 1980s. Ma'refat (Education) was formed in 1988, to voice social, cultural and political grievances. Also, the Ruberu (Face to Face) group emerged from the Komsomol (youth union), which was more of an independent political group. Ashkara (Openness), a literary circle based in Dushanbe with members from different areas of the country, functioned 'outside of the Communist Party, questioning the monopoly of state power and its shortcomings and seeking ways of asserting an independent culture, especially through the promotion of the national Tajik language. These organisations brought issues surrounding economic disparity into the public arena and raised questions relating to individual freedom and expression. They could be considered as the pioneers of non-governmental initiatives carried out by civil society during the last phases of the Soviet break up' (Boboroyov and Heap 2003a: 15).

Development of NGOs and other organisations was interrupted by the most severe period of fighting in the civil war. After 1994, there was a phase where public workers formed initiative groups and associations that were seen as NGOs and 'served the people' (Boboroyov and Heap 2003b: 41). These were often funded as part of the humanitarian relief effort and, like other 'initiative groups' across the region, were not necessarily registered. The Tajik study cites Mullojonov who states that after 1994 most of the political resistance groups became NGOs, thereby agreeing not to interfere in 'political issues and state affairs' (Boboroyov and Heap 2003b: 41). The study also states that the government in this period, 1994–97, did not understand the purposes of NGOs. Recent interviews carried out by INTRAC in Dushanbe with representatives of NGOs noted that a national conference held in 2002 on social partnership which the President attended marked a turning point in the Government's understanding and acceptance of the NGO sector. This was followed up with awareness-raising workshops at *oblast* and *raion* level.

In more recent years, INGOs have been establishing local NGOs (a strategy which is generally being followed by INGOs in other parts of the world). This is especially true in the areas most ravaged by the civil war, in the Khatlon *oblast* and Tursundoza and Kofarnihon districts. Newer local NGOs are also emerging. These are often established around the vestiges of the Soviet public organisations and clubs at local level. Thus a group of new Community Development Centres (CDCs) are almost all based on local committees of the old Komsomol of Tajikistan, which had buildings available. UNDP facilitated the development of the CDCs at the end of the 1990s, and the centres are also supported (usually in kind) by the local authorities. Where the CDCs can access funds, usually from international donors, they work on particular projects. However, as the Tajik study states, 'the CDCs themselves remain dependent upon international initiatives ... they work spasmodically on projects for which they receive funds.' It further states that the CDCs do not operate in the same way as NGOs – they 'lack the strong motivation and understanding of NGOs', and have a 'traditional (Soviet) way of doing things'.

Uzbekistan

In INTRAC's first mapping report of the NGO sector in Uzbekistan in 1998 (Garbutt and Sinclair 1998), the authors noted that there were two main types of NGO. Firstly there were the ten Republican NGOs which had been established by the President, which all had a minimum of eight branch offices covering all regions of the country. The other type were the 'grass-roots' NGOs which registered with the Ministry of Justice. The report also states there were other forms of public association, which it did not classify as NGOs, for example farmers' associations, trade unions and boys' clubs.

The first type of organisation is based on the traditional Soviet form of public association. The examples given in the 1998 report illustrate this by citing both old-style public associations which had continued and modified their activities, and newly formed associations which operated in a very similar way, in that they were Government-sponsored. The report notes that these organisations often have very good relations with Government structures at national level.

The other category of NGOs identified in the1998 mapping is very different, in that they have been established without support from the State. But the support tends to come from external donors instead. In some cases, NGOs have been founded by motivated individuals who have identified a need amongst the population and then created an NGO to respond to this. The development of these organisations is then facilitated by donors. In other cases, donors have created NGOs where they are not able to find suitable partners to implement specific projects or programmes. The authors also note that:

> The NGOs are generally led by one strong personality, often a woman, have little staff back-up and tend to lose their staff to the higher paying international agencies (Garbutt and Sinclair 1998: 4).

These conclusions are largely relevant for the situation in the mid 1990s in the other Central Asian states, when donor support for NGOs came fully on stream.

Whilst donors wanted to work with 'bona-fide NGOs' and frown on those who work with GONGOs, the distinction is not always clear. Furthermore, organisations classed as 'bona-fide' do not instantly make perfect partners for donors. An internal INTRAC report on civil society and the political climate in Uzbekistan produced in 2003 suggests that many of the problems identified in the 1998 report remain:

> Very often the NNOs [non-governmental non-profit organisations] are led by one strong personality, often on a voluntary basis, with volunteers to help out. There is often little or no management back up. High staff turnover to the high-paying international agencies is normal ... Potential NNOs cannot become bona-fide NNOs until they have been trained and assisted (partly financially but mostly non financially).

But there are exceptions – for example, organisations that have successfully blended elements of the Soviet heritage (a secular, professional, well-educated population) with a readiness to take on new challenges and undertake programmes with a social benefit. The Business Women's Association of Uzbekistan is one such organisation, described below.

Case Study – Business Women's Association of Uzbekistan

This network is made up of 12 organisations, bound together in a loose confederation. Offices in Samarkand and Tashkent emerged shortly after independence, whilst others were created in the mid 1990s as the network sought to expand. Many of the organisations' founders and leaders are women who held positions of authority in the Communist Party and are thus very well connected. But along with their connections and experience they have managed to find a way to adapt themselves and their organisations to the environment of post-independence Uzbekistan. Part of their success derives from convincing the Government of the need for organisations that support women to set up business enterprises.

Representatives of the BWA mark a turning point in the fortunes of the organisation after a meeting between the head of the Tashkent branch and the President in 1995. This seemed to help smooth the way for official recognition of the need for such bodies nationwide. This was also the year in which significant external donor funds began to be channelled to the Association.

Initially these organisations were set up to promote entrepreneurial opportunities for women, by providing training, assistance with business registration and information on issues such as taxation. The Bukhara BWA, for instance, has delivered training courses around the *oblast* on how to do business in a market economy and has received grants from over 20 international donors for this work.[3] It has also worked with the Bukahra *Hokimiyat* in co-ordinating a Government–NGO effort to support the local entrepreneurial sector. Some branches have also engaged in micro-crediting initiatives, generally in conjunction with external donors.

Whilst a number of the branches have maintained a focus on facilitating women, and now also men, in business, the BWA in Kokand has widened its scope considerably and now addresses a wide range of issues. Despite its name, it no longer has a specific focus on the promotion of women in business, although one of its declared goals is to promote women's participation in politics and the political decision-making process. INTRAC interviews held with staff members in late 2002 recorded six main programmes: 1) health 2) ecology 3) women 4) human rights 5) youth and 6) civic and humanitarian issues. Respondents explained that the BWA functions as a 'clearing house' for new ideas and that each part of the programme is covered by partner organisations: of the 60 NGOs in Kokand, the majority are BWA members. Once an NGO that worked directly with Uzbek women to help them register their businesses and obtain credit, the BWA in Kokand is now a national support organisation that channels external donor funds to other organisations in Uzbekistan, delivers training and liaises with international multi-lateral institutions. Whilst it could be criticised for losing its original focus, the BWA in Kokand has certainly provided an enabling environment for NGO development in the region.

[3] Akhmedova, Dilbar (1999). Interview with Director of the Business Women's Association, Bukhara, 26 October, by the Uzbek mapping report researchers.

Turkmenistan

In Turkmenistan the term NGO is still not commonly used, and this is linked to the very difficult environment for civil society groups in the country. INTRAC's 2003 mapping report states, 'Even the NGOs themselves prefer to call themselves Public Associations' (Buxton and Musabaeva 2002: 15). They continue,

> During our mission, we received from many NGOs the definite impression that calling such groups 'NGOs' at the very beginning of their development, as a new type of civil society organisation, was a mistake. According to this view, the choice of this term caused a negative reaction from the Turkmen Government which has lasted for many years and has proved very hard to change. Some NGO leaders have come to think that this was a mistake by foreign donor organisations who began talking about non governmental organisations without taking into consideration the national context and historical legacies in Turkmenistan (Buxton and Musabaeva 2002: 15).

Nonetheless, a limited number of registered NGOs do exist in Turkmenistan. Most of these managed to process their papers before 1997 when the Government's policy towards registration was not so restrictive. At the time of the mapping visit, voluntary groups pursued one of two main strategies: either to register as an initiative group under the auspices of one of the larger, Government-approved, organisations like the Women's Union or the Youth Union (see notes in the previous chapter); or to present their papers and thus show responsible intent. In late 2003 the Turkmenistan Government imposed further restrictions on public associations and religious organisations alike. The public activity of unregistered bodies was declared illegal and persons ignoring warnings about working in unregistered associations were threatened with criminal prosecution.[4]

Despite these serious problems, INTRAC was able to identify a slow but noticeable development of civil society groups. This included the work of another Government-approved association, the Union of Entrepreneurs (see case study in Chapter 5) and a small number of NGO or voluntary networks which operate with multi-lateral donors. For example, UNAIDS has funded ten target NGOs to undertake work on an HIV/AIDS programme. Working through branches of the Youth Union, these local-level NGOs undertake educational work with young people. UNHCR provides services to refugees in liaison with local NGOs, and UNICEF mother and child health programmes. Similarly, OSCE has been supporting a group of environmental NGOs.[5]

---

[4] See INTRAC internal political and civil society report, January 2004, and United Nations Integrated Regional Information Networks, December 2003 (www.irinnews.org).

[5] As in other countries of the region, environmental NGOs were considered to be one of the most advanced sectors.

Moreover, INTRAC's 2003 report noted changes in NGO thinking in the country, compared to a previous visit several years previously.

This time we noticed that many NGOs have started to differentiate clearly between public associations as successors of Soviet pro-government organisations uniting people by their interests or established mainly for information sharing, and the NGO as an absolutely new type of formation, representing the interests of particular groups in a particular field (Buxton and Musabaeva 2002).

However, an NGO round-table held by INTRAC in December 2003 heard examples of leaders and activists questioning Government officials and preparing information for a number of court cases where key NGOs were under threat of disbandment. Voluntary groups have developed a considerable ability to accommodate themselves to changing donor opportunities and interests. The Government is not happy with this, and new legislation has been designed to control these groups and if possible align them under sectoral ministries. The level of Government concern was directly related to the political content of NGO work. By contrast, work at the community level seemed to arouse less suspicion from the authorities.

Classifications and Numbers of NGOs

Despite the recognition of the 'fuzziness' of the definition of NGOs, people involved in civil society strengthening programmes in the region still talk of the 'NGO sector'. Each of the research reports looked at the various forms of classification of this sector, and attempted to give an idea of the size of the sector in their specific countries.

Given the legislative basis of public associations in all five countries, the official statistics include all sorts of organisations which would not necessarily be regarded as civil society organisations, such as commercial entities. In addition the official statistics include all the organisations that have registered, many of which may have only existed for a short period of time – an almost universal feature of the voluntary or civil society sector.

Thus, the State Statistical Agency of Kazakhstan had 6,796 public organisations registered in 2002. Franz et al. (2002) estimate that 44 per cent of these organisations are dormant – that is they are registered but not currently doing anything. In 2002 in Kyrgyzstan there were 2,500 officially public organisations registered with the Ministry of Justice. This figure will reflect NGOs registered at the national level. Kyrgyz organisations can also register at *oblast* and even *raion* level, and these will not figure in the Government's statistics.[6] A report from Tajikistan notes that there are fewer than 1,000 public associations registered with the Ministry of Justice. Quoting the Tajik academic Karimov, the report argues that 'not all these will be non-governmental, and some will be inactive due to scarcity of funds' (Boboroyov and Heap 2003a: 20).[7] The Uzbek research study states that there are over 3,000 public associations registered in Uzbekistan of which around 300 are central (All-Republican or branches of international organisations) (Abdullaev et al. 2003). Finally, it is impossible to get reliable Government data on the number of public associations in Turkmenistan, since the Ministry of Justice does not disclose the list of registered organisations to the general public. The Turkmen Mapping Report states, 'It is thought that 600–700 organisations may be registered, though this might include "public enterprises" (income generating units belonging to public associations, used for non-commercial purposes).' In reality, perhaps a fifth of this number are actively functioning.

The Kazakh study notes that, 'there are at least six types of NGO classification made by different agencies,'[8] and that these figures are not consistent with each other. Similarly, the Kyrgyz study states that data on NGOs, 'are not widely or easily accessible even for development workers and researchers. ... Domestic statistics on NGOs vary considerably ... it seems that civil society classifications are used by government and donors only' (Dissenova et al. 2002: 34).[9]

This last comment highlights the importance afforded by some donors to the creation of a plurality of organisations as part of a civil society strengthening programme. For example, the US agency Counterpart Consortium (which began its programme in Central Asia in 1994) maintains a database of organisations it classifies as NGOs in all five countries.[10] The figures for Spring 2004 are given below in Table 2. Organisations have been classified according to sectoral areas of work:

---

[6] Whilst registration at more local level will limit the geographical scope of an organisation's work, registration at the national level is free, and can be obtained relatively easily.

[7] The report continues, 'many have an agenda lacking in focus, and their programmes are so wide in intention and scope that they resemble government plans to address all the country's needs' (Boboroyov and Heap 2003a: 20).

[8] These agencies are: Central Asian Sustainable Development Information Network (CAS-DIN); Counterpart Consortium; the United Nations Development Programme (UNDP); the Public Foundation for Political and Legal Studies Interlegal; USAID; and the World Bank.

[9] The Kyrgyz report continues, 'In the case of the government, it is a bureaucratic and legal requirement for the administration's ... control and regulation of the third sector. In the case of donors, classifications may assist in the design of programmes or the measurement of the sector' (Dissenova et al. 2002: 34).

[10] See www.cango.net

the country offices select what they consider to be the most appropriate categories. These numbers are much smaller than the Government statistics, because Counterpart Consortium tries to select only those organisations it considers to be 'development NGOs'.

Table 2 Summary of NGO-type organisations in Central Asia

Sector	Kazakhstan	Kyrgyzstan	Tajikistan	Turkmenistan	Uzbekistan
Children/ youth	105	302	97	19	56
Health	87	129	44	15	46
Education/ science	83	212	87	13	38
Ecology	81		37	20	38
Disabled	75	126	48	9	74
Women	71	236	45	31	41
Business	52	145	31	4	-
Legal/ judicial	45	-	-	-	-
Human Rights	44	146	18	-	-
Artists/ artisans	43		50	9	36
Families/ pensioners	37	166	60	4	-
Ethnic/ cultural	19	35		3	20
Charities/ foundations	-	152	-	-	41
Agriculture/ farmers	-	128	-	16	-
Media	-	120	21	3	15
Social	-	-	-	-	17
Associations	-	-	-	-	50
Other	72	86	19	6	77

Source: NGOs listed on Counterpart Consortium Website, Spring 2004[11] (www.cango.net)

[11] It should be noted that NGOs which carry out work in a variety of areas may be listed under more than one sector. Therefore, totalling these figures would not be useful.

The Expansion of the NGO Sector

In essence, the pattern of NGO development across the region does not show huge differentiation. In all countries, some of the pre-independence, Soviet-style organisations continue to operate, either working along similar lines and closely aligned with the Government, or with some adjustment to the new economic and political climate. These organisations are especially prominent in Turkmenistan, Uzbekistan and to a lesser extent in Tajikistan. In Kyrgyzstan and Kazakhstan they also play an important role alongside the larger number of newly established NGOs. The advent of international donors and availability of funding for NGO-type activities has led to a major expansion of new organisations across the region, which fit the Western-style NGO mould better.

The ease with which donors can operate and NGOs develop correlates with levels of Government liberalisation. The more facilitative regime in Kyrgyzstan, for example, contrasts with greater repression in Uzbekistan and Turkmenistan. The civil war in Tajikistan, as has been noted, also slowed donor promotion of the sector. But although donor priorities are beginning to shift, with many withdrawing from Kazakhstan as its GDP per capita increases, there are similarities across the region.

Donors seem to have followed similar strategies across the region, and similar types of NGOs have emerged. Thus, the bulk of donor resources for the region coming from USAID and private foundations was initially concentrated on democracy promotion and civil society strengthening. Other international NGOs and bilateral donors had more of a poverty focus. Support was available for organisations that worked with vulnerable groups, and there was funding provision for institutions set up to facilitate business activity, raise awareness of human rights, give legal advice and promote democratic governance. Pressure groups and professional associations were also supported. In Tajikistan, the priority was post-war conflict resolution, humanitarian aid and reconstruction.

One conclusion regarding the NGO 'sector' that the reader gains from the research reports is of a set of organisations that are still fairly isolated. As one example among many, the Kazakh mapping report describes a women's support centre with Dutch and private foundation funding that was established to help survivors of sexual violence and harassment. Whilst it acknowledges that the Centre has achieved a great deal in a short space of time, there are a number of caveats regarding its sustainability and external linkages. Thus, although the NGO had in theory set up official channels for collaboration with the law enforcement bodies of Almaty through the Ministry for Internal Affairs, exchanging information with the Ministry and its city department was proving to be difficult. Furthermore, the report notes that the Centre lacked communications with other NGOs and was in effect competing for donor support with other women-focused groups (Dissenova et al. 2002: 35).

This reflects one of the biggest problems for the new NGO sector: its dependency on donor funding. As noted in the discussion of the discrepancy around numbers on NGOs above, many of those registered are inactive. This is often because they have been formed to undertake specific projects, or have managed to win grants for start-up initiatives, but have then not managed to secure follow-up funding. INTRAC's liaison with civil society groups across the region uncovered considerable dissatisfaction with donors, arising at least in part from the over-dependent relationship in which NGOs find themselves. For example, at a workshop on donor–civil society relations held in 2002, participants noted the lack of co-ordination among donors, the prevalence of short-lived donor 'fads', poor consultation and feedback mechanisms, the distance of many policy makers from the realities of the region and a lack of transparency in the selection of NGO partners.

When small, newly established organisations begin chasing relatively limited grants for one-off projects, it is inevitably almost impossible for them to stay close to their original mission (if this was clearly defined) or their constituency (if they had one). Thus there are many examples of NGOs who have 'read' the local situation and also the donor possibilities successfully, broadening their remit in order to access funding for different types of project. One such example can be seen in the work of an NGO in northern Kyrgyzstan. Its original mission was to provide social security and lending assistance to vulnerable population groups, especially the women and young people of the province, and to improve the status and capacities of these groups. The NGO has undertaken activities in this regard by providing charity assistance to vulnerable groups and setting up some credit lines. However, in the late 1990s, the organisation implemented a UNDP supported project to rehabilitate water pipe networks and has undertaken environmental projects and campaigns. It has come to work on poverty issues more generally and is seeking to set up a centre for regional business promotion (Baimatov et al. 2002: 37–8).

This example shows an NGO that is obviously highly successful at raising funds from international donors and implementing projects. But the example also illustrates the potential pitfalls by which, in the process of ensuring continuity of funding, a group can lose touch with its original remit and target group. This is a common criticism of the sector in Central Asia, and indeed of the donors that support it. This is not to say that all organisations have acted in this way; quite the opposite, there is a mass of success stories detailed in the reports, only a few of which we have space to reproduce in this publication, which show organisations demonstrating clear commitment to target groups and specific areas of work.

The Work of Civil Society Support Centres

Beside the 'thematic' programmes of donors, it is important to note the establishment of a Central Asia regional network of generic civil society support, funded by USAID and implemented by Counterpart Consortium.[12] This work has been extremely influential.

Counterpart Consortium itself identifies three stages of its work in the region. Phase one (from 1995) introduced the idea that problem-solving through independent organisations was a viable option for Central Asian countries; the second phase began in 1997 and emphasised the role of NGOs in strengthening democratic civil society and in fostering citizen participation in decision-making processes; phase three began in 2000 and built on the previous two phases but shifted its emphasis to establishing a geographically dispersed network of over 30 civil society support centres through five Central Asian countries.

Initially the organisation combined training and information provision activities with small-scale grant-giving programmes. There was a great demand for the training provided, and the courses were gradually rolled out, following the same modular format across all countries, by contracted local trainers. In the early 2000s it remains true to say that the majority of people involved in urban-based NGOs have been on Counterpart courses. As a result of its outreach, the organisation has become one of the principal 'messengers' in the region about the expectations associated with the development of civil society. Once the *oblast*-based civil society support centres (CSSCs) were established, they became an important tool in reaching 'untouched' geographical areas, and the basis for a community outreach programme.

Counterpart Consortium is currently involved in an exit strategy, or localisation strategy, for the countries with more advanced sectors. The idea is that the support centres will eventually become self-sufficient and be able to fundraise independently (for example, it is stated in policy documents that these centres should be able to make direct applications for funding to USAID) in order to carry on grant-making and training work. However, the environment in Turkmenistan, where Counterpart continues to be the main support organisation for NGOs, is not sufficiently advanced for it to consider withdrawal.

In Uzbekistan, too, the organisation is recognised as having played a leading role in developing the NGO sector; some observers even regarding it as having had a type of monopoly on the sector. And, whilst some NGO staff regard Counterpart Consortium training as being too standardised and rather simplistic, it is recognised as having played a crucial role for 'beginner' and 'middle-level' NGOs.

---

[12] In 2003, the CSSC programmes in Uzbekistan and Tajikistan were contracted to another US based INGO, IREX.

Many NGOs are grateful for to Counterpart Consortium for helping them to launch activities and for continuing to support and promote them.

The Rise of Local NGO Support Organisations

In some cases, the capital based or *oblast* level CSSCs were established by Counterpart in partnership with indigenous NGOs. Many observers consider these to be among the most successful centres, because the partner organisation knew the locality and the needs of organisations located there. Some of the organisations already featured in the case studies for this book have successfully managed Counterpart centres – for example, Centre Interbilim in Bishkek and Osh, Kyrgyzstan. The generic information and training services operated alongside the specialised activity of the NGO. Among many examples which could be noted here are the Bukhara Information and Cultural Centre (Uzbekistan), which maintains close links with craft, cultural and tourism associations, as well as running the city's civil society support centre; and Foundation for Tolerance International (Kyrgyzstan), which combines work on prevention of community and cross-border conflict in Fergana Valley with maintenance of two centres in Batken *oblast*.

By the late 1990s, a number of NGOs across the region found themselves sufficiently experienced to take on the role of support organisation to newer organisations. These larger, well-established NGOs had met the criteria for external donors' civil society strengthening programmes when they first came to work in the region. At this time, in order to put their programmes in place, donors had identified existing NGOs that were working as pressure groups, and encouraged the establishment of others. These organisations have now come to serve as the model for NGOs in the region. The Kyrgyz study outlines some of their most common characteristics and strengths:

The term NGO in Kyrgyzstan usually refers to a non-governmental voluntary network working predominantly in an urban setting ... covering 'advanced' issues as the NGO practitioners say. These tend to be concerned with human rights, civil society and democracy building, good governance, social protection, decision making and transparent elections. It is very common for an urban NGO to recruit highly qualified members. ... As a rule, urban NGO staff possess specifically academic and research backgrounds due to previously held lecturing and teaching positions at universities and scientific agencies (Kyrgyz study).

Gradually these NGOs have evolved as higher-level intermediary or support organisations. Some were leaders in their own geographical area, others established head offices with outlying branches (like for example the Business Women's Association network in Uzbekistan); others again provided special information or training services to the sector. In many cases they gradually began to work with donors to channel grants to smaller groups in outlying or rural areas. However, once clearly exercising the role of a donor intermediary, such NGOs run the risk of orienting themselves more towards their donors than their supposed target groups.

A report from Tajikistan (Mirzoeva 2003b) notes that while these leading organisations have their advantages in that they are often set up by sectoral specialists or experts, there is a tendency to think that 'only the centre is able to formulate an awareness of social problems related to communities.' Sometimes they do not have a great deal of knowledge or information about local rural situations. Thus, 'only a limited number of NGOs have branches and representatives in local communities.' The report gives the example of a Tajik NGO, which managed to organise more than a hundred seminars and training workshops during the first four years of its activities, 'but still the problems of people and communities are little understood and acknowledged, no more than when the organisation first began. This is a characteristic of the system which rewards talk over action' (Boboroyov and Heap 2003b: 52).

Conversely, it is clear that for NGOs and support organisations alike, success breeds success. Meeting objectives and being able to show impact will encourage other donors to pledge support for further work. It is in this way that 'market leaders' began to appear across the region (with the exception perhaps of Turkmenistan) during the 1990s, and have further established themselves and begun to create networks in the first years of the new century. One such NGOSO is ASTI in Tajikistan, described in the case study below.

Case Study – ASTI

In Tajikistan, the Association of Scientific and Technical Intelligentsia (ASTI) was set up in the second city Khujand in 1995. Its main areas of activity are education, poverty reduction, micro-credit, social programmes, information and consultancy. They recently added gender issues to their wide remit, and have a new education and strategic studies programmes. The former undertakes research on poverty issues and civil society development whilst the main foci of the education programme are civic education, agriculture and family planning.

The Tajik report states that the organisation has become one of the strongest NGOs in Central Asia. ASTI has now established two Agencies for the Support of the Development Process (ASDP) that work in three target *raions* of the Khujand *oblast*. These function as implementing partners in these areas. Local trainers and other staff of these agencies analyse community needs and feed back to ASTI to identify how to implement its policy in the districts.

Funded by an array of donors from both the former Soviet Union and Europe, ASTI works to build up relations with local government first at *oblast* level, then with *raion* authorities and finally at the community level. But as well as working directly with communities, ASTI works to meet the needs of 15 local NGOs. It provides financial support to newly created organisations but focuses on training for more well-established NGOs. This training covers issues such as organisational management and activity planning through advanced development education.

In Kazakhstan, the situation with regards to 'market leader' NGOs is a little different, in that the economy, geography, political situation and donor focus have perhaps not provided an environment where NGO support type organisations would thrive and find a niche. Certainly, international donor pressure has been directed towards the democracy promotion agenda. Nevertheless, there are a number of organisations that stand out, and would be regarded as 'mature' organisations in the region itself, because of the high-profile nature of their work. One example is the Eco Centre in East Kazakhstan that grew out of the Nevada-Semipalantisk movement, that works in the area of environment and produces a widely read newsletter. A case study of two well-established NGOs working in Almaty (Baspana and Moldir) is to be found in Chapter 3.

Sustainability of Civil Society and NGOs

As alluded to above, the quality and vitality of civil society also affects its degree of sustainability. An ambitious and widely known attempt to measure this is provided by USAID's Sustainability Index. During the last few years USAID has been carrying out an annual assessment in 30 countries of Eastern Europe, the Commonwealth of Independent States and Central Asia. At present this is one of the most developed tools in the region for an overall evaluation of NGO efficiency. The index uses seven variables: the country's legal environment, organisational potential, financial status, advocacy, service delivery level, infrastructure and image of public institutes. Sustainability is scored on a scale from seven to one, assessed with a focus group consisting of NGO experts who evaluate the USAID programme's impact in each country.

The problem about using this method, as recounted by USAID's democracy programme director at an INTRAC conference, is that while in some areas a very detailed estimate is made, nonetheless experts (particularly where the issues are new or not fully worked through in the sector) tend to give too high an evaluation of civil society development in their countries. As a result a picture is presented where the sustainability level in Turkmenistan is estimated to be higher than that of, for example, Poland, even though it is widely understood that the civil society development levels in these countries differ greatly. In other words, whilst a quantitative comparison between countries is potentially interesting, in practice a reliable comparison is very difficult to achieve.

In recent years, USAID has also been using a special tool, the 'NGO Thermometer', to measure specific areas of change. The difference from the Sustainability Index consists in target group selection. In each of the five Central Asian states target NGOs are identified by civil society support centres – ten in each region (or city), working in different areas, are chosen. Every year USAID measures the changes in these organisations.

NGO Collaboration

This chapter has not tried to hide the fact that in some respects the NGO sector in Central Asia is somewhat disparate and isolated. Certainly, the struggle for survival and the drive to access donor funding may have contributed to an atmosphere of competition. This is only partly counter-balanced by many positive efforts by the same donors to encourage co-operation and the sharing of experience – for example among grantee NGOs working on the environment, with women, youth and health issues.

Although NGOs across the region have been criticised for being 'donor driven' and led by external agendas, NGOs have struggled over the decade of the 1990s to establish common ground and a value base from which to initiate collaboration. Recently, a more cohesive sector has begun to emerge, certainly in Kazakhstan and Kyrgyzstan. In these two countries, organisations with very different backgrounds have worked together to lobby government over legislative and human rights issues, for example, and have established forums and platforms that have actually functioned as spaces within which NGOs can discuss critical issues and articulate opinions and criticisms of government policy. In Kyrgyzstan, the two large groupings of NGOs, the Association of NGOs (a pro-government grouping), and the Coalition of NGOs (initially set up by the US's National Democratic Institute for International Affairs, NDI) have begun to work together on social, community and poverty issues, organising important public events and information fairs for the sector. This type of joint working was unheard of until relatively recently. As such, NGOs are maturing according to their country's needs and priorities and are beginning to step beyond the donor agenda, initiating activities and collaboration on issues of concern independently of external pressure. These developments will be discussed further in Chapter 8.

Conclusion

This chapter has identified developments in the civil society sector since independence, which has largely been characterised by the emergence of NGOs, the majority of which are funded by American and European donors and private foundations. Not surprisingly, considering the economic context of the transition period, these organisations have come to depend extensively on continued funding from external donors in order to survive. Many smaller NGOs appear to have shifted their goals and original aims in order to access funding lines from these actors, and have been criticised as a result and described as 'donor driven'. However, these local-level organisations are often the only hope that poor communities have to maintain basic infrastructure, and access to certain services.

This chapter also documented the emergence of higher-level intermediary organisations. These support organisations have done much to open up the civil society sector in their respective countries. Going beyond service provision for target groups, they have liaised with government to implement projects. They have also undertaken lobbying activities to improve the environment for civil society in general and invested further in the sector as a whole by providing training and consultancy to improve the work of other NGOs. It should be noted, however, that these highly successful actors have also drawn a degree of criticism. Their success is partly derived from their ability to work with foreign donors. Some commentators have noted that professional, urban-based NGOs are becoming the sole interlocutors of these external actors. Some have gone so far as to say that the language they use and the concepts and jargon they employ are only comprehensible to other NGOs and the donors who originally introduced this language. These critics go on to suggest that any effort to broaden the outreach of their message is confined to the idea of PR and of selling a concept, rather than establishing a grass-roots constituency.[13]

Whilst these criticisms are at the more extreme end of the spectrum, there is a general acceptance that many urban-based NGOs, particularly those that have risen up through the aid chain, have either lost touch with their target groups or never established a full understanding of the needs of poor and marginalised groups, especially in rural areas. Without a strong non-governmental sector in place, new NGOs springing up post-independence had few examples on which to model themselves. In general, they evolved as a rather urban group of organisations, staffed by highly educated, multilingual professionals, many of whom were women who had been squeezed out of the public sector.[14] Whilst their motivation is not in question

---

[13] These ideas were expressed at the Fifth Annual Central Eurasian Studies Society Conference held in Boston, Massachusetts in October 2003.

[14] For further discussion see Garbutt 2003.

here, it is clear that engaging with poor communities, especially in rural areas, has been a challenge for many of these NGOs. This has had an impact on their ability to become involved in community development projects, and has problematised interaction with their target groups at the grass-roots level.[15]

INTRAC would therefore argue that, since the research reports were completed, a 'new phase' of NGO development and donor activity has begun, as the latter focus on greater engagement with target communities and give increased attention to the problems of development and poverty in rural areas. The result, as will be shown in the next chapter, is a drive to implement community-based development projects and an increase in the occurence of community-based organisations and other local level groups.

---

[15] Many NGOs in the region are now addressing this issue. ASTI, for example, has undertaken extensive research into rural poverty, livelihood strategies and migration.

CHAPTER 7

New Developments Since Independence: The Focus on the Community

Donors and the Commitment to Poverty Reduction

As shown in the last chapter, many of the first programmes funded by US and other large donors in Central Asia were focused on civil society strengthening. These programmes directed support to emerging pressure groups that were forming around specific issues. The availability of funds for such groups encouraged more, similar groups, to emerge. Most of these early groups were urban-based, and with limited knowledge about or connection to the problems of rural areas.

The limitations of these groups, together with the international donor community's renewed focus on poverty, have led to an increased desire to fund more rural, community-based initiatives. The World Bank requires governments to produce Poverty Reduction Strategy Papers (PRSPs) in order to access concessional development assistance. These are supposed to be country-driven documents which indicate the country's ownership of policies. The setting of the Millennium Development Goals by the world's industrial nations has seen a publicly stated commitment to a reduction in poverty, and there is now considerable pressure on the donor community to meet these targets. There is also a recognition that, after the break-up of the USSR, the slide into poverty of the majority of its former population was much more acute than anticipated.

At least as important for US donors working in the Central Asian region is the link between poverty, social unrest and the growth of radical forms of Islam.[1] USAID-funded conflict mitigation programmes were already in operation in the Central Asian states in the 1990s, as incidents in Osh at the start of the decade had alerted external agencies to the real possibility of communal violence, especially in border areas, that could destabilise the region. However, the events of September 2001 in the US sparked what USAID has described as the 'rapid roll-out' of community investment schemes aimed at conflict prevention.[2] High levels of poverty and inequality also have negative implications for the development of democracy, which remains a priority for the US. Finally, there is also pressure on the US Government, especially in Uzbekistan and Kyrgyzstan, to undertake higher profile development activities as a type of payment in-kind for the use of military bases at Khalkhabat and Manas that have played a role in the 'war on terror'. As such we see the USAID-funded INGOs focusing on the community, and launching a number of multiple project programmes in potential 'hot-spot' areas such as the Ferghana Valley and the southern Uzbek *oblasts* of Kashkadarya and Surkhandarya that are close to the Afghan border.

There are therefore a number of factors behind the greater focus on community development initiatives, besides the realisation that many Central Asian NGOs were out of touch with poorer rural communities.

Community-Based Organisations

Populations in Central Asia are predominantly rural and these populations can have very high densities in the more fertile farming regions, particularly in Uzbekistan. The majority of poor people in Central Asia are found outside of the cities, and whilst there are poor groups of people located in and around urban centres, the bulk of poverty-focused work by the international agencies is being undertaken in rural areas. Donors, over approximately the past five years, have shown an increasing interest in funding organisations that work with the poor in these areas. Some of the USAID-funded INGOs are moving towards work with more locally rooted NGOs that engage with poor rural communities, setting up three-way projects with community groups and local governments. Some examples of this are discussed below – Counterpart Consortium's Mahalla Initiative Programme and Community Outreach Programme, and Mercy Corps' Peaceful Communities Initiative. Details of the NGO intermediaries involved in some of these projects are to be found in the

---

[1] There is both national and international concern over the appeal of more radical groupings such as the Islamic Movement of Uzbekistan and Hizb ut-Tahrir.

[2] USAID press release, 11th July 2002. www.state.gov/p/eur Accessed 31/12/03.

case studies in the previous chapter.

Not all the USAID-funded community programmes work with local NGOs, however. The Community Action Investment Programme, known as CAIP, is being implemented by Community Habitat Finance (CHF) and Mercy Corps directly with community groups, mainly in rural areas. This approach has been taken by the multi-lateral institutions also, who are planning, or already undertaking large-scale programmes of grass-roots development, working directly with communities and local self-governing bodies, with a far smaller focus on NGO intermediaries. The World Bank's Community Driven Development (CDD) initiative is one such example. UNDP has been engaged at the local level for a considerably longer time, with, for example, environment and water projects in the Aral Sea area of Kazakhstan and with the poverty component of its Social Governance Programme across Kyrgyzstan.

Clearly, since the end of the 1990s, the region has witnessed a growth of donor-funded community development projects. Related to this has been an increase in the use of the term 'community-based organisation' (CBO), as opposed to NGO, and a rise in the number of groups that refer to themselves in this way. However, understandings and employment of the new terminology are not standardised, as was the case previously with the term 'NGO'. The current situation is one where local, rural groups are encouraged to form an 'initiative group' to deal with a particular issue. These then tend to be identified by donors as CBOs. Donors do not necessarily require these organisations to register, and in Kyrgyzstan, for example, they can remain as informal groups and associations, registered locally at the office of the *ayil okmotu*. In Uzbekistan, groups are obliged to register in order to operate legally since CBOs are not recognised in law. In Kyrgyzstan, despite the option of remaining informal, registration can be attractive to CBOs, especially if their income is significant or they feel the need for formal recognition.[3] Once registered, they are defined as NGOs and it may be easier for them to address certain issues. In some areas, practitioners are trying to make a clear distinction between NGOs (urban-based, specialist, more aware of the civil society agenda) and CBOs (rural-based, closely linked to the target group), but in practice the situation is more confused.

Research was carried out for UNDP in 2003 with INTRAC facilitation in Kyrgyzstan and Uzbekistan for a project assessing the ability of community-level

---

[3] In Kyrgyzstan, a law has been in place since 2002 that allows for the creation of local organisations to work within a defined territory to implement 'initiatives of local significance'. Giffen and Buxton (2004) suggest that while community organisations are given a lot of freedom in comparison to Uzbekistan, there should be space for informal, unregistered entities that act as an entry point for citizens into civil society and development processes.

groups to engage in pro-poor policy making. The project documentation employs the term 'community-based organisation', but the assessment found that the term was not well understood. It is becoming more familiar within the NGO sector in Kyrgyzstan, largely due to UNDP's work at community level with this type of group. In Uzbekistan, where there are fewer international development programmes, and where the research was carried out by an institute which was not particularly familiar with 'development speak', there was general discussion about what community-based organisations might be. It was concluded that these could range from religious organisations, to residents' associations, *mahalla* committees and initiative groups (Giffen and Buxton 2004).

In general, however, the donor community focuses on organisations originally set up as' initiative groups'. This term, which was current in Soviet times, signifies a group of people who come together to work on a particular problem, and is widely used across the former Soviet Union to describe the organisations and groupings that are emerging locally to deal with local problems. These groups are often associated with community initiatives to repair or reconstruct village infrastructure (such as roads, bath houses, schools, water supplies), all of which began to need attention at the end of the 1990s after ten years without maintenance. For instance, there has been a proliferation of funding for maintenance of water supplies, and many of the donor-funded programmes relating to water will involve the establishment of Water Users' Committees, another form of CBO. As noted in Chapter 4, where traditional practices or fundraising mechanisms are familiar to local populations, they will be incorporated into community development programmes.

As has been noted, community organisations are very often set up by external actors, and heavy donor dependency means that these organisations often disband once funding ceases. This is not always the case, however. Research carried out for UNDP on the potential for CBOs to participate in pro-poor decision-making has shown that it is not unusual for them, especially in Kyrgyzstan, to evolve into other types of organisation, and to move from involvement in repair of infrastructure projects to work on other issues affecting the local population. Giffen and Buxton's (2004) synthesis of this research notes that actors in the region identified a trend in which CBOs that were initially established as self-help or mutual-help groups are quite likely, over time, to diversify their activities and develop, particularly into micro-credit agencies, but also into NGOs, wider associations, or even start undertaking small business. They are sometimes supported in these endeavours by foreign donors. In some areas of rural Kyrgyzstan, the term 'village self-help group' seems to be synonymous with micro-credit provision.[4] The research goes on to note, however, that this type of change in organisational direction throws up a number of difficult choices for CBOs and NGOs in the region:

It is particularly important that these options and their implications are ... thoroughly thought through. This especially concerns the choice between prof-it-making or charitable aims and activities and between an economic or social focus. Related to this is the issue of mission and representation. As new money is pumped into existing community development programmes, many CBOs are being asked to represent larger constituencies and to go beyond their orig-inal 'initiative'. Many will readily agree to carry out larger pieces of work as a way to alleviate local poverty as well as get funds to prolong the life of their organisation. The question, however, is whether this will distort their aims and structure and their true community character and base (Giffen and Buxton 2004: 4–5).

The fact that this transition towards the economic sphere is seen as 'natural' sug-gests a very different understanding of the role of community organisations on the part of the original researchers, compared with Western understandings of this organisational form as voluntary and non-profit-making. But the focus on commu-nity-level initiatives that generate income, ensure credit or undertake rehabilitation activities is one that can be seen across Central Asia and the former Soviet Union and is not particularly surprising, considering levels of poverty and unemployment in the region. This move from 'development' to income generation is perhaps less jarring for a Central Asian observer. During the Soviet era, social capital was built up through the workplace and regular employment was the key to social inclusion. There was a clear link between networks generated through the workplace and income generation. It could be argued that with the sudden onset of unemployment and poverty, involvement in NGOs or community organisations is seen as a new way to build up social networks that can be used to generate income through busi-ness enterprise.[5] Some Western observers might find an emphasis on income gener-ation at the expense of 'typical development' based on values as distasteful, but this would be an obvious example of a normative approach to civil society development.

---

[4] The UNDP research on CBOs in Kyrgyzstan states that too many international donors are involved in setting up credit unions, and that there are examples of the same people being members of more than one group. (Kalmykova, cited in Omuraliyev et al. 2002). The study further states that in most cases initiative groups were set up by local people, to form a credit union. 'This is the main reason for widespread family-governed credit unions ... it is normal, especially in the rural and remote areas, for a credit union to include family members on the Management Board, Credit Committee and Supervision Committee, whereas the credit unions in the central or urban areas tend to elect the Management Board by a General Assembly of members. In the future, it is expected that rural credit unions will increasingly elect their officials.'

[5] Conversation with Jane Cooper, AKF, Dushanbe, August 2004.

As will be shown below, UNDP has taken the lead in the region by supporting CBOs to develop on their own terms, rather than dictating how they should function or what they should do. The Mountain Societies Development Support Programme of the Aga Khan also distinguishes itself by concentrating on the need to build the capacities of local organisations to bring about pro-poor change in rural areas.

Donor Strategies

At present, the large majority of international NGOs working at the grass-roots level in Central Asia are USAID funded. Those with the widest outreach are currently Mercy Corps, Counterpart Consortium, Soros, IREX and CHF. The manner in which these agencies work is very similar across the region. Sometimes, village residents make the first contact with a donor agency through a local support centre or office; on other occasions, the donor will approach local government officials or other local figures, with a request for contact within a particular village or cluster of settlements. Consultation meetings are then held at village level to ascertain the extent to which there is interest in undertaking a project – this frequently involves installing or renovating infrastructure which has lacked maintenance since the break-up of the Soviet Union (gas supply, irrigation or drinking water systems, road and school repairs, for example). The next stages involve needs assessment, during which participatory techniques are used at further meetings where community members are divided up into separate groups of men, women and young people. Consultations are also held with villagers to design the project, based on results of participatory exercises, and to elect members to a 'community initiative group' or 'action group', who will mediate between the donor and the villagers, helping to mobilise their input. The community generally has to raise a percentage of the cost of the project and it is at these meetings that those assembled also decide on the type and amount of their contribution. Very often, this will be delivered through voluntary labour.

In the push to implement community development projects in accordance with these guidelines, there was initially a tendency amongst some agencies to ignore the complexity of Central Asian society – the kind of traditions and structures described in Chapter 4. However, in response to criticism, in recent years, donors have sought to involve individuals in their community-level projects who fulfil traditional positions of responsibility within the village and to promote pre-Soviet forms of community mobilisation.

In the late 1990s, Counterpart Consortium established its Mahalla Initiative Programme (MIP) in Uzbekistan, in which NGOs are encouraged to develop three-way partnerships with *mahalla* committees and community groups, who then make a joint application for grants from Counterpart. The idea is that the three stakeholder groups work together to undertake participatory community appraisals (PCA) to prioritise needs, followed by community action planning (CAP) and project implementation. Research from Uzbekistan would suggest that often, it is the NGOs which initiate this type of activity and take on responsibility for project management, with community members and the *mahalla* committee acting essentially as implementing partners. However, there are examples of *mahalla* committees approaching NGOs having heard about the possibility of funding.[6] In some cases, as will be shown in Chapter 8, the *mahalla* committee takes the lead in project planning and implementation.

Based on the lessons learnt from the Mahalla Initiative Programme in Uzbekistan, Counterpart developed its Community Outreach Programme for the whole of Central Asia, delivered through the network of local civil society centres described in the previous chapter. Whilst involving similar principles and using the same tools, the programme acknowledges that initiatives may come directly from communities (often those that are already active). As such it does not insist that CBOs or initiative groups work with a registered NGO partner, or register formerly themselves. In both cases there is a heavy emphasis on community participation through voluntary labour.

One example of this type of programme in action can be seen in the work of Alga, an NGO based in the north of Kyrgyzstan that works in rural areas. It selects the communities it plans to work with according to the criteria suggested by Counterpart Consortium for its Community Outreach Programme. One of the key criteria is the readiness of the community to participate in development initiatives. In one typical example, Alga helped with the establishment of a village initiative group, and then helped the group organise a general meeting in which residents discussed their priorities for improvements to their environment. In this case, it was decided to rebuild a sports hall for the school's 220 pupils. Alga then helped the initiative group to apply for funding from Counterpart Consortium. The application was successful, and the local male residents undertook building work, while women prepared food for them. Alga have worked in this way in many villages across Chui *oblast*.

In cases where mediating NGOs are involved, the onus is upon them to ensure that the aims of the projects and the planned input of the community are adequately communicated to the community members themselves. INTRAC research in Uzbekistan examined a Counterpart Consortium Mahalla Initiative Programme in the south of the country, where it was clear that very little trust had been built up between an urban-based NGO, the *mahalla* committee and a newly formed

---

[6] Interview with B. Fozilhujaev, Kokand, March 2003.

initiative group. As a result, implementation of the seemingly simple infrastructure project stalled from the start as rumours abounded as to the nature of the project and the aims of the NGO.

Problems of trust, awareness and mobilisation are commonly found, however, when foreign-funded donors arrive in rural villages and try to engage community members in project planning and implementation activities. This is shown in the following examples of infrastructure and community development programmes in the region.

Community Water Projects

Water is a key resource in Central Asia. Settlements on the plains of the region are centred around irrigation ditches or *aryks*. In densely populated farming areas, particularly in the Ferghana Valley, the problems of access to water have occasionally threatened to provoke inter-communal or cross-border violence. The problems are compounded by a history of over-exploitation and poor management of the resource. This is one area that donors have been keen to tackle and initiatives have been launched across the region in rural areas to repair and install pipelines and pumps, provide drinkable water and set up water users' committees to ensure the maintenance of infrastructure and the management of water services.[7]

Case Study – Water Users' Unions in North Kyrgyzstan

One such project has been undertaken across the *oblasts* of Naryn and Talas in northern Kyrgyzstan. This mountainous area has traditionally received less investment than other parts of the country. Communications are difficult and levels of poverty are higher in these *oblasts*. The project aimed to improve drinking water provision and set up Community Drinking Water Users' Unions or CDWUUs and was funded by the World Bank and the UK's Department for International Development (DFID).

This programme is particularly interesting as it highlights some of the attitudes towards working at community level and the tension between the civil society strengthening agenda and the drive for poverty reduction. In the early stages of the project, there were very uneven levels of involvement in the water project even between villages which, to the outsider, appeared to have similar problems surrounding the provision of drinking water. INTRAC research in two pilot villages in late 2002 in Naryn *oblast* highlighted these discrepancies (Tashbaeva 2002).

---

[7] Access to clean drinking water is one of the Millennium Development Goals.

Water provision for Village A came from an underground source. Changes in the water table over the previous ten years meant that the source was now flowing close to the graves in the village cemetery. The village suffered from high incidence of viral hepatitis and residents were aware of their need for an improved water source. Hearing about the proposed drinking water project, and without waiting for external mobilisation, village leaders established an initiative group, registered their CDWUU and were able to raise the five per cent contribution to costs from the community within nine months. This is quite an achievement in itself, considering the cash-poor nature of the area. This money came from salaries, pensions and family benefits, and village leaders suggested that they might even be able to raise more. The CDWUU have taken steps to ensure that all their funds are managed transparently and that the Union is accountable to the community. The researcher noted the high level of women's involvement in the CDWUU. As a result of these initial efforts the village was the first to undertake a water project.

In contrast, Village B, visited during the same research trip, showed very low levels of interest in and awareness of the drinking water project. This despite the fact that the water source used by villages ran close to the public toilets and had caused a number of infectious diseases amongst children and adults. Village B was selected by the local authorities to take part in the project pilot without consultation or awareness-raising activities with the villagers themselves. Lack of trust in the authorities was clearly demonstrated by villagers during a meeting held with the researchers. The local elders demanded that the water supply be provided first, before villagers contributed the five per cent of project costs. They also suggested that it should be the state providing them with this resource. Attempts to gauge the opinions of other groups in the village failed as they simply deferred to the statements of the *aksakals*.

It became clear both to the INTRAC researchers and consultants to the project that it could not be assumed that villages in need of improved drinking water would necessarily become involved in the project in the way that Village A had. The key problem was raising community contributions towards project costs. However, with a change in management and in focus, with far greater emphasis on community mobilisation, the fortunes of the programme began to change. It is now positively evaluated by consultants who are working on it. Rather than being an infrastructure initiative run by engineers, the programme privileges the civil society aspect of water provision as well, and levels of community engagement are much improved. Critically, issues such as relationships between the communities and local government are being addressed, and the CDWUUs are being given training so that they continue to manage the service once the project is completed. There are already examples of 'knock-on' effects that have been generated as a result of positive experiences with the work of CDWUUs, with communities discussing the possibility of repairing other elements of village infrastructure and becoming involved in small business ventures. There have been suggestions that these Unions could federate so as to improve their ability to stand up to the local self-governance structure who are trying to claim ownership and control over these water projects.

Djamankulova (2004) writing with regards to water projects in Kyrgyzstan praises this particular initiative for its 'bottom-up' approach. However, she notes that often, key roles in project formulation are played by government agencies, international experts, the private sector and NGOs rather than community players themselves. The involvement of the local self-governing bodies, the *ayil okmotu*, is particularly sensitive. Their assistance is often needed to initiate mobilisation, since they are able to provide data on living conditions and existing infrastructure in target areas. The legacy of Soviet bureaucracy, however, means that these structures are not always happy with the autonomy given to CDWUUs and other similar bodies to charge for water supply and manage its provision.

Conflict Prevention

The examples of the Counterpart Consortium and Kyrgyz water project programmes above have infrastructure provision as their principle aim, with in the latter case some commitment to the strengthening of local people's organisations. Other donors involved in community development in the region also focus on the way in which competition for access to resources can spark violence, as mentioned above in the case of water, and state conflict prevention as a key motivating aim for work at community level.

One such initiative is the UNDP's Drinking Water Supply Project, set up to enhance 'social peace within the framework of preventive development in South Kyrgyzstan' (Djamankulova 2004: 5). UNDP has acknowledged the way in which water use can cause tensions between communities. For example, household waste and livestock from an upstream village can pollute drinking water sources for downstream villages. For UNDP, working on water systems means more than infrastructure provision, as it aims to find solutions to broader socio-economic problems such as a reliable drinking water supply and a decrease of tension connected with water that can be exacerbated by ethnic factors.

Concerns with ethnic and cross-border tensions associated with access to resources have also been taken up by Mercy Corps in the Ferghana Valley where it is implementing its Peaceful Communities Initiative (PCI), in conjunction with the Business Women's Association of Kokand. Mercy Corps staff conduct participatory rural appraisal for needs assessment in villages that they decide meet the criteria for the project. Projects (planned to take around three years) are then developed on communities' priorities, and again they often involve water. One particular characteristic of this programme is that it aims to undertake cross-border work by pairing up villages across borders in a single project. (In practice this is often quite hard to achieve and is not popular with the Uzbek authorities.) It also works in villages where the majority of the population is not of the titular ethnicity. Along with infrastructure improvement the projects should involve joint social events, festivals, drama and sports competitions, and young people are especially encouraged to become involved.

The Community Action Investment Programme (CAIP) that is also being rolled out on the Uzbek side of the Ferghana Valley by Mercy Corps (as well as in Tajikistan and Turkmenistan) and by CHF in southern Uzbekistan, also refers to the problem of social tension in its policy documents. As explained in a CAIP document produced in Uzbekistan,

> The goal of CAIP is to build social stability and alleviate sources of conflict in key areas of Uzbekistan through improved community access to infrastructure and economic opportunities. CHF and CI plan to assist communities to democratically elect a management structure that will lead community dialogue and collective action processes, resulting in multiple self- and CAIP-funded projects over a three-year period.
>
> This highly participatory process, when coupled with the community contribution requirement, generates a sense of pride and sustainable ownership of project outcomes. The links to and coordination with the activities of other key stakeholders, particularly local government and neighbouring communities will help to build a more open, democratic culture (CHF 2002a: 10)

However, compared to Mercy Corps' PCI, CHF appears to put less emphasis on operationalising conflict prevention in CAIP. CAIP is more orientated towards the installation of infrastructure and there is no provision within it for social initiatives, despite the social goals expressed in the quotation above. According to CHF's evaluation document (CHF 2002b) there is a heavy focus on training interventions at the start-up stage of individual projects, but this tends to be technical in nature. Training delivered is largely oriented towards organisational issues such as operational protocols, roles and responsibilities for the Community Initiative Councils (CICs), human resource and financial planning and project management skills. There is also some technical assistance training for procurement and project monitoring. In general, CAIP appears to be geared towards concrete and quickly visible quantifiable results, as can be seen from evaluation documents. The emphasis on successful implementation of infrastructure can be seen in the programme's working method: initially it provides very small amounts of money for village projects. If these are completed on time and according to guidelines, then larger grants are made.

It is not clear from the information on the project available how the training interventions and the projects implemented through CHF's CAIP will contribute to conflict prevention in the region. Overall, the potential for Community Initiative Councils (CICs) to be both project implementers and local civil society actors does not appear to be exploited, nor are local NGOs widely involved in CHF's CAIP programme. Whilst it is acknowledged in their semi-annual report that local NGOs could contribute to CAIP's objectives, their proposed input appears to be primarily linked to training interventions. Relations with the local authorities are also downplayed in the report. It is noted that 'local government leaders on occasion have also been asked to attend [training on community mobilisation] to develop understanding of and support for CAIP process and objectives' (CHF 2002b: 8). However, their input is not standardised throughout the programme. It would appear that for CHF's CAIP project, engagement with local government is viewed as a way of achieving sustainable cash flows for CICs. The report provides details of one particularly active CIC as a case study:

> Currently [Village Q] and CAIP are implementing a 1,600 metre medium-pressure gas project. [Village Q] has seen how this will positively effect [*sic*] their village so they have decided to provide another 1,280 metre of low-pressure gas pipe themselves. ... Now the community is investigating the possibility of using additional donors to provide heating boilers and radiators for the village school. They have been very active in contacting the government and are currently working out a contract with the government and trying to find additional donors along with convincing the community to invest (CHF 2002b: 16).

Mercy Corps, which is undertaking CAIP in the Ferghana Valley, has produced a paper on its involvement in the region, both through CAIP and the PCI discussed above. In this document there is more focus on the civil society element of infrastructure work, as noted in this passage:

> Based on assessments, contextual analysis and lessons learned in development practice, both CAIP and PCI staff have concluded that the programs can be assumed to be contributing toward conflict prevention if they meet the following four criteria, which are also measures of strengthening Civil Society:
> • Increased shared resources between and within communities and the skills to manage them sustainably.

- Increased positive contact and sustained relations between and within communities, both general and individual.
- Increased knowledge and understanding between and within communities.
- Communities develop, adopt and take ownership of new problem-solving skills (Mercy Corps 2003: 4).

Mercy Corps shows more of a focus on social interventions, although it acknowledges that, whilst these are stand-alone events in themselves in PCI, and serve to improve inter- and intra-community relations, in CAIP they are 'a mechanism to facilitate and strengthen the process of implementing infrastructure projects' (Mercy Corps 2003: 21). Despite use of the term 'civil society' in the report, there is very little in the discussion to suggest that in either project the groups established in communities have the capacity or are encouraged to act within the broader arena, beyond neighbouring villages, to take the interests and needs of their members to the local authorities. The type of relationship that is fostered is based on government 'rubber stamping' of projects.

> CAIP and PCI are designed to help facilitate greater linkages and communication between communities and the government authorities at the municipal and regional level. CAGs [Community Action Groups] must obtain the necessary approvals before projects are implemented and although PCI and CAIP staff know it would be quicker if they were to negotiate the approvals themselves, they believe it is essential to build these relationships between CAGs and the government authorities. Many communities claim that they received no visits from the municipal authorities before the programs started working in their communities, but now report that because of the PCI and CAIP infrastructure and social projects, there has been increased government communication and attention paid to their village or Mahalla (Mercy Corps 2003: 26).

Mercy Corps does acknowledge the importance of advocacy, however, and suggests that lack of engagement with local government may in the long term reduce the sustainability of their interventions. These issues will be discussed in more detail in the following chapter.

Community-Based Organisation Capacity Development

Whilst somewhat absent from CAIP and PCI, the emphasis on the need to build the capacity of local-level organisations is very clear in the position of the Mountain Societies Development Support Programme of the Aga Khan Foundation, working in Tajikistan. The main goal of the programme is 'to contribute to the laying of the foundations for self-sustaining social and economic development in the regions where it operates'. In order to achieve this, the programme works to establish Village Organisations (VOs) to plan and implement holistic development strategies for rural communities. The purpose of the programme is, crucially, to:

> strengthen the capabilities of Village Organisations to manage their own resources at the village and households levels, to increase their standard of living and to play an active role in developing civil society in Tajikistan (Abdulalishoev et al. 2004: 6).

It is clear from internal documents produced by the programme that it is driven by the commitment to strengthen the *capabilities* of these organisations. Its approach is one of long-term capacity building, and the Aga Khan Foundation is known for its extended stays in the countries in which it is involved: generally upwards of 15 years. Part of the programme of work with Village Organisations involves participatory evaluations of their organisational development, looking at the full range of their functions, including partnership, women's participation, attendance at meetings and financial management, and asking members (a minimum of 80 per cent of households must be members of the VO for it to be established) to evaluate its work. Whilst these participatory methods may sound the same as those employed by other international organisations working in the region, it would appear that the Aga Khan encourages analysis that is much more in-depth, and more challenging. Village residents are asked to think through issues of gender roles of both men and women, and to acknowledge differences in levels of poverty and inclusion within village societies.

Perhaps key to the Aga Khan Foundation approach is the idea that the Village Organisations are both a means to promote local development through a range of interventions surrounding agriculture, livestock, training, infrastructure and credit, as well as an end in themselves, in that these organisations provide a forum for increased dialogue and social cohesion amongst members. However, what is not clearly set out in policy documents is the relation between these organisations and local self-governing bodies (*mahalla* committees) or *Jamoat* authorities. Whilst the Tajik Government are clearly on board with the Aga Khan Foundation as an institution, and have acknowledged its key humanitarian interventions of the mid 1990s that were crucial to the survival of isolated populations in Gorno Badakshan, they are now also supportive of the Mountain Societies Programme. However, the presence of government officials at village meetings appears to be more symbolic of overall acceptance, rather than to promote engagement for joint development processes. The lack of a clear idea of how the Village Organisations will interact with local government does appear to have created some tension. Again this will be explored further in the next chapter.

UNDP, in its work across all seven *oblasts* of Kyrgyzstan, takes a different tack. Within the framework of its Social Governance Programme, it has rolled out its poverty alleviation component in 140 villages. The key focus is on setting up self-help groups, many of which have then gone on to co-operate with a World Bank funded micro-credit provider, the Kyrgyz Agricultural Finance Corporation, to provide loans to members. UNDP has also provided 'micro-grants' for infrastructure projects to improve village environments. Whilst there is still a focus on service provision within the project, there are also other clearly stated overriding programme aims that take wider issues of poverty and inequality into account.

> The social aspect [of UNDP's poverty reduction programme] comprises a wide range of social issues including poverty alleviation, social services and protection, as well as strengthening of and support to civil society as a channel for poor people's participation and advocacy for human rights (UNDP 2003: 2).

The authors would argue that this support for activities such as lobbying and advocacy is very important, as is creating strong links with local government. The priority of the link with government certainly sets UNDP's work aside from some of the other community development initiatives described in this chapter.[8]

In general, the poverty component's approach, rather than focusing on project implementation, is more geared towards the establishment and organisational development of village-based self-help groups. UNDP chooses not to define specifically the composition or activities of these groups. Using the language of empowerment and promoting poverty reduction through community mobilisation, the organisation privileges an approach that 'allows people to form groups they are comfortable with and to muster up support so that they can collectively raise themselves out of poverty' (UNDP 2002: 10). They note further that:

> Once mobilised, people can choose by themselves the directions in which they wish to move to address the causes of their deprivation. Experience has shown that poor communities do not need to be led, as opportunities emerge; they will produce their own leaders and set their own directions (UNDP 2002:10).

The approach of UNDP is for self-help groups to be federated within an umbrella Self Help Group Association (SHGA) which unites them at village level. It is these associations that help the individual groups to take up wider roles for themselves,

---

[8] As a recent World Bank report on community-driven development initiatives in Central Asia has noted, 'Consistent with its mandate, UNDP consistently collaborates with national and local governments as well as community based organizations' (Peabody et al. nd: 8).

by facilitating their registration as legal entities in different spheres: as credit unions, co-operatives and NGOs that work on rights protection, lobbying and social issues.

> Self-help group association is a civil society organization established by SHG members residing in the same village and non-members representing the community. In many cases the SHGA steering committee is selected through consensus or elections. The committee conducts meetings once in a month and whenever it is needed. The main functions of an SHGA are to monitor programme activities in the village and address community development needs. ... SHGAs collaborate with local government and other institutions to address community problems, needs and mobilization of resources. SHGAs are also actively involved in identification of the poor and mobilization of self-help groups, monitoring of credit use and repayments (UNDP 2001: 23–4).

UNDP's approach also shows much more of a mainstreamed gender focus. Whilst CHF's CAIP project, for example, stressed the percentages of women involved in its Community Initiative Councils, UNDP attempts to go beyond this somewhat Soviet-style quota system to address more analytically the problems surrounding the full involvement and participation of women and younger people in its programme.

Community Groups as Civil Society Actors

In the discussion of civil society in Chapter 2, the challenge posed by the 'alternative' approach (opening up new agendas for participation and democratisation) and the concept of 'public space' were given some prominence. The question here is how traditional community groups, such as those developing from the pre-Soviet or Soviet tradition or formed in the 'initiative group' model, can move from their initial grass-roots role to a wider and deeper engagement with society. The issue for international agencies is how to provide an enabling environment for such groups by both emphasising good relations with government, and putting in place umbrella bodies responsive to their demands and needs.

The authors would argue that, for local organisations to develop into fully fledged civil society organisations, it is important for them to begin to engage with other bodies outside their immediate target group or geographical area. This move onto a wider stage, in turn, will demand considerable development from CBOs in terms of their activities, structure, governance, membership and general understanding of their role. Within definitions of the concept of civil society, the idea of representation of interests is almost always present. A wholly inward-looking organisation, however, is unlikely to be representing the interests and priorities of its members' needs to others. As Roy (2002: 31) has argued with reference to traditional savings groups, these closed circles are purposefully *apolitical*. However, much contemporary community development rhetoric has its roots in a highly *politicised* debate around participation and empowerment. Despite this, in practice in Central Asia, donor approaches to community development often give more weight to infrastructure provision than the empowerment and wider participation of community group members.

Peabody et al. are highly critical of actors engaged in grass-roots level development that fail to engage with government:

Many CDD practitioners perceived government agencies to be irrelevant or obstacles to CDD and have largely bypassed them in CDD initiatives, fearing that government involvement would result in elite capture and the exclusion of vulnerable groups (Peabody et al. nd: 14).

The authors draw attention to the fact that 'inattention to governance and the enabling environment limits the impact of CDD efforts, stymies initiatives and threatens the sustainability of CDD impacts' (Peabody et al. nd: 14). As they note, not involving government bodies in these initiatives allows the authorities to divest themselves of responsibility for issues such as rural water supply, for example.

However, the stress that these World Bank authors place on relationships with government appears to come from a more instrumental concern for successfully implemented projects. Theirs has an echo of the efficiency argument for community-driven development, as mapped out by Dongier et al. in the World Bank's CDD sourcebook in which empowerment is seen as a bonus of well-designed projects:

CDD is an effective mechanism for poverty reduction, complementing market- and state-run activities by achieving immediate and last [*sic*] results at the grassroots level ... CDD has also been shown to increase the efficiency and effectiveness of poverty reduction efforts. Because it works at the local level, CDD has the potential to occur simultaneously in a very large number of communities, thus achieving far-reaching poverty impact. Finally, well-designed CDD programs are inclusive of poor and vulnerable groups, build positive social capital, and give them greater voice both in their community and with government entities (Dongier et al. 2002: 5).

Peabody et al. concede that 'CDD initiatives are also effective vehicles to simultaneously strengthen both local governments and civil society' (nd: 4), but they do not do much to develop their thinking on the civil society component of community development in their report.

Some of the international donor organisations working on grass-roots development do stress that they are encouraging community groups to engage in dialogue. This might suggest a role for community organisations as representatives of their members, but closer reading of reports and policy documents shows that this dialogue is often limited to the village or district level. Whilst in the interests of sustainability, some of these organisations are being taught how to find resources from international donors or from government, this appears to be understood as fundraising, rather than as lobbying and advocacy. Training for these groups does teach them to understand the needs of those with whom they share an environment, but these needs and interests are then most often presented to donors in order to receive resources, rather than used in negotiation with government, to press the authorities to uphold the rights of their members and to deliver on their commitments to the local population.[9]

Indeed, an analysis of the way in which the majority of INGOs work at the grass-roots level with community initiative groups, action groups or initiative councils suggests that strengthening these organisations as a component of local civil society is far from a priority. This is somewhat surprising, considering the emphasis American donors, in particular, have placed on the 'civil society for democracy promotion' agenda. Whilst civil society support centres are in place at *raion* and *oblast* level across the region, their grant-making facility and training initiatives, as expressed by one INGO employee in Tajikistan, are creating a core group of private development consultancies that are able to apply for grants and undertake projects. This type of body is quite different from a membership oriented community-based organisation, or an NGO working in the interests of poorer populations.

INTRAC is not alone in believing there to be a lost opportunity to connect the civil society agenda and the promotion of community development initiatives. Some analysts within the World Bank have questioned the nature of that institution's drive for grass-roots level work and have implied that there is a disjuncture between its rhetoric and practice. In their critical review of community-based and community driven development, Mansuri and Rao (2004) argue that the World Bank, by promoting the civil society agenda, and within it, an emphasis on participation, has adopted a politicised rhetoric. Drawing on the observations of Sarah White (1996), they note that:

---

[9] These issues were tackled in INTRAC's analytical skills training programme, run for NGO representatives in Kyrgyzstan, Kazakhstan and Uzbekistan during 2002–2004.

Power relations in the wider society within which participation occurs have to be taken into consideration. In some cases, the state may have to support broad-based redistributions of power for community projects to be really successful. This suggests that community-based and -driven development projects must be seen as part of a shift toward a broad-based participatory and decentralized system of governance (Mansuri and Rao 2004: 46).

They go on to note that it is not clear how this can be achieved, but that, 'Participation in the absence of state facilitation can result in a closed village economy, which limits the possibility for improved public action' (Mansuri and Rao 2004: 47). For these authors, community development cannot exist in a vacuum or in a closed apolitical space.

The questions must be: Are donors which implement community-driven and community-based development projects in Central Asia, including the World Bank, concerned to promote this improved public action? Is this even a goal? Peabody et al. (nd.: 22) state that CDD approaches include training for intermediaries and some community group members, and clarify the areas in which these are most often delivered. They put these into three categories: (i) ideological (forming a community group, promoting co-operation), (ii) functional (planning and prioritising) and (iii) technical (maintenance of project infrastructure). Reports on training delivered by CHF's CAIP project back up this statement. Public action appears to be absent from many community development capacity-building interventions.

Whilst White (1996) argues convincingly that for community-level projects to function they must acknowledge and often work to change wider power structures, Earle (2004a) has noted that aspects of the World Bank's CDD programme suggest an attempt to depoliticise the development process. Reducing the role of local and domestic NGOs to that of contractors, so that they do little more than provide certain services, may well prevent them from expressing the type of vocal dissent that they are often known for across the world. Cynical voices from within the World Bank have also suggested that far from being 'demand driven', CDD is 'supply driven demand driven development', implying that any aims to empower communities comes second to the overall goal of disbursing resources.

In their defence, all the main donors working in Central Asia stress the need to undertake participatory needs assessments and facilitate participatory community planning. But attempts to encourage wider democratic participation beyond the formation of initiative groups and project planning are not common. However, INTRAC's research into the type of participatory activity that does take place suggests that in some cases 'participation' may well amount to little more than perfunctorily performed exercises, and is perceived by local trainers and NGOs as a hoop that must be jumped through, or a box to be ticked on a blueprint plan for engaging with communities. In general, it could be argued that an approach to work with community groups that delivers training in standard packages that are geared almost exclusively towards the implementation of a planned project does not aim to build the capacity of these local organisations to be much more than project implementers. The Aga Khan Foundation's approach to community group capacity building is cutting edge for Central Asia in this regard. But overall, engagement in the public sphere and public action in the interests of community members is not a high priority for donors. Whilst community development projects clearly provide tangible benefits for many poorer and marginalised rural villages, we regard the lack of attention to the potential wider strategic role of community organisations as a missed opportunity.

Conclusion

In general, there is an identifiable trend, beginning around the end of the 1990s, for donor-sponsored development activities located at the grass roots. There are a number of factors that might explain this in Central Asia, and beyond, including donor concerns with the spread of radical Islam, local-level conflict exacerbated by limited access to resources, continuing high levels of poverty that have not much improved after more than a decade of so-called transition and the fact that many NGOs in the region have 'floated up' to the middle ground, and are out of touch with key target groups.

Donors' approaches are almost always couched in the language of participation, and involve the setting up of local-level organisations to prioritise and plan development interventions. However, closer inspection of the forms of participation and the type of training given to these new community groups shows marked differences between donors. At one end of the spectrum, donors appear to be concerned principally with infrastructure provision, and community groups are formed so as to install infrastructure and implement a project formulated with reference to an externally designed blueprint. At the other end of the spectrum are donors that concentrate on developing the capabilities and capacities of local-level organisations so that they become representative and sustainable institutions that are able to promote village development on their own terms.

It should be stressed, however, that the key to development and sustainability of community development initiatives is an acknowledgement of the wider environment in which local-level organisations are operating. For community-based organisations to emerge as civil society actors, there must be an effort to engage with other actors, particularly with the state authorities, in a way that promotes the interests, needs and priorities of the organisations' members. It would appear that the politicised component of community development interventions has been played down in donor approaches to grass-roots level work in Central Asia. Whilst many rural communities have benefited from better access to resources, improved infrastructure and often an introduction to participation through involvement in some village-level decision-making processes, without a move towards public action, these activities will, on the whole, remain localised and inward-looking. The next chapter develops these ideas by looking at the spaces for wider participation that are emerging in Central Asia.

CHAPTER 8

Civil Society and State Relations

Whilst the neo-liberal view of civil society, which has provided the basis for most international donor agencies' models, suggests that civil society groupings should be independent from the State, the authors would argue that in reality this view is too simplistic. Not only does the history of Central Asian states suggest that it could be inappropriate to insist on separation between civil society groups and the State, but also many of the most exciting developments and innovations are to be found in some of the collaborative work between civil society groups and State structures.

The first chapter of this book addressed the idea of the 'public sphere', privileged in some of the literature on civil society as a forum in which civil society organisations can carve out a space for themselves to bring about positive change and work towards goals of social justice. For example, Howell and Pearce (2001) argue that support for the public sphere is perhaps the most useful way to promote civil society. They argue that within this space, there is an opportunity for a strong public that interacts with government, and can work with it on a level footing for the common good. These authors see the potential of democratic, developmental states, in which the government plays a key role in promoting development, by responding to debates and new ideas brought out in the public sphere. On this point of the public sphere they comment,

> If donor civil society programs strengthen this they are useful and relevant. If they use money and power to promote one vision over any other, they are likely to be negative and counterproductive (Howell and Pearce 2001: 13).

Despite the potential of the public sphere, Chapter 7 noted that some local projects are so tightly focused that community-level projects have not been sufficiently equipped or encouraged by the donors to engage with other actors and operate within this space. Edwards comments that,

> Theories of the public sphere provide a powerful framework for interpreting the role played by civil society in social change, though their implications are often ignored by the neo-Tocquevillians or reduced by donor agencies to preserving the institutions of the independent media and building the communications capacities of NGOs (Edwards 2004: 58).

Edwards argues that this is often because of the conservative tendency to view associations in a neutral role of counterweight to the State. Furthermore, donor approaches often appear to reflect an idea that simply by existing associations will be fulfilling this function as a check on the State. This essentially gives them the role of maintaining power relations that already exist and denies them the potential to search for alternative forms of development and governance. This lack of attention to the public sphere is not always the case and this chapter provides examples of fruitful co-operation between the sectors as well as campaigning and advocacy initiatives. Even so, in general relations between non-governmental actors and the State in Central Asia are characterised by ambivalence.

This chapter draws on another set of short research papers written by local experts to inform INTRAC's Central Asia programme. This was a series of 'political and civil society' reports, created to ensure that INTRAC's capacity-building programme was both informed by processes and changes within the external environment, and wherever possible found opportunities to support civil society organisations in their efforts to improve legislation and relations with government. Legislation affecting NGOs and NGO–State relations were two recurring themes in the reports; a third related to freedom of information and the media.

NGOs, the Media and the State

On the one hand, at the highest level, the presidents of the Central Asian republics have voiced support for the work of NGOs and have created official bodies that recognise and ostensibly work with civil society organisations. For example, in Kazakhstan, the Government has set up a department within the Ministry of Information, Culture and Public Accord that oversees *oblast* and city-level councils that serve as information, education and support centres for public associations, including NGOs. In late 2003, a republic-wide Citizens' Forum was held to discuss the role of non-governmental actors. The Forum was addressed by the

President who acknowledged the important role played by civil society and international donors alike in supporting social and other issues in the difficult first decade after independence.

Similar public displays of support and recognition have been seen in Tajikistan, where a round-table discussion between the President, over a hundred domestic NGOs and a number of representatives of *Hokimats* was held in June 2002. According to the academic Karimov, this has had some impact on relations between NGOs and the Government, and has generated a greater degree of confidence in each other, on both sides.[1] When interviewed, Zokirov stated of this meeting that it demonstrated how representatives of the third sector are inclined to be sympathetic to the position of the State. His position is that the NGO sector can become a destructive force and threaten stability, if it is not supportive of the state's social programmes.[2]

In Kyrgyzstan, recognition by the state for the role that the non-governmental sector plays in the country has been in place since the mid 1990s, and was certainly a contributing factor to the accolade 'Central Asia's Island of Democracy' that Kyrgyzstan held for a while. However, the President's quip that the country 'produces NGOs like the Netherlands grow tulips' casts doubt on the seriousness with which he views these organisations, and by the early years of the new century the Government's commitment to democracy was being put seriously to the test. High levels of poverty remain a threat to democracy and State–civil society relations across the region. Furthermore, undemocratic practices continue and the decaying state apparatus is inefficient. In Kyrgyzstan the tragic killing of demonstrators in the southern *oblast* of Jalal-abad in early 2002 led to large-scale protests at the community level and the national mobilisation of civil society groups on issues such as press freedom and the right to demonstrate. The sacking of the Government by the President was one step in a series of only partially successful measures to placate the opposition; and in a complex situation some NGOs developed a clearly anti-government line. Later, NGOs united in a Civic Forum to campaign against the referendum proposals which took Kyrgyzstan towards a combined presidential-parliamentary system, and against corruption and dynasty-building in the regime.

Events external to Central Asia, as well as those within it, often have a significant impact upon NGO–State relations in the region. Thus, in Uzbekistan the Government has become increasingly wary of the work of NGOs following the role of civil society organisations alongside political groupings in the 'Rose

---

[1] Interview with S. Karimov, Dr Shamsiddin, Country Representative, Academy of Education Development (AED), Dushanbe, 7th November 2002, by Tajik mapping researchers.

[2] Interview with Zokirov, Dushanbe, 2001.

Revolution' in Georgia in 2003 and the 'Orange Revolution' in Ukraine in 2004. These events were widely cited as the real reason for the closure of the Soros Foundation office in Uzbekistan in 2004 during a re-registration process brought in by the Government for all foreign donors. The new regulations made it much more difficult for INGOs to transfer funds to local organisations. This move was also prompted by the country's role in the 'war on terror' and the reality of terrorist attacks inside the country. The political and civil society report comments on the atmosphere at the time:

> Most NGOs feel that they have no options and all this pressure will make them even less able and willing to be involved in political life. Among other intentions, the government wants to be pro-active in preventing civil society groups from becoming politicised and having a real voice in shaping social policy (Salimdjanova 2004: 3).

Religious groups and human rights organisations and other NGOs with a rights focus have come under particular pressure from the Government. Some NGOs have been accused of supporting the radical Islamic organisation Hizb-ut Tahrir. At one point, there were suggestions that all NGOs with photocopiers would have their copying monitored, to ensure that they were not being used to produce anti-Government, pro-Islamic propaganda.

Another tendency was noted by Salimdjanova (2004):

> The government is trying to create a lot more pro-government NGOs. Many have already been created with similar names and missions to other NGOs. These NGOs receive good coverage in the central press.

This process has also been noted in an INTRAC political and civil society report for Tajikistan, which referred to Committees for District Development in the northern Sogd province. These carry out programmes with funding and support from UNDP, the Japanese Government and Soros Foundation:

> The other NGO sub-type ... is a Committee on District Development (CDD). In this case the CDD is completely composed of the local authority leaders; sometimes leaders of 2–3 jamoats and district services may be included as well. At the same time they are registered in the Ministry of Justice as NGOs and they have their own seals, name and bank accounts, and use UNDP and other international grants for their activities. The goals and tasks of these committees completely mirror the goals and tasks of the corresponding local authority institutions (Davlatov 2004: 5).

The phenomenon of pro-government NGOs is not new in Central Asia. Alongside the Soviet-era organisations which have survived and re-established themselves, there are many newly created organisations – the large, well-funded foundations which support children, for example – in which the President's wife often plays a figurehead role. However, in the more strictly controlled environments of Uzbekistan and Turkmenistan, the governments have explicitly stated their aim to organise NGOs, if possible grouping them under the tutelage of a relevant ministry. In Uzbekistan, new regulations in 2004 required all women's NGOs to review their mission statements and re-register, leading Salimdjanova to comment: 'This further supports the thesis that the government has decided to organise the NGO movement and take as much as possible under their control' (Salimdjanova 2004: 3).

Some analyses of civil society include the media as one of its component parts. While this book has not addressed this area, it is clear that newspapers, television, radio and other media play a key supporting or restricting role for civil society. In all the countries of Central Asia there is a continued struggle to open up, maintain or push forward the boundaries of the free and independent media. NGOs are one of the main groupings that confront the state on this issue, giving voice to citizens' frustrations and articulating their demands.

The closure of newspapers and fining of individual reporters for slander of political figures and civil servants is, unfortunately, a feature of life in all countries of Central Asia. This has been well documented by international agencies such as the OSCE, Human Rights Watch, Freedom House and others. The radical or alternative local NGOs are often able to link directly to international civil society partners working on similar themes or issues. Thus Weinthal (2004) shows how environmental NGOs in Kazakhstan have short-circuited their own 'representative' government to make international alliances.

The cases of Uzbekistan and Kyrgyzstan highlight the 'hard' and 'soft' lines adopted by government towards NGOs and the media in the region, although abuses continue in all countries. In Uzbekistan, INTRAC's political and civil society reports note the absence of independent newspapers, the self-censorship practised by journalists, and the relative lack of success of international programmes, such as Internews and Eurasia Foundation, to make significant progress in the facilitation of a free press. By contrast, in Kyrgyzstan, the political and civil society report of February 2004 documents attempts to set up a self-regulating media council:

According to the *Russian Newspaper in Kyrgyzstan*, the proposed Media Council could become a buffer between the pro-government and independent mass media at a time when there are major tensions between them. The Media Council's goal would be to protect rights and freedoms of the Press and mass media in Kyrgyzstan, and to carry out initial investigations prior to court actions. ... Despite continuing division over whether the Media Council will help stem the flow of court cases involving the media, or will turn out to be one more punitive body serving the interests of the Government and attempting to control and circumscribe the development of the non-governmental sector and society as a whole, both sides gave public support to the Council (Bialeva 2004: 1).

Participants at a conference, 'Power and the Press in Kyrgyzstan', held in Bishkek in October 2003, warned that conflict between State power and the press is obvious, and tends to come to a peak with the approach of elections. Therefore, 'in the foreseeable future the likelihood of the above branches of power to draw closer to each other remains open to question' and mutual attacks could quickly discredit the self-regulating council.

Access to the media for NGOs in Central Asia is variable. Some independent NGO activities and events do get press coverage (in Turkmenistan this applies only to the Government-oriented NGOs). However, access is problematic for those working in controversial areas or promoting views considered oppositional by Government. Human rights is a sensitive area. The Kazakhstan political and civil society reports note that organisations such as the Kazakhstan Bureau for Human Rights and the Helsinki Committee are powerful in terms of political influence. The author, commenting on rights-focused groups, notes,

Although they are not numerous, their voices are distinct and heeded. They exert considerable influence on social and political processes which [echoes] the high pressure on the Kazakhstan government [exerted by] western states in the area of human rights (Sakhanov 2003: 3).

However, the public and information space won by such groups is inevitably hotly contested.

Collaboration between Civil Society Groups and the State at Local Levels

Whilst presidents and government officials may demonstrate support or ambivalence to, or suspicion of, the activities of the civil society sector, the question remains as to how, or indeed whether, these attitudes translate into practice at the different administrative levels of the State structure. INTRAC research would suggest that, in general, relations are easier at the local level, but again, a co-operative working environment will often depend upon the knowledge, understanding and personality of particular office holders, both those working in administrative bodies and staff members of civil society organisations. In some cases, lack of understanding of the work of NGOs or community groups means that their actions are met with fear and hostility by government officials or are not taken seriously.

Familiarity with the organisational form of old-style public associations or 'official NGOs' (more often known as GONGOs) can facilitate relationships with government bodies. A source from the Central Asia Regional Ecological Centre in Atyrau in the north-west of Kazakhstan, near the Caspian Sea, noted that 'officials tend to misunderstand the role of NGOs and are hesitant to consider the civil society sector as a real and permanent part of society'.[3] However, the local government structures will provide funds for the Women's Council and for occasional charitable activities and events such as the annual festival for disabled children. Other NGOs in the area have found it less easy to get funding. The Ecological Centre further notes that unregistered initiative groups were less likely to be taken seriously by officials in the region.

Despite these expressions of resistance and suspicion, instances of government collaboration with newer style organisations are increasingly to be found at local levels in all countries in the region. Even in Turkmenistan, NGOs and unregistered initiative groups can operate with some freedom at local level, even though at national level the State remains hostile:

> Most NGOs we met during our visit informed us that in many cases the government either refrains from interfering in NGO activities or simply ignores them, especially at the local level ... . Many NGOs think that the government is gradually becoming more neutral – it is not helping, but it is not creating as many obstacles as before (Buxton and Musabaeva 2002: 18).

A more actively facilitative attitude towards the work of civil society organisations is found elsewhere in the region, generally where the local authorities have been impressed by initiatives and activities. In the past, public associations would have received support from local state structures, in the form of office space or other assistance in kind. Newer NGOs can get this sort of assistance where their work is seen to be useful. Since the collapse of many State-provided services such as kindergartens, youth facilities, culture houses and other entities, there are large numbers of empty buildings which local authorities can offer to these newer organisations. As a result in Tajikistan, many Village Development groups have been housed in former Komsomol buildings. In Bukhara *oblast*, Uzbekistan, various service-provision NGOs have been given office space by the local *Hokimat*. In the Nookat region of Kyrgyzstan, an enterprising NGO called Chernobyl has been provided with land where it has built an office, and been given a larger piece of land nearby on the understanding that the NGO will transform this into a park for the

---

[3] Personal conversation with Izembergenovea, 2000.

town. Mostly these arrangements seem to be rent-free or at minimum cost.

This type of local-level collaboration has been encouraged further by the recent donor trend towards funding community activities. Local government offices at *raion, oblast* and village level now realise that the activities of initiative groups and others can bring in international donor money for infrastructure projects, relieving the pressure on their budgets and bringing kudos to the local authorities.[4] Indeed, in an INTRAC interview, one *ayil okmotu* in Osh *oblast* admitted that he saw this as the main function of such initiative groups. However, the arrangements do not stop there: some donors' funding procedures require that there is support provided, at least in kind, from the local authority. For instance, in 2002–2003 the Soros Foundation in Uzbekistan invited applications for project funding from NGOs working together with local levels of government. The initiative of Counterpart Consortium to bring the *mahalla* into grass-roots development processes is discussed below.

Much of this local-level work is connected with repair and reconstruction of village infrastructure, since roads, water supplies, communal buildings and other facilities have all suffered from lack of maintenance since the collapse of the Soviet Union. As a result, there are many examples of village-level groups, initiative groups or established NGOs applying for funding to repair such structures. The more advanced NGOs, which have set themselves up as support and resource centres, are in a position to help newer groups make applications for funds. Most local levels of government see the advantages in supporting such groups in their applications. The NGO Chernobyl in Nookat has developed a standardised 'contract' form which local groups can use to draw up their agreements with the local *akimat*, and the local *akimat* itself has created a position for a full-time official to be responsible for developing such agreements with local groups.

Social Partnership

Beyond tolerance or fairly passive encouragement, there are other ways in which the state engages with civil society actors in Central Asia. There is much talk in the region of 'social partnership' and the term is increasingly being used by NGOs. The Copenhagen Centre defines social partnership as:

---

[4] For example, in the southern *oblast* of Batken in Kyrgyzstan, the international donor income received in 2002 by the NGO Foundation for Tolerance International was said to exceed the provincial government budget. Their work involves a range of activities including infrastructure repair, community development, education and conflict prevention.

People and organisations from some combination of public, business and civil constituencies who engage in voluntary, mutually beneficial, innovative relationships *to address common societal aims through combining their resources and competencies'* (emphasis added) (Nelson and Zadek 2000).

Counterpart Consortium, in the training module it runs on social partnerships throughout the former Soviet Union, employs the following definition:

Social Partnership is a collaboration among NGOs, the private sector and government to solve community problems in a sustainable way (Counterpart Consortium Training Materials).

The focus of both definitions is on finding solutions for communities through the joint work and effort of organisations from different sectors. However, the emphasis of interpretation of the term 'social partnership' in Central Asia and other parts of the former Soviet Union is rather different from Western understandings. The drive for social partnerships in the West is, in the face of the declining welfare state, centred on the need to find new approaches to old problems. The idea is that new energies can be unleashed through joint collaboration and that 'joined-up' thinking (between different government departments, agencies and the voluntary sector) can help define appropriate policies to meet the needs of those sectors of the population regarded as 'socially excluded'. Such joined-up approaches are variously defined, in the literature in the West, as 'interagency', 'interprofessional', 'whole systems' and 'holistic approaches'.

In the countries of the former Soviet Union (and Central and Eastern Europe), interpretations of the term 'social partnership' focus more strongly on the development of collaborative service delivery mechanisms between the newly independent public, private and civil society sectors (in the context of a collapsed welfare state). Even NGOs that have well-defined and agreed visions and missions tend not to have a strong local constituency, and struggle to think about how they would finance their work if international donors were to leave. Their tendency is to see social partnership as an opportunity to receive funds from the State. Local authorities, in their turn, have responsibilities, some of which are relatively new, and inadequate funds to meet these responsibilities. Whilst some local authorities in Central Asia are still very wary of NGOs and CBOs, as noted above, there is also an increasing number interested in commissioning NGOs to provide services.

Between April and July 2002 a series of round-table discussions on social partnership was held in 12 regions of Uzbekistan and the Republic of Karakalpakstan. These discussions were attended by representatives from the city and regional *khokimiats*, the departments of the Ministry of Justice and taxation, *mahalla* committees, the private sector and NGOs (including INTRAC and the International

Centre for Non-Profit Law). Experiences to date of collaborative working and social partnership were discussed, as were legislative problems.

The documentation of these discussions shows that there are many examples of joint working between NGOs and State structures, but that these tend to be based on informal agreements. Successful co-operation was noted particularly in the Ferghana Valley, where NGOs are strongest and have a good image and where relationships often depend on strong personal networks. There were also good examples of co-operation between NGOs and the state in Samarkand Region. In Termez region (Surkhandarya *oblast*), NGOs generally had to obtain a letter of agreement from the *Khokimat* as a basis for their co-operation. Elsewhere, in cases where the State took the initiative to work in partnership, this co-operation tended to be with State-established organisations rather than with NGOs. Examples of partnership with business were also found – often a form of arm-twisting by local government to force major local enterprises to fulfil their social responsibilities.

Experience in Kazakhstan provides a contrasting illustration of how social partnership is being developed in a country that has taken market reform further. Recent work to draft a new law in Kazakhstan on contracting out public services[5] sets out the future framework for NGO–State relations and demonstrates that the Government recognises that NGOs play an important role in 'solving social problems' in Kazakhstan.[6] The new law will introduce a set of procedures which will facilitate open and transparent mechanisms of State support to the NGO sector. This will involve asking NGOs to tender for work alongside private sector organisations, and will also establish criteria according to which NGOs will be able to participate in the tendering process. There is increased talk of the need to develop social partnerships to tackle social issues.

The point here is that the Government is openly recognising the contribution being made by NGOs in areas of social development, and would like to encourage the establishment of more NGOs, especially in rural areas. CASDIN[7] (an INTRAC partner in Kazakhstan) has undertaken research on examples of contracts piloted in the northern part of the country; these ranged from business information and

---

[5] The local term for state contracting is 'state social order' or *sotsialny zakaz*.

[6] See for example the Programme of State Support to NGOs for 2003–2005. The documentation around the introduction of the draft papers, 'On the conception of state support of NGOs in the Republic of Kazakhstan' from January 2002, talks of the rapid increase in NGOs, their support from international organisations, their experience and expertise in working in 'problems of the social sphere', the need to encourage the establishment of NGOs in rural areas and the need to establish principles of social partnership.

[7] CASDIN – Central Asia Sustainable Development Information Network, based in Almaty.

advice services, to a city rubbish collection service and delivery of coal to older people in rural districts. It also cited cases where the Government has expressed an interest in partnering with NGOs, recognising that these actors may have better expert knowledge and newer ways of working. Examples include improved techniques for rehabilitating drug abusers and better technology for working with disabled people. Interestingly, the Government's documentation also expresses the need for training of State officials on developments within the NGO sector. It mentions seminars for officials at different levels of State administration, exchange of experiences and participation of workers from international agencies.

The funding for work done under the new national *sotsial'nyi zakaz* agreement will come from both central and local budgets. The first grants were received at the time of the Civic Forum in Autumn 2003. Many NGO leaders expressed concern that the legislation would result in the rapid creation of new organisations, established in order to tender for work. The challenge will be to ensure transparency in the awarding of contracts and the provision of support so that NGOs are able to deliver on government requirements and undertake socially useful work. Currently NGO law in Central Asia does not allow government grant-making to NGOs, and this no doubt helps to explain why so many NGOs are ready to enter the contracting arrangement.

In summary, whilst there are examples of joint working between the State authorities and local-level civil society organisations, this support seems to represent what is essentially a technocratic approach to the development of relationships between the sectors. The 'social partnership' debate is increasingly focused on issues around contracting. This emphasis does not recognise the wider strategic contribution that can be made by NGOs and anecdotal evidence suggests that those working on 'safe' issues, generally involving service delivery, are more likely to find support than those that could potentially challenge authorities or local traditional structures, such as human rights groups, for example. However, the vast majority of NGOs and other civil society organisations regard these developments as hugely important, anticipating that the ability to tender for State contracts will provide secure sources of funding for the future, plus improved public legitimacy.

Spaces for Participation

The first chapter of this volume referred to the work of Gaventa (2003) and discussed his identification of three types of 'spaces' – closed, invited and created – within or around which citizens and their organisations relate to the State. The following sections of this chapter will use this framework to examine some of the experiences of civil society–State relations in Central Asia.

We would argue that the examples of service contracting above represent a type of collaboration that relates most closely to the 'closed' space. The possibility of negotiation of common aims and agendas is curtailed by the nature of the relationship, in which local authorities decide what needs to be done, and NGOs and other organisations tender for the opportunity to carry out the work. In this type of situation, it would appear there is little opening for civil society organisations to gain any immediate leverage over State bodies. But as Gaventa goes on to note, spaces for participation are fluid and are constantly 'opening and closing through struggles for legitimacy and resistance, co-optation and transformation'. Cornwall (2002), discussing a similar typology, notes that spaces can be used tactically and strategically or even undermined by actors, in order to open up opportunities for different types of deliberation. In theory, Central Asian civil society organisations could, through contracting, raise their profiles and development relationships and skills that they can then use to have greater strategic influence on the type of work they undertake.

Moving on to the idea of 'invited' space, there are different examples of this type of relationship between civil society and the State. The most visible of these are the civil society consultation processes of the World Bank's CDF (Comprehensive Development Framework) and PRSPs (Poverty Reduction Strategy Papers) that have been carried out in Kyrgyzstan and Tajikistan. These new aid paradigms, which channel funds through the recipient country's budget, promote decentralisation strategies and require civil society groups to be involved in relevant discussion and consultation forums, are driving a different type of collaboration between the NGO/CBO sectors and different levels of government. PRSPs are a component part of the CDF, and in Kyrgyzstan a National Poverty Reduction Strategy (NPRS) has been drawn up.

Kyrgyz civil society organisations were initially somewhat wary of giving implicit consent, through their participation in the drawing up of the NPRS, to a process that they believed would further increase the country's debt burden. However, according to Salmorbekova (2004), representatives of Kyrgyz civil society took an active part in the development of mechanisms for the implementation of the strategy, and the consultations that were carried out have come to be valued by members of the civil society sector. In an INTRAC interview, a representative of Counterpart Consortium in Kyrgyzstan stated that participation had been of very high quality, and that the CDF documents were much influenced by debate. However, civil society stakeholders have not been involved in any coherent or co-ordinated way in the implementation of the resultant poverty reduction strategies, and, according to the Counterpart Consortium interviewee, there is a real need to put pressure on policy makers to put these strategies into practice. Currently, the CDF secretariat is establishing a structure for the monitoring of the process.

It would seem that, while the initial design process is considered to have been a success, doubts have been raised as to the way in which the poverty reduction strategy will be implemented. Salmorbekova notes that,

> there is no evidence of active cooperation, partnership and participation in the implementation of NPRS and CDF, which is a weakness in the implementation of the strategy. Roundtable participants on monitoring and evaluation of NPRS expressed their dissatisfaction with the coordination between the civil society and the government in the implementation of the NPRS; there is insufficient information on the implementation of the strategy, no transparency of financial resources, which makes it difficult to carry out monitoring of the implementation of the strategy (Salmorbekova 2004: 10).

She goes on to argue that the Government lacks knowledge of how to approach cooperation with civil society and sees widespread and continued adherence by public officials to the Soviet method of working. She believes that the real catalyst for dialogue in the development of the NPRS came from international organisations. This dialogue is not evolving, and she states that 'the majority of the population still views itself as lacking the right to express its opinion and promote its interests. The population is used to being subordinate to the authorities' (Salmorbekova 2004: 10).

Giffen and Buxton (2004) note that a similar process will be carried out by the Uzbekistan Government with the assistance of the World Bank and Asian Development Bank in order to 'improve people's "living standards"'[8] although it is not clear how much civil society this will involve. They do query, however, the potential for local-level groups across the region to participate and contribute in these types of fora, even if national NGOs and civil society groups are involved in discussion of strategies. In particular, there are few established channels of communication from the community level to the 'centre', and civil society organisations at national level are not generally representative of a wider constituency.

This type of consultation process is perhaps the epitome of the idea of an 'invited' space in that collaboration of civil society organisations is actively sought by the State. However, the emphasis here is on consultation, and dialogue is kept framed within a certain agenda that has already been decided upon by the Government and the World Bank. These processes fit Cornwall's description of 'bounded spaces':

> Only certain members of the public are able to participate within them. Their purposes, mandate and remit tend to be circumscribed by the agendas of

---

[8] The existence of 'poverty' is not officially acknowledged in Uzbekistan.

implementing agencies, and are rarely, if ever, open to negotiation by citizens who are invited to take part in them. The role of such institutions and initiatives in securing legitimacy for intended policy directions rests on forms of discursive closure that bound what can be discussed and frame the versions that emerge (Cornwall 2002: 18).

This guiding of agendas by external agents can be seen elsewhere in Central Asian development initiatives. For example, in late 2004 Counterpart Consortium launched phase 2 of its Civic Advocacy Support Programme in Uzbekistan, which will provide training on lobbying and campaigning activities and strategies for NGOs. However, the range of advocacy topics for which training is available has been decided in advance by Counterpart, reflecting how the organisation believes Uzbek civil society should operate. This is an example *par excellence* of normative civil society strengthening programmes, where training on advocacy is itself limiting the space within which civil society may be able to act in the future.

Other examples of externally encouraged collaboration between the sectors can also be seen to fit within the 'invited' space classification of participation. Cornwall (2002: 24) explains these spaces as ones where 'people (as users, as citizens, as beneficiaries) are invited to participate by various kinds of authorities, be they government, supranational agencies or non-governmental organisations' in an effort to widen participation. For example, the Mahalla Initiative Programme, also promoted by the international NGO Counterpart Consortium, attempts to involve local authorities in community development initiatives. Here the donor invites joint applications for project funds from different stakeholders. As such, in theory, this should promote some negotiation of common aims between the local authorities, community groups and NGOs. It should be remembered that participation and discussion will most likely be limited to the immediate practical aims of project implementation.

Cornwall (2002) has noted that collaboration in invited spaces can blur the distinction between State and citizen. In Central Asia, there are some very interesting examples of initiatives where the difference between the State body and the civil society organisation becomes hard to distinguish. In these cases, it is not clear who is inviting who to participate. This relationship is further complicated by the fact that local self-governing bodies, particularly the *mahalla* committee in Uzbekistan, are often considered to be part of civil society. Two examples are given below as case studies.

Case Study – *Mahalla* as Community or Government Organisation?

Whilst the *mahalla* committee in Uzbekistan is labelled as a self-governing body, as noted previously, it is responsible for the distribution of the State's targeted social benefits. There is also continued government control over appointments to key positions within the committee and the chairman receives a State salary. Concerns have been raised about the way in which the *mahalla* committee is being drawn increasingly into the State apparatus (Kandiyoti 2002). Nevertheless, the institution has its roots in community mutual assistance and neighbourhood co-operation. It is therefore difficult to gauge whether civil society organisations that work with the *mahalla* committee are exerting leverage over State authorities.

INTRAC research into one initiative sponsored by Mercy Corps in a city in the Ferghana Valley produced some interesting findings on the nature of relations between community organisations and the *mahalla*. As part of the CAIP initiative, Mercy Corps had established a Community Action Group to oversee a project designed to undertake a number of improvements to infrastructure in *mahalla* U. The first of these had involved repairs to the roads, after which attention was turned to repairing the roof of the secondary school and making improvements to the sanitation system. It was not the first time that residents of the *mahalla* had been involved in activities geared towards installation and repair of infrastructure. Since the early 1990s they had also built a mosque, improved the kindergarten and linked up the *mahalla* to the gas supply. These activities had been funded by the population itself, along with contributions from the *mahalla* committee and other sponsors (often local business people). This type of collaboration was therefore not new to either the population of the *mahalla* or to the representatives of the *mahalla* committee.

Fozilhujaev (2003) notes that the *mahalla* committee located in *mahalla* U benefited both from a committed and hard-working chairman, and from a core group of 'activists' who were elected by the community and served both as advisors to and a check on the chairman. Out of the nine activists, six had also been elected to the Community Action Group, but rather than function separately to the *mahalla* committee, the researcher found that the finances for the projects were being managed in the traditional way, and that the activities connected with the implementation of the project were being carried out by the *mahalla* committee chairman, in collaboration with his advisers and assistants. An INGO staff member explained that they had tried to create something new for the *mahalla* as a community, but that the residents and activists continued to act in a way that was familiar to them.

The virtual takeover of the project by the *mahalla* committee could be regarded as worrying if it were thought that the project had been co-opted by a government body. However, the opinions of residents seemed to be that it was the chairman's job to undertake this type of activity, that he was conscientious, responsive to his constituents and, importantly, as a resident had loyalty to the *mahalla*. Here the researcher asserts that considering the experience and expertise of the *mahalla* committee, there was no need to establish a separate community group to oversee the project. Without further research, it is not possible to ascertain the extent to which the residents of the *mahalla*, particularly women, were able to express their opinions on the project, either through the women's subcommittee or the central functions of the committee. However, this case is an interesting example of the blurring of barriers between civil society and State. Stevens also expresses support for the potential synergy of the *mahalla* committee and civil society, noting that 'too narrow a focus on creating "pure" civil society organisations that work in isolation from the state and lamenting the co-option of the *mahalla* is to miss out on the potential for synergy' (Stevens 2003: 4).

In a twist on the idea of invited spaces, research by the Mountain Societies Development Support Programme (MSDSP) of the Aga Khan Foundation[9] documents cases of *mahalla* committees in its programme areas of Tajikistan that voluntarily disbanded or merged with MSDSP's Village Organisations (VOs), ostensibly in order to prevent duplication of local development tasks. The conclusions and recommendations made by the researcher attest that the merger is not desirable for the goals of the MSDSP. However, the rich qualitative data provided in the rest of the paper suggest a much more nuanced situation in which many positive results have arisen out of this merger.

Case Study – Village Organisations and *Mahalla* Committees, Tajikistan

Abdulalishoev et al.'s (2004) research suggests that the *Jamoat* (the local authority at *raion* level), has been pushing for the merger of the Village Organisations with the *mahalla* committees so as to bring the well-funded VOs under local government control and to mask the *Jamoat's* own inability to provide services and respond to needs. There is clearly a danger of co-optation if government bodies take over a project, and this is a concern for Aga Khan who are very keen to promote democratic decision-making and transparency, but research in a number of villages provides evidence of positive aspects of this merger.

---

[9] Research was undertaken by a staff member as a requirement for completion of INTRAC's Analytical Skills Training Programme.

The researchers point out that the *mahalla* committees have never been particularly influential in the parts of Tajikistan where the MSDSP is working, and that in a number of villages residents were unaware of the existence of the *mahalla* committee, or felt it was not an important player. It was also noted that where mergers occurred, this was often at the request of the villagers themselves. The researchers warn that at times the *Jamoat* can have undue influence over the appointment or election of VO leaders, but this is not necessarily always the case, as other examples are given of villagers resisting these appointments, or removing leaders at a later stage. The extent to which VOs are expected to promote and deliver government policy in the absence of the *mahalla* committee is not consistent. In some cases, this is undertaken by school directors or other people of standing in the village.

The research documents positive influences of the structure and working practices on merged leadership. One VO leader, who still considers himself a *mahalla* committee chairman, was quoted as saying 'I continue my work but now with more responsibilities and in a structured and documented way'. This assertion is backed up by respondents in other villages who refer to improved working practices, including minute taking at meetings, improved accountability and greater financial transparency, where the two organisations had been merged. The same leader quoted above went further, stating:

> Before people considered me a representative of Jamoat in the village and now they know me as a representative of their community in the government, ... and even outside of their community representing the community interests (Abdulalishoev et al. 2004: 12).

This last comment is suggestive of a highly positive, if unforeseen, outcome of the work of the MSDSP. In many of the cases documented, the merger of organisations seems to have brought villagers, their participation and their influence into the structures of governance. This has opened up opportunities for the VOs to act within the public sphere, even though, as discussed in the preceding chapter, this was not a stated aim of the Programme. The question remains as to whether, with a merger, the VOs can ensure that their valued ways of working – including space for women's full participation, transparency, accountability and greater focus on female-headed and other vulnerable households – can be maintained. If these aspects can be sustained into the future, beyond an initial merger of the two types of organisation, then this approach should surely be sanctioned and developed by the MSDSP, rather than so resoundingly criticised by the researchers.

Achieving government recognition of the worth of civil society actors, and an acknowledgement of the views and interests that they represent, is one way for these actors to begin carving out spaces for more in-depth participation and engagement. It is quite possible that the VOs that are closely integrated with the local authorities are able to create a more influential space for themselves at higher levels of government.

Another example of this type of gradual progression towards increased levels of space for participation can be seen in the case of the NGO Umut, operating in the town of Balykchi, at the western end of Lake Issyk-Kul in Kyrgyzstan. This town was built up as a transport hub and around the fishing and fish canning industry, most of which has now collapsed. Balykchi now suffers from high rates of unemployment and the decline of its infrastructure and services. The NGO Umut (Hope) was established in the early 1990s, initially formed around a project to clean up the town. It worked with *kvartal* (block) committees, mobilised volunteers and achieved noticeable results. Fired by the success of this activity, the NGO proceeded to identify new areas of work.

Case Study – NGO Umut

Staff of the organisation describe their relationship with the local authorities as a 'journey'. At first, when approached with lists of problems and proposals to solve them, the town's government officials declared that there was nothing they could do to help. Having decided to focus on problems faced by older people, whose needs were not being addressed by any other bodies, they began an awareness-raising venture amongst the population and government structures. Early impact was achieved by presenting their findings at a town meeting through a 'social video'. This also helped to ensure participation in other more general research looking into priority issues for the town.

Building on its research, Umut set up a centre for pensioners, where they could come for advice, particularly relating to benefits and the payment of utility bills. This model then developed into two strands, both of which are now quite large-scale. The first of these strands of work focuses on establishing self-help groups for pensioners, revolving around small micro-credit schemes and income generation activities. They are also provided with a centre where they can meet to receive medical attention and meals. The other strand involves a network of advice centres (funded by the Eurasia and Soros Foundations) that have been set up across the city. Each of these advice centres works closely with the police department, the local *aksakal* (elder), and the local authority. They are staffed by lawyers and legally trained volunteers who provide advice on housing, utilities and documentation, often for pensioners. Other problems that are often presented at the centre involve child truancy and unemployment. The centres' staff try to find solutions to problems but can also make demands of higher authorities and have in the past taken

---

issues to the national parliamentary deputies.

In each area where there is an advice centre 'small social committees' have been set up. These committees are made up of representatives from the advice centre staff, the local *kvartal* committees, elders, police and other residents. They meet to discuss the types of problem brought to the advice centres and additional ways of providing assistance. A 'large social committee' has also been established by the NGO where representatives from the small committees meet, and which is also attended by NGO and local authority leadership. There are ambitious discussions and plans about extending the support network. Umut is now involved in even more long-term planning projects with the town's authorities.

The *Akim* (mayor) of Balykchi is a supporter of Umut, and he and the NGO's leader often speak to plan further projects. The *Akim*, who was interviewed as part of this research, stated that it was not a secret that the State structures cannot solve all of the city's problems alone. He had been impressed by the activities of Umut but admitted that in the late 1990s the local authority had been 'afraid' of NGOs, in that they expected to receive criticism from them. In their turn, the authorities had been critical of NGOs that 'made a lot of noise, but did not do much'.

Clearly, Umut is concerned to maintain a positive working relationship with the local authority. The NGO's leader was alert to the potential difficulties that could ensue from collaboration, particularly around sensitive issues of the public's perception of NGOs as 'more advanced' than local government, in terms of ability to develop project plans and access outside funding. However, she emphasised the importance of involving the local authority, which has the responsibility for provision of basic services to the population, but does not have the funds to do it. The local authority had been crucial in developing the new structures and providing premises where possible. Encouragingly, many of the newer officials in the authority had shown themselves to be open to working with the NGO sector, rather than seeing it as an opposition group. The exciting thing about Umut's work is the organisation's vision of a locally developed approach to resolving some of the problems faced by the town's population. It is an entirely home-grown model developed together with the local authority.

Both Gaventa (2003) and Cornwall (2002) stress that spaces for participation are fluid, and can change. In the examples of the *mahalla* committees engaging with non-state actors in both Tajikistan and Uzbekistan, there appears to be potential for a creation of more profound spaces for the input of organisations' members. Cornwall identifies other types of space that, rather than blur the distinction between citizen and State, 'come to depend upon and qualify' this distinction.

Rather than arenas for participation *with/in* the state, these are spaces in which citizens act *without* (both outside and in the absence of) and *on* it. These are spaces which are more often chosen than offered. They can be 'sites of radical possibility' (Cornwall 2002: 20–21, emphasis in the original).

These spaces can be carved out by the work of activists, or social movements, and provide the opportunity for popular protest and resistance and can be a way of achieving leverage (Cornwall 2002: 22).

In some cases, advocacy and monitoring forums that involve joint working by NGO sectors have been sponsored by external donors. The Soros Foundation in Kazakhstan has helped to establish a high-profile network of NGOs to monitor the oil industry. The environmental lobby in Kazakhstan is well established and is able to take on high-level campaigning very effectively. For example, in 2003 a campaign launched to ban the import and burial of nuclear wastes was successful and the Government withdrew its plans.

There are also cases of collaborative working within the non-governmental sector in Central Asia that can be seen as a step towards the types of action described by Cornwall above. These are particularly noteworthy as they are examples of 'indigenous' organising, undertaken by NGOs working as a sector, autonomously, and beyond the donor agenda. In an earlier section we referred to the Civic Forum in Kazakhstan, which was addressed by the President. This event was also the culmination of a campaign by the newly created NGO 'platform' that brought together a very diverse group of organisations to lobby against proposed NGO legislation. During the Forum the President yielded to pressure and withdrew the draft law. However, the debate continues within the sector as to whether NGO–state relations and, in particular social contracting arrangements, are truly satisfactory.

In Kyrgyzstan, advances by NGOs campaigning around the deaths of protesters in Jalal-Abad in 2002 led to further joint lobbying on proposals to change the Constitution, in early 2003. Many civil society groups played an active role in the commission that reviewed possible changes, but were then disappointed by a referendum that was called at short notice and put forward less radical proposals. By contrast, Salmorbekova (2004) notes successful examples of civil society participation in the development and lobbying of draft laws in the Kyrgyz Parliament. In 2003 two laws were adopted following pressure from women's NGOs including the collection of 30,000 signatures: the law 'on social and legal protection from domestic violence' and the law 'on gender equality'. Salmorbekova states that this is the first time in the history of Kyrgyzstan that NGOs have exercised their constitutional rights in this way, through a people's initiative. It also led to one of the first examples of social contracting in Kyrgyzstan: the commissioning of NGOs to set up a network of women's crisis centres in provincial areas.

In Tajikistan, Sharq (2004) note that the UNDP's 'Women in Development' programme that began in 1995 has fostered a type of women's NGO movement in the country that has also had strong support from the state. Since then, the Government has clarified and implemented a gender policy. However, this same review suggests that there is a lack of strategic co-operation and political co-ordination amongst civil society organisations in the country. Their donor dependency is also cited as a barrier to better co-operation.

Conclusion

Working with the idea of different types of spaces for participation of citizens and their organisations within state structures, this chapter has identified the different ways in which civil society organisations in Central Asia engage with the state. At one level, the autocratic and even repressive nature of the political climate would appear to make this type of participation very difficult. It would seem fair to assert that much Government decision-making is done behind closed doors in a closed space, to which ordinary citizens and civil society are not privy. However, there are also examples of Governments opening up for consultation with civil society through PRSP processes, and other discussions on livelihoods and well-being, although this has often been in response to pressure from the international financial institutions and Western governments.

These types of process have been categorised by Gaventa (2003) as 'invited' spaces, in which the boundaries for discussion are set in advance by controlling institutions. Here, to refer back to the discussions of Chapter 1, there is little opportunity for civil society groupings to make decisions about the type of dialogue they would like to have, and the way in which they would like to see development unfold. In some cases, donor-encouraged forms of participation are based upon limited forms of consultation or brief technical collaboration. There are also financial incentives for local government to work with NGOs and CBOs in order to access external funds, along with a perhaps contradictory drive on the part of these organisations to diversify their own funding away from international donors.

Nevertheless, civil society organisations can gain much from their involvement in these types of invited spaces. This can include recognition from government and other bodies and better networking with other similar organisations. It is also a chance to develop skills and influence that can be used to deepen participation on future occasions.

The nature of local-level authorities in Central Asia, particularly in Tajikistan and Uzbekistan, also creates interesting opportunities for community groups and NGOs to engage in potentially fruitful participation. This is because in some cases, traditional (although perhaps partially co-opted) institutions such as the *mahalla*, are considered to be both part of the State, and part of civil society. The cases referred to in this chapter show a blurring of the boundaries between the sectors, positive examples of improved working at local level, and the chance for citizens to extend debate and prioritisation of their needs into the governance structures.

Finally, increasingly, in countries with more developed non-governmental sectors, organisations are moving beyond competition to find locally acceptable and useful ways of working together on pressing issues. NGO platforms and campaigning activities are a step towards dynamic and influential forms of participation, through which government is forced to listen to and consider alternative viewpoints, and is pressurised to be more accountable to its citizens.

Conclusion

Chapter 1 of this volume raised the question of how external actors can build or develop the capacity of civil society without distorting its character or dynamics. The opening chapter also flagged up the problem of using the concept of civil society in twenty-first-century Central Asia, when it originated in the Enlightenment period in Europe and was then developed by academics and policy makers in Europe and America. In creating and funding such programmes, the challenge is for Northern or Western agencies to avoid too narrow a definition of the term 'civil society', and prevent favouritism in the choice of local partners or recipients of resources. Throughout this book, the contrast has been made between neo-liberal approaches to civil society promotion, that have a tendency to view civil society organisations as an instrument, or means to an end (for example creating a pluralistic society, rolling out infrastructure programmes), and more alternative approaches which try to build upon the situation on the ground and use people's involvement in civil society as a way to promote goals of social justice, empowerment and voice.

This publication has tried to echo the alternative approach to an understanding of civil society by acknowledging and investigating a broad range of influences on the development and dynamics of the sector. Thus chapters of this volume were dedicated to Soviet and pre-Soviet forms of social organisation, and their continued importance for Central Asian people today, as well as the constraints of political systems and the economic situation facing the region. Inevitably, this publication has looked into the role of more recently created NGOs and community-level organisations, but it has also considered how these types of groupings and institutions are maturing into representative bodies that play a role beyond practical work with immediate target groups and beneficiaries.

As has already been noted, much cynicism has been voiced by analysts of the emergence in Central Asia of locally owned and driven civil society organisations and activities. Certainly, during the 1990s, there was a tendency amongst donors to create NGOs from scratch that would be able to implement their projects and manage bureaucratic reporting requirements. As a result, established local ways of working and socially embedded institutions and groupings were often overlooked. However, the authors would argue that partly as a response to criticism coming from within the region, external actors have begun to realise and act upon the potential for collaboration and engagement with traditional practices and institutions. Whilst the authors of this book welcome these developments and the move towards acknowledgement of the role and importance of 'communal' civil society, we would argue that these cannot be adopted uncritically as a new vehicle for poverty reduction, social mobilisation or conflict prevention. Any approach to work with civil society must involve adequate analysis of power and gender dynamics that cut across communities and organisations.

As the civil society sector in the region matures, examples of collaboration and joint initiatives between different actors are increasing, particularly in advocacy and lobbying work. Significantly, many of these have occurred without the impetus from external donors. This is an encouraging sign that civil society organisations are finding ways to work together and give voice to the needs and opinions of their members and interest groups within the public sphere. The groundswell of popular protest against alleged fraud in the Kyrgyz parliamentary elections in spring 2005 and the revolution that followed are also signs of growing confidence amongst local civil society in its own potential as a force for change.

INTRAC's Central Asia Experience: Developing the Capacity of Civil Society

Acknowledging the complex nature of civil society, both as a concept, and as a reality on the ground, INTRAC over the past decade has attempted to undertake dispassionate and effective civil society capacity-building initiatives in Central Asia. This began with the NGO-focused programmes in the mid 1990s and continued with a wider civil society strengthening programme, fully funded by the UK Government's Department for International Development (DFID) from 2001–2004. These programmes benefited from the promotion of close links between research and capacity building and between theory and action. In the pages of this book the reader is regularly pointed towards studies and papers that have been developed with the help of local writers and experts. These are not just the Civil Society Mapping Reports funded by ESCOR, but also the community development case studies and the political and civil society reports undertaken as a contribution to INTRAC's Central Asia Programme. In Chapters 2–5, we reviewed the ESCOR reports and their contribution to our understanding of the emerging third sector as well as the pre-Soviet civil society heritage of the region and the important Soviet-era formations and experience. Alongside this empirical work, in addition, the local researchers helped INTRAC to understand something of the overall Central Asia 'take' on civil society, a distinctive viewpoint which has many elements. One of these is an emphasis on the 'communal' – the community and family networks that underpin society; another, shared with the other countries of the former Soviet Union, is a strong set of expectations from the State, a willingness to work closely with its institutions and a tendency not to see 'public' associations as necessarily completely autonomous from government.

Clearly INTRAC's programme work in Central Asia gained a great deal from the various concurrent research initiatives. But it also put something back: one of the successes of the 2001–2004 programme was an analytical skills training programme (ASTP) for NGOs. The rationale behind the development of the ASTP for the region was that analytical skills were not often to be found outside of research institutions and state statistical agencies, and that these bodies were not readily providing policy-relevant information needed by civil society activists.[1] INTRAC provided a five-module training workshop series, starting from research skills, proceeding through key development concepts (poverty, gender, participation) and ending with advocacy.[2]

A second advantage which INTRAC enjoyed was the opportunity to experiment with a comprehensive, multi-level regional programme in Central Asia. At the start of this second phase of INTRAC's work, several key challenges were defined for this programme. One related to the scale and complexity of the work – how to do capacity building at the individual, organisation and society levels, in five nations moving away from the Soviet State socialism development model. A second, linked issue concerned the political dimension. While there are strong arguments in favour of political impartiality for civil society organisations, if civil society capacity development is conducted within an 'ideological vacuum', this will prevent it from being embedded in public life. As such it will neither foster nor occupy a public space. A third issue was the need to move beyond the world of NGOs and to work with other types of civil society organisations – in this case, with community associations of different kinds.[3]

This model of institutional development meant a multiple approach; first, linkages between NGOs, government, donors and communities, and second, a focus on partnership with indigenous NGO support organisations (NGOSOs). Thus the objectives of the programme – to build the sustainability of NGOs, to increase the variety and quality of services offered by them, to deepen the critical thinking of staff in the sector, to develop effective ways of working with communities – were all to be achieved through collaboration with experienced local partners. These activities and events were backed up by an active information and translation programme. As a result, ICAP partners and trainees built up their ability to provide

---

[1] Simon Forrester, 'Enabling Analysis: Enhancing Civil Society's Role in Development', in *Ontrac* 24, Central Asia Edition, May 2004, p. 4.

[2] ASTP was run in Kyrgyzstan and Tajikistan in 2002–2004. All participants committed to writing a mini-research study and there were some impressive results. For example, a comparison of urban and rural self-help groups in Kyrgyzstan and Kazakhstan, a report on problems in access to primary school in a village in Jalalabad *oblast*, Kyrgyzstan (which led directly to the opening of new facilities), and a study of the cotton sector in Tajikistan – asking 'who gains'?

[3] See Garbutt (2003).

consultancy, training and research services for a range of donors. They were also able to tailor ICAP materials to their own work and to translate them into local languages.

Listing these tangible successes is, however, much easier than reaching any conclusions as to the extent to which civil society has achieved its potential in Central Asia and is 'vibrant, independent and effective' (as defined in ICAP's overall project goal). A number of chapters in this book point to the challenges faced by many organisations, including internal weaknesses, the difficulties in establishing and maintaining relationships with government and the over-dependence of NGOs on external donors. An evaluation of INTRAC's Central Asia Programme noted:

> Over the life of the project, many NGOs have demonstrated growing maturity: with examples of coalition-building such as the coalition of NGOs which successfully derailed a draft NGO Law in Kazakhstan and a number of NGOs setting up local branches. However, the majority of NGOs continue to be urban based, and most continue to be strongly leader-oriented and to lack formal governance structures. In most countries little attention has been paid to issues of financial transparency.

The issue of sustainability was raised throughout the Central Asia programme. INTRAC's lead trainer on the other main multi-module series, the education and training support programme (ETSP), noted that: 'A sustainable NGO is one that has a reasonable prospect of continuing to function and to develop over the medium term (three to five years) and to work productively with its target group'. To do this, the organisation has to do 'meaningful work', develop external contacts and not rely on one foreign donor.[4]

Capacity-building issues with community-based organisations are different, however. While they have the advantage of being close to the community, have better understanding of local needs, and easier access to local resources, these organisations are often directly vulnerable to the widespread conditions of poverty, powerlessness, information 'hunger', and isolation. ICAP's third annual conference, entitled 'Community Development in Rural Areas of Central Asia', identified a number of priorities for the improving of work at this level. These included enhancing the role of communities in poverty reduction programmes, improving capacity building for CBOs and local government, strengthening the gender approach in community development, further development of self-help groups,

---

[4] Chris Wardle, 'Re-Thinking Sustainability', in *Ontrac* 21, May 2002, p. 6. Between 1999-2003, ETSP ran in four countries of the region: Kyrgyzstan, Kazakhstan, Uzbekistan and Tajikistan.

micro-credit programmes and community investment funds, and the consolidation of community empowerment networks in the region.[5]

For leading NGOs in the region, one of the most attractive opportunities offered by INTRAC's programmes was the chance to 'enter the international NGO/development arena' and to put Central Asia on the map. Learning generated from shared experiences with partner organisations in the region has fed into INTRAC's work worldwide, on issues such as monitoring and evaluation, civil society involvement in PRSPs, and community development. These insights have made an important contribution to INTRAC's programmes of publications, conferences and workshops. The authors hope that in turn INTRAC's engagement in Central Asia has brought a wider understanding of the potential composition, role and scope of the civil society sector.

Civil Society – a Contested Space

Despite the wealth of informed and expert contributions to this book, we offer it to readers sure in the knowledge that not all will accept the concepts or agree with the arguments put forward in it. Furthermore, the civil society environment is fast-moving, and inevitably much of the information about individual organisations goes quickly out of date; we experienced this problem in presenting earlier versions of the ESCOR mapping reports to local audiences. We have tried to ensure that this publication presents fresh information and impressions and hope that the emphasis on different types of civil society organisation and activity makes this a balanced book.

This book has analysed civil society in Central Asia from both a regional and individual country perspective. It should be stressed here one last time that the approach and attitude of the state is crucial to the way that civil society will evolve and develop. This is one of the many areas where the countries of the region are diverging. Development in Kazakhstan is strongly influenced by the market; in Turkmenistan and Uzbekistan it is State-led; whilst Kyrgyzstan and Tajikistan are largely aid-dependent. The governments of these states vary in strength and authoritarianism. This affects civil society in a complex way, and is of particular importance when, as recently, donors are concerned to engage with government on poverty reduction programmes.

One of ICAP's most ambitious events was the 2003 regional conference, 'Who Benefits? The Monitoring and Evaluation of Development Programmes in Central

---

[5] Report of the third annual INTRAC Central Asia conference, 'Community Development in Rural Areas of Central Asia', Osh, Kyrgyzstan, April 2004, ed. Anne Garbutt, pp.13–17.

Asia'. Informed by the experience of civil society in the consultation process and implementation of development programmes, this conference asked how civil society could begin to set its sights higher in terms of influencing development policy and programmes and queried how government and international agencies will respond to greater pressure from civil society.[6] Whilst it is clear that states continue to see NGOs in an instrumental way – they can leverage money from donors or undertake service provision work at the local level, the role of civil society in these activities affords it a high profile and feeds back into the democratic process. NGO leaders go into politics, and attend public budget hearings; the results of development programmes are discussed at election time and in between. In other words, government is not unaffected by the activities of civil society.

The popular revolution in Kyrgyzstan in March 2005 was a more dramatic example of civil society impacting upon the State. Civil society organisations that encouraged resistance to the regime are now having to take some responsibility for the ensuing confusion and must reassess their role in a changing political environment. It is not yet clear how events in Kyrgyzstan will impact upon civil society relations with the State in neighbouring countries.

Will the states in Central Asia be able to cope with an 'alternative', groundbreaking politicised civil society sector? In a sense the sector has been evolving in this way since independence in 1991. Whatever one's views of the Soviet and capitalist periods (and most agree that the former was exhausted and inefficient, and the latter primitive and inequitable), in retrospect it is possible to see that the 'transition' period was always going to be a time of experiment, imitation, confusion and conflict. As this publication has shown, despite some attempts to establish a blueprint for civil society development, the sector has undergone a similar process of experimentation during this period. As a result, the civil society sector that has emerged in the region is heterogeneous, and defies neat categorisation. What is clear is that spaces are emerging for alternative visions of the future, and that it is only through empirical research that the dynamics of the sector can be adequately analysed.

---

[6] INTRAC 2003 regional conference, 'Who Benefits? The Monitoring and Evaluation of Development Programmes in Central Asia', Charles Buxton, INTRAC OPS No. 42, p. 5.

Glossary of Central Asian Terms

(Please note that some of these terms are Russian/Soviet rather than Central Asian)

Akim	mayor
akimat	see *Hokimat*
aksakal	(white beard) elder, local imam
artel	co-operative, group of workers within one specialty
aryk	irrigation ditch
ashar	voluntary labour by the community for the community
assar	see ashar
aul	mobile village
avlod	traditional institution regulating community relationships
awlad	identity group
ayil okmotu	Kyrgyzstan equivalent of *mahalla* committee
basmachi	group of rebels who sought to create pan-Turkic state in the 1920s
fond	foundation eg Public Union Foundation
gap	(to talk) local savings group or private dining club/entertainment
gashtak	(taking in turn) as *gap*
guzar	community or geographical area
hakim	see *Akim*
hashar	see ashar
Hokimat	government authority at *oblast* level
jailoo	pastures
Jamoat	local authority at *raion* level
kelin	daughter-in-law
khokimat	see *Hokimat*
kolkhoz	collective farm
Komsomol	Young Communist League (Soviet)
kvartal	block (apartment block or residential area)
mahalla	community or geographical area
mahalla committee	self-governing body
navruz	national holiday to mark end of winter
oblast	provincial, regional (level)
qawm	identity group
raion	district (level)

sotsial'nyi zakaz	instrument used by state to finance NGOs (and private sector organisations) to provide services
sovkhoz	state farm
subbota	Saturday
subbotnik	unpaid labour groups on Saturdays (Soviet)
tois	large-scale community celebrations
Umid	(hope) a foundation to support gifted youths' studies abroad
velayat	see *oblast*
Yntymak	contribution of money for community celebrations

Bibliography

Abdulalishoev, K., Hojimamadov K., Zevarshoeva, N., Ghiyosov, E. and Nabotova, Z. (2004) *Merger of Village Organisations and its Influence on the Local Communities*. Dushanbe: Policy and Evaluation Unit, Mountain Societies Development Support Programme of the Aga Khan Foundation. Draft.

Abdullaev, S., Abdullaeva, O., Heap, S. and Tatybayev, A. (2003) *Taking the Pulse of Civil Society Development in Uzbekistan*. Oxford/Tashkent: INTRAC/FACT.

Adams, L. (2004) 'Cultural Elites in Uzbekistan: Ideological Production and the State' in Jones Luong, P. (ed.) *The Transformation of Central Asia*. Ithaca, New York: Cornell University Press.

Akiner, S. (1997) 'Between Tradition and Modernity: the Dilemma Facing Contemporary Central Asian Women' in Buckley, M. (ed.) *Post Soviet Women: From the Baltic to Central Asia*. Cambridge: CUP.

Akiner, S. (2002) 'Prospects for Civil Society in Tajikistan' in Sajoo, A. (ed.) *Civil Society in the Muslim World*. London: IB Tauris.

Aksartova, S. (2003) 'Donors and NGOs in Kyrgyzstan: Trust, Mistrust and Social Networks'. Paper presented at the Central Eurasian Studies Society Fifth Annual Conference, 2–5 October, Harvard, Cambridge, Mass.

Anderson, J. (1999) *Kyrgyzstan: Central Asia's Island of Democracy?* Amsterdam: Harwood Academic Publishers.

Arkoun, M. (2002) 'Locating Civil Society in Islamic Contexts' in Sajoo, A. (ed) *Civil Society in the Muslim World*. London: Tauris.

Asian Development Bank (2002) *Asian Development Outlook 2002*. Turkmenistan: ADB.

Babajanian, B. (2004) 'Poverty and Social Exclusion in Tajikistan'. Paper prepared for the World Bank, Europe and Central Asia region.

Babajanian, B., Freizer, S. and Stevens, D. (2005)'Civil Society in Central Asia and the Caucasus' in the Special Edition on Civil Society in Central Asia and the Caucasus, *Central Asian Survey*, forthcoming.

Baimatov, B., Stakeeva, B. and Heap, S. (2002) 'Civil Society in the Kyrgyz Republic'. Oxford: INTRAC unpublished report.

Bialeva, C. (2004) 'Political and Civil Society Report for Kyrgyzstan'. Bishkek: INTRAC.

Boboroyov, H. (2003) *NGOs and Social Partnership for Community Development in Tajikistan*. Dushanbe: unpublished report.

Boboroyov, H. and Heap, S. (2003a) 'Civil Society in Tajikistan'. Oxford and Dushanbe: INTRAC report. February draft.

Boboroyov, H. and Heap, S. (2003b) 'The Development of Civil Society in Tajikistan'. Oxford and Dushanbe: INTRAC report. May draft.

Boboroyov, H. and Heap, S. (2003c) 'Developing Civil Society on the Periphery'. Oxford and Dushanbe: INTRAC report. Draft.

Buxton, C. and Musabaeva, A. (2002) *Turkmenistan NGO Mapping Report*. Bishkek: INTRAC unpublished report.

Carley, P. (1995) 'The Legacy of the Soviet Political System and the Prospects for Developing Civil Society in Central Asia', in Tismaneanu, V. (ed.) *Political Culture and Civil Society in Russia and the New States of Eurasia*. New York: ME Sharpe.

Chambers, S. and Kymlicka, W. (2002) *Alternative Conceptions of Civil Society*. Princeton: Princeton University Press.

Chandoke, N. (1995) *State and Civil Society: Explorations in Political Theory*. New Delhi: Sage.

CHF (Community, Housing, Finance) (2002a) *Community Development Assessment*. Tashkent: CHF.

CHF (2002b) *Community Action Investment Programme Semi-Annual Report: 2 May–22 November*. Tashkent: CHF in collaboration with Counterpart International.

Cornwall, A. (2002) 'Making Spaces, Changing Places: Situating Participation in Development'. University of Sussex, IDS: Working Paper 170.

Csaki, C. and Tuck, L. (2000) 'Rural Development Strategy: Eastern Europe and Central Asia'. Washington: World Bank. Technical Paper 484.

Davlatov, K. (2003) 'Political and Civil Society Report for Tajikistan'. Dushanbe: INTRAC. August.

Davlatov, K. (2004) 'Political and Civil Society Report for Tajikistan'. Dushanbe: INTRAC. February.

DCCA (2003) 'Self-Help Groups' Role in Solving Livelihood Problems for Socially Vulnerable Populations: Preliminary Research Summary Data For Kazakhstan & The Kyrgyz Republic'. Bishkek: DCCA.

Delehanty, J. and Rasmussen, K. (1995) 'Land Reform and Farm Restructuring in the Kyrgyz Republic'. *Post-Soviet Geography* 36 (9): 565–86.

De Toqueville, A. (1994) *Democracy in America*. London: Everyman.

Dissenova, S., Heap, S., Ibrayeva, A., Kabdieva, A. and Sharipova, D. (2002) 'Civil Society in the Republic of Kazakhstan'. Oxford/Almaty: INTRAC/KIMEP.

Djamankulova, K. (2004) 'Exploring Community Mobilisation through Rural Water Projects'. Bishkek: INTRAC unpublished paper.

Dongier et al. (2002) 'Community Driven Development', in *The PRSP Sourcebook*. Washington: World Bank. (http://www.worldbank.org/participation/CDD1.htm accessed 2 June 2005).

Earle, L. (2002) 'Rural Livelihoods in Independent Central Asia: Agricultural Restructuring, Gender and Civil Society'. Geneva: UNRISD unpublished paper.

Earle, L. (2004a) *Community development in Kazakhstan, Kyrgyzstan and Uzbekistan: Lessons Learnt from Recent Experience*. Oxford: INTRAC Occasional Paper No. 40.

Earle, L. (2004b) *Civil society support: Is community development the way forward?* INTRAC: Oxford. (http://www.intrac.org/pages/jordanconferencepapers_abstracts.html conference background paper, accessed 2 June 2005).

Edwards, M. (2004) *Civil Society*. Cambridge: Polity Press.

Eurasianet (2002) 'Poor Drinking Water Seen as the Source of Typhoid Outbreak in Tajik Capital'. Posted by J. Bennet, 24 October, (http://www.eurasianet.org).

FACT Social Research Agency (2003) *Community-Based Organisations in Uzbekistan*. Tashkent: FACT.

Falkingham, J. (2000) 'A Profile of Poverty in Tajikistan'. London: Centre for Action Against Social Exclusion (CASE), London School of Economics (LSE).

Falkingham, J. (2004) 'Inequality and Poverty in the Former Soviet Union'. Presentation at the Centre for Euro-Asian Studies, University of Reading. 3 November 2004.

Fathi, H. (1997) 'Otines: the unknown women clerics of Central Asian Islam'. *Central Asian Survey*, 16 (1): 27–43.

Fitchett, D. and Owen, G. (2002) *Microfinance Sector Assessment Tajikistan*. Soros/CGAP.

Fowler, A. (1997) *Striking a Balance: A Guide to Enhancing the Effectiveness of Non-Governmental Organisations in International Development*. London: Earthscan/INTRAC.

Fozilhujaev, B. (2003) 'Mahalla Initiatives Case Study'. Tashkent: INTRAC unpublished document.

Franz, I., Shvetsova L. and Shamshildaeva, A. (2002) 'Development of Non-Governmental Sector in Kazakhstan', Part I. Almaty: Institute for Development Cooperation.

Freizer, S. (2004) 'Central Asian Fragmented Civil Society: Communal and Neoliberal Forms in Tajikistan and Uzbekistan', in Glasius, M., Lewis, D. and Seckinelgin, H. (eds.) *Exploring Civil Society: Political and Cultural Contexts*. London and New York: Routledge.

Garbutt, A. (2003) 'Civil Society Strengthening in Central Asia' in Pratt, B. (ed) *Changing Expectations? The Concept and Practice of Civil Society in International Development*. Oxford: INTRAC.

Garbutt, A. and Heap S. (2003) 'Growing Civil Society in Central Asia. INTRAC's first Central Asia regional conference'. Almaty, Kazakhstan, 13–14 June 2002. Oxford: INTRAC Occasional Paper No. 39.

Garbutt, A. and Sinclair, M. (1998) 'NGOs in Uzbekistan: A Mapping Exercise'. Oxford: INTRAC.

Gaventa, J. (2003) 'Towards Participatory Local Governance: Assessing the Transformative Possibilities'. Paper prepared for conference 'Participation: From Tyranny to Transformation', Manchester, 27–28 February 2003.

Gellner, E. (1994) *Conditions of Liberty: Civil Society and its Rivals*. London: Hamish Hamilton.

George, A. (2001) *Journey into Kazakhstan – The True Face of the Nazarbayev Regime*. Lanham, Maryland: University of America Press.

Giffen, J. and Buxton, C. (2004) 'CBOs and the Elaboration of Pro-Poor Policy: Lessons Learnt from Research and Consultation in Georgia, Kyrgyzstan and Uzbekistan'. Bishkek: INTRAC unpublished paper.

Government of Tajikistan (2002) Poverty Reduction Strategy Paper.

Hanafi, H. (2002) 'Alternative Conceptions of Civil Society: A Reflective Islamic Approach', in Chambers, S. and Kymlicka, W. (eds.) *Alternative Conceptions of Civil Society*. Princeton: Princeton University Press.

Handrahan, L. (2001) 'Gender and Ethnicity in the "transitional democracy" of Kyrgyzstan'. *Central Asian Survey* 20 (4): 67–496.

Handrahan, L. (2004) 'Hunting for Women: Bride-Kidnapping in Kyrgyzstan'. *International Feminist Journal of Politics*, 6 (2): 207–33.

Horton, V. (2002) *Assar: Handbook for Self-Help Groups*. Voluntary Services Overseas.

Howell, J. and Pearce, J. (2001) *Civil Society and Development: A Critical Exploration*. Boulder: Lynne Reinner.

Ikramova, U. and McConnell, K. (1999) 'Women's NGOs in Central Asia's Evolving Societies', in Ruffin, M. H. and Waugh, D. (eds.) *Civil Society in Central Asia*. Seattle: University of Washington Press/Center for Civil Society International.

Ilkhamov, A. (2001) 'Impoverishment of the Masses in the Transition Period: Signs of an Emerging "new poor" Identity in Uzbekistan'. *Central Asian Survey*, 20 (1).

International Crisis Group (2001) 'Tajikistan: An Uncertain Peace'. Osh/Brussels: ICG Asia Report No. 30.

Jones Luong, P. (2004) *The Transformation of Central Asia: States and Societies from Soviet Rule to Independence*. Ithaca: Cornell University Press.

Kandiyoti, D. (1998) 'Rural Livelihoods and Social Networks in Uzbekistan: Perspectives from Andijan'. *Central Asian Survey*, 17 (4) 561–78.

Kandiyoti, D. (2002) 'Agrarian Reform, Gender and Land Rights in Rural Uzbekistan'. Geneva: UNRISD Programme Paper.

Kangas, R. (1995) 'State Building and Civil Society in Central Asia', in Tismaneanu V. (ed.) *Political Culture and Civil Society in Russia and the New States of Eurasia*. New York: ME Sharpe.

Kazakhstanskaya Pravda (2001) 'Some Arrived, Some Left: Statistical Data on Migration in Kazakhstan', 5 January p. 4.

Kramer, M. (2002) 'Should America promote a liberal, democratic Middle East?' Weinberg Founders Conference, The Washington Institute for Near-East Policy. www.martinkramer.org accessed February 2005.

Kudat, A., Peabody S. and Keyder, C. (2000) *Social Assessment and Agricultural Reform in Central Asia and Turkey*. Washington: IBRD/World Bank.

Kuehnast, K. and Dudwick, N. (2004) *Better a Hundred Friends than a Hundred Rubles?: Social Networks in Transition – the Kyrgyz Republic*. Washington: World Bank.

Makarova, E. (1999) 'Paradoxes of Development in Soviet and post-Soviet Central Asia: With Special Reference to the Role of the Mahalla in Uzbek Cities'. PhD Thesis: University of Manchester.

Manor, J., Robinson, M. and White, G. (1999) 'Civil Society and Governance: A Concept Paper'. University of Sussex: Institute of Development Studies unpublished paper.

Mansuri, G. and Rao, V. (2004) 'Community-Based and -Driven Development: A Critical Review'. Washington: World Bank Policy Research Working Paper 3209.

Mardin, S. (1995) 'Civil Society and Islam', in Hall, J. (ed.) *Civil Society: Theory, History, Comparison*. Cambridge: Polity Press.

Melvin, N. (2000) *Uzbekistan: Transition to Authoritarianism on the Silk Road*. Amsterdam: Harwood Academic Publishers.

Mercy Corps (2003) *Ferghana Valley Field Study: Reducing the Potential for Conflict through Community Mobilization*. Mercy Corps Central Asia.

Mirzoeva, G. (2003) 'NPO "Modar" – eto shto sorok djenshin'. *Vecherny Dushanbe* 10 (274), 7 March.

Narayan, D. with Patel, R., Schafft, K., Rademacher, A. and Koch-Schulte, S.(2000) *Voices of the Poor: Can Anyone Hear Us?* New York: Oxford University Press.

Narbekova, B. (1999) *K Issledovaniu "Traibalizma" v Kazakhskom Obshestve; Soveremennii Mir: Issledovaniya Molodikh*. Almaty: Soros Foundation. Summer University. Karzhy-Karazhat.

Nelson, J. and Zadek, S. (2000) 'Partnership Alchemy: New Social Partnerships in Europe'. The Copenhagen Centre.

Olcott, M. B. (2001) 'Revisiting the Twelve Myths of Central Asia'. Washington: Carnegie Endowment for International Peace, Working Paper.

Omuraliyev, N. A., Biyalieva, Ch. S. and Balabai, V. N. (2003) 'Strengthening the Capacity of Non-governmental and Community-Based Organizations to Facilitate a More Active Involvement of Civil Society in the Development and Implementation of National Poverty Reduction Strategies on Local and National Levels in Central Asian and Caucasian Countries'. National Academy of Sciences of the Kyrgyz Republic.

Padamsey, S. (2000) 'Community Development Advisor's Initial Mapping Report for Kazakhstan'. Almaty: INTRAC report. Draft.

Peabody, S., Kuehnast, K. and Rana, S. (not dated) *Critical Issues for Scaling up Community Driven Development in Central Asia*. Central Asia CDD Working Group.

Ponomarev, V. (1994) *Third Sector Development in Kazakhstan*. Almaty: Interlegal.

Pratt, B. and Goodhand, J. (1996) *Institutional Development of NGOs in Central Asia*. Oxford: INTRAC.

Putnam, R. (1993) *Making Democracy Work: Civic Traditions in Modern Italy.* Princeton: Princeton University Press.

Putnam, R. (1995) 'Bowling Alone: America's Declining Social Capital'. *Journal of Democracy* 6 (1).

Roy, O (1999) 'Kolkhoz and Civil Society in the Independent States of Central Asia', in Ruffin, M. H. and Waugh, D. (eds.) *Civil Society in Central Asia.* Seattle: University of Washington Press/Center for Civil Society International.

Roy, O. (2000) *The New Central Asia: The Creation of Nations.* London: IB Tauris.

Roy, O. (2001) *L'Asie Centrale Contemporain.* Paris: Presses Universitaires de France.

Roy, O. (2002) 'Soviet Legacies and Western Aid Imperatives in the New Central Asia', in Sajoo, A. (ed.) *Civil Society in the Muslim World.* London: IB Tauris.

Sajoo, A. (2002) (ed.) *Civil Society in the Muslim World.* London: IB Tauris.

Sakhanov, N. (2003) 'Political and Civil Society Report for Kazakhstan'. Almaty: INTRAC. March.

Sakhanov, N. (2004) 'Political and Civil Society Report for Kazakhstan'. Almaty: INTRAC. March.

Salimdjanova, T. (2004) 'Political and Civil Society Report for Uzbekistan'. Tashkent: INTRAC. February.

Salmorbekova, Z. (2004) 'Review of the Publications and the Role of Civil Society in Poverty Reduction'. Bishkek: INTRAC. September draft.

Seligman, A. (2002) 'Civil Society as Idea and Ideal', in Sajoo, A. (ed.) *Civil Society in the Muslim World.* London: IB Tauris.

Sharq (2004) *Review of Publications on Poverty Issues and Civil Society Role in Poverty Reduction.* Dushanbe: Sharq.

Sievers, E. (2003) *The Post-Soviet Decline of Central Asia.* London: RoutledgeCurzon.

Sinclair, M. (2004) 'Center Interbilim's work in NGO capacity building, advocacy and lobbying at the local and national level'. Impact assessment report prepared for Center Interbilim.

Smith, S. (1999) *Labour Issues and Trade Unions in the Kyrgyz Republic.* London: Know How Fund.

Stevens, D. (2003) 'Mahallas and NGOs: In search of Civil Society and Synergy in Uzbekistan'. Paper presented at the 4th Annual Conference of the Central Eurasian Studies Society, Cambridge, Mass. Draft.

Tabyshalieva, A. (2000) 'Revival of Traditions in Post-Soviet Central Asia', in Lazreg, M. (ed.) *Making the Transition Work for Women in Europe and Central Asia*. Washington: World Bank.

Tashbaeva, C. (2002) 'Report for DFID October–December 2002'. Bishkek: INTRAC unpublished report.

UNDP Regional Bureau for Europe and the Commonwealth of Independent States (1999) *Regional Human Development Report*. www.undp.sk/Reg_progs/Human_dev.asp, accessed June 2002.

UNDP (2000) Human Development Report for Tajikistan.

UNDP (2001) 'Empowering Grassroots Organisations for Poverty Alleviation in Kyrgyzstan: Experiences of the poverty alleviation component'. Annual Report of UNDP Social Governance Programme. Bishkek: UNDP.

UNDP (2002) 'Social Governance Programme Annual Report'. Bishkek: Government of Kyrgyz Republic and UNDP.

UNDP (2003) *Changes in Target Villages*. Bishkek: UNDP.

Weinthal, E. (2004) 'Transnational Actors, NGOs and Environmental Protection in Central Asia', in Jones Luong, P. (ed.) *The Transformation of Central Asia*. Ithaca: Cornell University Press.

White, S. 'Depoliticizing Development: The Uses and Abuses of Participation'. *Development in Practice* 6(1): 6–15.

Whitlock, M. (2002) *Beyond the Oxus: The Central Asians*. London: John Murray.

World Bank (2000) *Making Transition Work for Everyone: Poverty and Inequality in Europe and Central Asia*. Washington: The World Bank.

Index